FEMALE INNOVATORS AT WORK

WOMEN ON TOP OF TECH

Danielle Newnham

Apress®

Female Innovators at Work: Women on Top of Tech

Danielle Newnham
London
United Kingdom

ISBN-13 (pbk): 978-1-4842-2363-5   ISBN-13 (electronic): 978-1-4842-2364-2
DOI 10.1007/978-1-4842-2364-2

Library of Congress Control Number: 2016959788

Managing Director: Welmoed Spahr
Acquisitions Editor: Robert Hutchinson
Developmental Editor: Laura Berendson
Editorial Board: Steve Anglin, Pramila Balen, Laura Berendson, Aaron Black, Louise Corrigan, Jonathan Gennick, Robert Hutchinson, Celestin Suresh John, Nikhil Karkal, James Markham, Susan McDermott, Matthew Moodie, Natalie Pao, Gwenan Spearing
Coordinating Editor: Rita Fernando
Copy Editor: Kim Burton-Weisman
Compositor: SPi Global
Indexer: SPi Global

Distributed to the book trade worldwide by Springer Science+Business Media New York, 233 Spring Street, 6th Floor, New York, NY 10013. Phone 1-800-SPRINGER, fax (201) 348-4505, e-mail orders-ny@springer-sbm.com, or visit www.springer.com. Apress Media, LLC is a California LLC and the sole member (owner) is Springer Science + Business Media Finance Inc (SSBM Finance Inc). SSBM Finance Inc is a Delaware corporation.

For information on translations, please e-mail rights@apress.com, or visit www.apress.com.

Apress and friends of ED books may be purchased in bulk for academic, corporate, or promotional use. eBook versions and licenses are also available for most titles. For more information, reference our Special Bulk Sales–eBook Licensing web page at www.apress.com/bulk-sales.

Any source code or other supplementary materials referenced by the author in this text is available to readers at www.apress.com. For detailed information about how to locate your book's source code, go to www.apress.com/source-code/.

Printed on acid-free paper

Apress Business: The Unbiased Source of Business Information

Apress business books provide essential information and practical advice, each written for practitioners by recognized experts. Busy managers and professionals in all areas of the business world—and at all levels of technical sophistication—look to our books for the actionable ideas and tools they need to solve problems, update and enhance their professional skills, make their work lives easier, and capitalize on opportunity.

Whatever the topic on the business spectrum—entrepreneurship, finance, sales, marketing, management, regulation, information technology, among others—Apress has been praised for providing the objective information and unbiased advice you need to excel in your daily work life. Our authors have no axes to grind; they understand they have one job only—to deliver up-to-date, accurate information simply, concisely, and with deep insight that addresses the real needs of our readers.

It is increasingly hard to find information—whether in the news media, on the Internet, and now all too often in books—that is even-handed and has your best interests at heart. We therefore hope that you enjoy this book, which has been carefully crafted to meet our standards of quality and unbiased coverage.

We are always interested in your feedback or ideas for new titles. Perhaps you'd even like to write a book yourself. Whatever the case, reach out to us at editorial@apress.com and an editor will respond swiftly. Incidentally, at the back of this book, you will find a list of useful related titles. Please visit us at www.apress.com to sign up for newsletters and discounts on future purchases.

The Apress Business Team

To Mama. I miss you.

Contents

Foreword

Technology is at the heart of most of the exciting innovations that will transform our world over the next fifty years. But women, who make up fifty percent of the global population, are still woefully underrepresented in technology innovation and entrepreneurship. Today, women comprise less than 25 percent of the technical workforce and startups with female founders make up less than 7 percent of venture-backed enterprises.

One important way to change this worldwide trend is through inspirational role models. Young students and young women considering a career in technology are heavily influenced by visible role models. But all too often, there aren't enough women technical leaders to look up to.

This book highlights extraordinary role models by telling the stories of twenty women with very diverse careers, inspiring anyone who is considering technology as a career where they can have impact. What is important about these stories is the breadth of experience, from early programming pioneers like Dame Stephanie (Steve) Shirley, to well-known technology and business entrepreneurs such as Judy Estrin and Lynda Weinman. It includes stories of technology innovators like Radia Perlman and Manuela Veloso, plus many extraordinary technology and business leaders. The stories include advice on what made them successful, such as finding mentors and focusing on business solutions.

Danielle Newnham brings their stories to life and helps the reader get to intimately know each of these women. Take your time and read the stories—learn and enjoy!

—Telle Whitney
President and CEO
Anita Borg Institute

About the Author

Danielle Newnham is the founder of The Junto Network, an online network for tech entrepreneurs, featuring interviews with inspirational tech founders and innovators. She is the cofounder of Tease and Totes, an online store for women and children. She was on the founding team of ubinow, a mobile apps agency in London. Newnham was named one of the Top 10 Tech Writers of 2015 by LinkedIn. She is the author of *Mad Men of Mobile* (CreateSpace, 2013), a collection of interviews with mobile pioneers and entrepreneurs.

Acknowledgments

A huge thank you must first go to the incredible women I interviewed for this book, who graciously gave so much of their time. And to the women I interviewed but couldn't include. You are all inspiring and I promise to keep telling your stories.

I would like to thank my sister, Natalie Bardega, for her unwavering support and help while I wrote this book. And Joshua Newnham, who I met at my very first startup and who continues to inspire me. I am also thankful to him for handing me a copy of *Founders at Work*, which I still credit for making me fall in love with this industry and its creators.

I thank Jessica Livingston for writing *Founders at Work* and for all she does for women in tech.

A huge thank you to Telle Whitney of the Anita Borg Institute for taking time to write the foreword. It was an honor to have you involved. And to Marc Andreessen for the recommendation.

Thanks to the Apress team, especially Robert Hutchinson for giving this book the green light, and Rita Fernando, Laura Berendson, and Kim Burton-Weisman for helping to make it a reality.

Thank you to all those who helped contribute to this book by offering names of women I should speak to or for coordinating interviews, including Dex Torricke-Barton of SpaceX, Sonal Chokshi of Andreessen Horowitz, Sharon Kempner, Lynn Hart, Lu Firth, Juliana Rotich, Samantha Walker, Sean Obedih, Nikki Klein, Marty Cooper, James Chase, Sunanda Krishna, Leslie Wilkinson, and Charlotte Morisetti.

To all those working tirelessly to increase diversity in tech—you're appreciated. What you are doing now will turn the tide and create a better future for us all.

To the many men who continue to champion women in this industry. Keep up the good fight. It might not make you popular within certain groups but we need your help to fight this. We are all in it together and we appreciate you, too.

Thank you to my wonderful son, Benjamin Edison. You are the shining light in my life and I loved reading the chapters to you. Thank you for listening so intently and for the many questions you asked. I appreciate it.

Finally, I want to thank every reader who takes this book and does something with it. Whether you use the stories as inspiration to get you where you need to go or whether you share them with others to help guide them. I hope you find the chapters within this book as useful, inspiring, and as important as I do. Thank you.

Introduction

In July 2006, I walked into the office of my very first tech startup and fell madly in love with the industry. Much like today, startups revealed a window into the future, which was, and still is, hugely exciting to me. That first startup worked on personalized search, NFC (near field communication), mobile payments, and mobile phone applications—all of which were several years ahead of their time. And although that company ran out of funding and closed down, as many do, I really enjoyed my time there and the experience taught me some valuable lessons. But there was something that bothered me. There were too few women.

Two years later, I joined the founding team at ubinow—a mobile apps agency set up by two members of the previous company's mobile team. And the lack of women in the industry became even more apparent, especially when we started looking to hire more developers. This was not because women didn't exist in tech, because they do. The issue was about visibility; a problem that persists today.

So I started to wonder, "How can we change this?" This, in turn, led me to ask, "Where are the stories about women doing well and thriving in this industry?" They were nowhere to be found. The press wasn't covering women, the startups weren't hiring women, and the industry wasn't promoting women. So how could we possibly attract more or even retain those women already here if we did not champion them? I started conducting some research and began to uncover a treasure trove of female innovators. The more I discovered, the more I asked myself, "Why haven't these stories been told?"

If one looks at the history of computer science, the overriding images of its creators have nearly always been men, despite some of its earliest innovators being women such as Ada Lovelace. Added to that, around the time that computers started arriving in our homes in the mid-1980s, advertising for personal computers mainly targeted boys. Magazines, films, and books at the time also focused on young males being the creators and consumers of tech, so the narrative shifted away from female programmers and focused almost entirely on men. And this was around the same time that the field saw a significant decline in the number of women taking courses in computer science.

But I knew that if more people learned these stories, they would be inspired too—and that by sharing them, we might have a better chance of changing the face of tech, in terms of its history, as well as its future. And these stories deserve to be told, so I decided to include some of them in this book. In *Female Innovators at Work*, I interviewed twenty inspiring women in tech; some just starting out but many with years of experience behind them. All are stories of women innovating. Each woman tells a different story about her personal journey, but there are some commonalities that are fascinating.

The first trait I found true for all was the unwavering grit and determination to succeed, often a trait built upon from childhood. Most would argue that all entrepreneurs share this trait—and they would be right. But what I find especially fascinating are the struggles that these women faced and how they used adversity to rise above it all. This includes Brenda Romero, who having been ostracized by her peers as a teen, decided to always "be one better." And Ramona Pierson, who came back from death's door to prove wrong the doctors who said she'd never thrive; she did just that and far more. And Judith Klein, whose father, an Auschwitz survivor, told her, "As a Jew, you must do even better than everyone else if you mean to get anywhere." These women had a steely determination to make it, no matter what.

Another interesting commonality is how mission-led many of the startups are. This leads me to believe that with women at the helm, we will see an increasing number of tech-for-social-good businesses, which is something the world needs more of right now. Examples in this book include Majora Carter, who founded StartUp Box to both empower and improve the opportunities for young people in low-status communities such as her own, in South Bronx, New York. And Yasmine Mustafa, a refugee who fled Saddam Hussein's regime in the 1990s and later founded ROAR for Good after learning her neighbor was raped on her doorstep in Philadelphia. And Judith Owigar, who both set up two organizations: AkiraChix to encourage more women into tech in Kenya, and JuaKali to change the face of manual labor. And Gwynne Shotwell, who is working with Elon Musk to realize a shared vision to save humanity and colonize Mars.

So why tell these stories now? The simple answer is because they should have been told already. The longer answer is that as the advancement of technology continues at an exponential rate, it has become necessary for our tech workforce to be as diverse as those it is being built for. The industry requires more skilled technologists, with different backgrounds and experiences, to take on the ever-increasing roles being created. And consumers and companies need a diverse range of workers building solutions for all.

In 2015, Intel pledged a $300 million budget to a "Diversity in Technology" initiative that aims to tackle both its own workforce diversity, as well as that of the tech industry in general. And they are not the only technology company looking to make a change. Facebook, Google, and other major players are also stepping up. They understand that it is the diverse workforces of tomorrow that will help shape the future of innovation and drive the next revolution.

And tech's ability to empower and drive change makes it the perfect field for female innovators to lead in order to create a better world. So I hope that the stories inside this book inspire, inform, and encourage the next generation of women in tech. Because tech needs you. It needs all of us.

As you read, please dive in, dig deep, and allow these stories to inspire you on your own journey. As women, there has never been a better time to stand up and to finally be counted.

Lynda Weinman

Cofounder, Lynda.com

A pioneer of online education, Lynda Weinman cofounded Lynda.com, one of the first and leading online learning platforms, with her husband and business partner, Bruce Heavin, in 1995.

Following the success of her early best-selling web design books, which included the first-ever industry book, Designing Web Graphics (Pearson Indiana, 1996), Lynda set up a school with Bruce before identifying a gap in the market for classes being taught via online tutorials, which became Lynda.com. The subscription business has since grown to host more than 250,000 tutorials, reaching more than 4 million learners looking to improve their business, creative, and technology skills. In 2015, Lynda.com was acquired by LinkedIn for $1.5 billion.

Danielle Newnham: Can you tell me about your background? What was your childhood like and how did it shape you as an entrepreneur?

Lynda Weinman: My mother says I was precocious, which I think just means I was curious. I was active and interested in things. I also had a very tough childhood because my parents split up when I was three and it was an acrimonious divorce. I was the oldest, so I felt responsible for my siblings and was kind of caught in the middle. I was maybe the most aware of what was happening, so whilst it was a blessing to be the oldest, it was maybe the beginning of when I started to become responsible for other people. When you run a company, part of what you are taking on is the responsibility of other people's lives or livelihoods, customer's experiences, and so on. There's a big element of willing to be responsible for others involved, and so I can see that that was shaped very early on.

© Danielle Newnham 2016
D. Newnham, *Female Innovators at Work*, DOI 10.1007/978-1-4842-2364-2_1

Also, I didn't really have any parental support because my parents were involved in their own frustrations and they weren't very attentive. At a certain point, I actually lived with my grandparents for a period. They didn't want me and my brother and sister to live with them so there was a lot of turmoil when I was young and I didn't feel I had security around me. So I think that made me fiercely independent, which was also a positive trait in business, despite being painful as a young person.

Newnham: And what was school like? I have read many people close to you say that you were always an educator and a great teacher.

Weinman: Well, I was a straight-A student until things got really tough at home. I moved in with my grandparents when I was in Kindergarten and first grade. I had loved school and did really well, but then my home life started to deteriorate. For instance, when we moved from my grandparents into my dad's place with my stepmother, my stepmother made it obvious that she didn't sign up for raising us, so it definitely felt as though my brother, sister and I were not wanted. And as I got more developed, that became more painful to me. So I started to disconnect from school, and by the time I was in junior high, I was getting Cs and Ds when I had formerly been a straight-A student. I just didn't care anymore.

Then when I was in junior high, I read a book titled Summerhill [by A. S. Neill and Albert Lamb (Penguin Books, 1960)]. It was about a different kind of school that gave students responsibility for their own learning. It was more to foster self-motivation and critical thinking while putting the trust in the student and allowing students to craft their own curriculum. If someone wasn't interested in math, the idea was that there is no point in making them take a lot of math classes. It was a very different philosophy to public education, which is one size fits all and everyone should be good in every subject.

So I was fortunate and determined. I found a local progressive high school that was based on some of the principles of Summerhill. I also had a part-time job at a hotdog stand earning minimum wage, which was about $80 a month, so I convinced the headmaster to let me go to his school on my hotdog income.

Newnham: How old were you then?

Weinman: I was fifteen. And I was the only kid who went to this private high school and was paying for it myself. And then I went on to The Evergreen State College, which is also a progressive liberal arts college and based on a lot of the same ideas. You can create your own curriculum, you have student/teacher evaluations, and there are no grades. There were also interdisciplinary programs so if you were studying art, history, philosophy, and math, it might be interrelated. And everybody was in one group and talking about the interrelationships of subjects so I was incredibly fortunate to have that kind of education.

I was already a more responsible and self-motivated person than most, but, on top of that, I was really more desperate than others because I didn't have a family system to give me security.

Around the same time, which I think is pivotal in my story, is that I took a women's study class in high school right at the dawn of feminism. It was when Ms. magazine started and books were being published about feminism, which exposed me to the idea that I had been selling myself short in terms of what I could be. I could learn anything and I could be anything, but it was really up to me to decide what it was that spoke to my talents and my interests. It was okay to follow your own compass. And I don't think many people are taught that therefore it only becomes a realization much later in life. So I felt I really had a huge advantage, in a way, by having a really tough childhood. And also having had this experience with progressive education, which greatly shaped our company and the future of my own teaching style, and my interest in learning and helping people.

Newnham: What was your first job out of school?

Weinman: I actually fell into my first job out of college, which was a manager of and buyer for a little gift store. When I was twenty-three years old, I convinced my grandfather to give me money to start a store. I owned the store for about four years. I ended up losing all his money.

Newnham: Was it a lot?

Weinman: It was $20,000, which isn't much today but back in the early 1980s, that was a lot of money. I felt like it was the worst failure of my life and I would never want to own a company again. But, from there, I started doing things on my own. I had been buying a lot of clothes, shoes, and jewelry when I was the store buyer, so when I closed my store after four years, I started my own little clothing company. It was a wholesale business.

My boyfriend at the time had worked on the Star Wars movie. He was a CalArts student. George Lucas had hired all these CalArts students to work on Star Wars, and many of them ended up starting their own studios. And being at the very beginning of special effects, and because he was my boyfriend, I was helping him out. I started to learn how to operate the camera for him and then I realized that it was better pay than what I was doing selling my clothing, so I fell into special effects. I went off on my own and I eventually became a camera operator. And then I became a director. And then I was creating the special effects and filming them. I realized that because of my background and education, I could teach myself things and I could pivot and change direction really easily if I were open to learning new things and being quick on my feet. I was also always a good communicator and good at helping other people, and so I think that's one way that I made myself important—made myself wanted.

So I ended up working in special effects for about four years. That was right at the dawn of the personal computer, and in 1982, when the same boyfriend had bought an Apple II Plus, that was my first exposure to computers. He was really mad at me because I wasn't that excited about the purchase. To please him, I opened up the manual and I realized it was written for engineers, not for people. And so I just started teaching myself and got super passionate about it. Back in the very beginning when computers were new, it was a very unusual and exotic thing to be using a personal computer so I was really there at the beginning of personal computers and saw their potential early on.

Then I stumbled across the Mac in 1984 and my mind was blown. It was really the first good graphical user interface and so much fun. It was whimsical and I knew I had to have one.

Newnham: Fast-forward to starting Lynda.com. Can you tell me about how it began?

Weinman: I was a teacher at numerous colleges in Los Angeles, teaching what I would call digital arts: imaging and things like Photoshop, motion graphics, moving imagery on the computer, 3D and so on. I was starting to get teaching assignments and a lot of them were extension colleges for adult learning. Students did get credits but you didn't have to apply to be admitted and so it was more casual learning.

So I was teaching at American Film Institute, UCLA Extension, and the Art Center College of Design, and I was primarily teaching art students whose majors were film, product design, interactive design, graphic design, and photography. It was the late 1980s, so it was right at the dawn of the computer age when most people didn't use computers. For arts students, a computer background wasn't necessarily what was expected of them. In fact, it was a very new idea that artists would use computers.

Then around 1994 or 1995, I was still teaching at ArtCenter when I first saw the web and thought how fantastic this was going to be for my arts students because I could see how they could put their portfolios online as opposed to having to carry them around. And I thought about the new jobs my students would work on such as designing web pages as opposed to brochures.

I didn't know anything about web design but I was self-taught at computer graphics and everything else because it was so early on that there just weren't any other ways to learn it. I taught myself all about web design and realized that there was no good book on the subject. There were books on programming and HTML, but not on doing graphics and media. So I wrote a book that ended up really becoming the first book on web design for what I call "mere mortals," i.e., not computer scientists. The book had a slow start because the field was so new, but within about six months, it was clear that it was doing well. It went into multiple reprintings and became a best-seller.

The book ended up giving me my first exposure to passive income. I had always worked for every dollar I earned, so it was my first exposure to income where you make something once, but it can sell multiple times and so you earn more for no extra effort. And it blew my mind because I realized that I had the potential to write more books and reach a much larger audience than I was reaching as a college teacher.

The book was selling well which really encouraged me and my husband. He was an illustrator and doing a lot of magazine illustrations with clients all over the country. So we realized, "Maybe I can write books and he can continue his illustration career but we could live in a more peaceful place than Los Angeles." So we found a place in this idyllic little town called Ojai, California—population 8,000—and I left my position at ArtCenter and decided to devote full time to writing books.

But what happened was I ended up really missing face-to-face teaching, so my husband had this idea to rent a local high school with a computer lab over spring break and put an ad on Lynda.com, which was the URL for the book I had written. And the class did really well. We even had one person who came all the way from Vienna, Austria. People came from all over and it shocked us. It was the power of the Internet, which we all know now is a global platform. So it actually gave us the encouragement to start a physical school which was amazing. In the first year, it did so well that we were able to hire staff. We were making more money than we ever expected to and the books were selling really well and were feeding into the classroom.

We first called the school Ojai Digital Arts Center, but people knew the website as Lynda.com and everybody just called it Lynda.com anyway, so eventually we caved in and decided that's what we would call the business. Then the school continued and grew pretty large. We had thirty-five employees, sold-out classes, two different classrooms, and people coming from all over the world, including the Vatican. It was kind of mind blowing that every week, we would have someone come in from overseas.

In the beginning, it was me doing the teaching, and then my husband, Bruce, began teaching too. He started teaching the things he knew such as photography and design, and the demand for what we did just kept getting bigger and bigger. Bruce then pushed the idea of bringing on other teachers so it quickly went from me as an individual contributor, someone who wanted to teach and write, to me owning a publishing platform and a school that was bringing in a lot of other teachers. It opened me up to a teaching community, of which I had not been aware.

So the school was thriving, but then some bad things happened such as the dot-com crash and a rather severe downturn in our economy. And then there were the terrorist attacks on the twin towers, so people stopped flying. And all of those factors naturally impacted our face-to-face business.

But I had already started to make videos of lessons mainly because I had wanted to write a book on Photoshop for the web but my publisher had been against it because several other books had already been written on the topic of Photoshop so I had ended up making a video instead.

So enrollment in our school dropped off during this period of financial uncertainty and it hurt us very badly. So we decided to close the school and instead put our video lessons online. And we charged an online subscription of $25 a month. I think this was the start of 2002.

Newnham: What was the eLearning market like back then? Was anyone else offering a similar service?

Weinman: There was one other company, also charging $25 a month and they had a lot more traction than we did. But there were very few people in this space. There might have been more in different disciplines but in the technology world, there were very few. There were a lot of video companies who were doing videotape lessons and selling the videos like we were, but very few had moved online because that was still pretty early in online history. It was before broadband and sites like YouTube.

Newnham: Can you remember what the numbers were for your first year?

Weinman: Yes, it was very small and it disappointed us. In fact, we were not sure this business was going to work at all. Thirty people subscribed the first month and we were up to one thousand by the end of the year. My husband and I were actually talking about this recently when we were discussing the movie The Big Short. It's a story of people who saw a pattern. A few investors saw a dangerous pattern in the housing market that nobody else saw or believed in. Everybody had data to support that the housing market was strong but there were people who were quizzical enough and smart enough to spot that actually there was a really big weakness here. And, looking back on it now, just like that movie, I think my husband saw potential in what we were doing online when perhaps others didn't.

So we were disappointed but, if you think about it now, going from thirty to one thousand is a very big jump. It was generating $100,000 or so at the end of that first year, which is not small, but that seemed insignificant to us then because our other lines of business were already in the multi-millions—the book, business, and the school. Online was cannibalizing our existing CD and video sales because we were charging $150 for a single course and online was $25 per month for unlimited courses.

So my husband actually saw the growth as positive and by the second year, it was at two thousand subscribers. We had doubled and that was a wonderful growth rate. What company wouldn't want to double every year? But it was still a small amount of revenue and a small amount of membership compared to other subscription services that we felt we were competing with. So we didn't see it as a big line of business until about four years in. Looking back of course, the growth was actually exponential. It doubled each year, so two thousand, to four thousand, to eight thousand subscribers, and once it was eight thousand, it started to be a significant revenue driver. It still wasn't as significant as other lines, but it was enough to really be encouraging. And by year six or seven, it was a freight train because it just kept doubling.

Newnham: In terms of retention, how did you keep customers coming back? And what did you struggle with?

Weinman: Well, part of what I say to new entrepreneurs is that you have to get market validation—that what you are doing actually has value to people. And we had market validation in that we had a best-selling book. People liked the way we taught. My signature style for teaching was a lot of hand-holding, a lot of explaining, and a lot of demystifying technology. And that ended up being a very popular approach, whereas a lot of other technology writers were burying people in jargon and being more like the "guru" expert. I was more like your friend, Lynda. I was on a first-name basis. I'm friendly, and my books are friendly. And this was the same way we taught our classes, and why people loved our school, and why our school grew so well, and why we were sold out and had to hire other teachers.

So we had a lot of market validation. It was the same thing with our videos— people loved our teaching style, so really our retention was down to having a great product that people loved. It wasn't any more scientific than that.

In terms of challenges… There were questions we had to solve. How do we make the online video stream? How do we make the website have the right look and feel? And how do we have the right information? There was also the challenge of how to expand and scale. And what kind of new team we needed to bring in in order to do this.

There's always this tension where you have existing people who are really wonderful and loyal, and they learn on the job. And then you need to bring in people who have more experience, who have scaled companies before and done production before. And you need an HR department all of a sudden, and a finance department. And when you grow and grow, you find you get this person with an MBA you didn't know you needed, or wanted, because it's just part of growing a successful company. You need all these different disciplines and departments. And then you have to introduce hierarchy, and you have to have people reporting to other people, and then you have to have performance reviews, and every one of these things is a struggle and every one of these things is a new learning curve and a potential tension that you are interjecting into your formula.

Newnham: Was it always your mission to grow it into a big company?

Weinman: In the beginning, I never dreamed it would be big. It was kind of amazing to me when we had thirty-five employees. I just couldn't believe that. And then we started to realize we had a freight train. We didn't just have a successful company that was profitable and growing at a really nice clip, but we had a freight train that had unbelievable potential. I still believe to this day that there isn't a person of age who can learn the types of things we teach who wouldn't benefit from our service. So that's a big demographic.

Saying that, we did have a moment of reckoning where we could have stayed a mom-and-pop company or really take this tiger by the tail and ride it where it's supposed to go. I think we were scared but we felt like we were the right people and that we could get more of the right people around us and we could figure it out. We knew that we had the right vision—that's what we always felt very confident about. We understood how to teach in this very approachable and nurturing way, and we knew how to scale that idea. We knew how to pick great teachers and we knew how to pick the right subjects. We were industry insiders with a real concern for the learner whereas a lot of our competitors were not in it for all those reasons. So we had a really good competitive edge and a good vision for what we wanted to do.

Newnham: At some point, you started to get people interested in buying the company. Did you start conversations with investors at this point?

Weinman: No, we did not. We were so naïve. If you really think about our timing, we were at the very beginning of the dot-com boom when I wrote the book. A lot of our customers who were coming to the school were getting this new thing called venture capital [VC] funding. We had already self-funded our company and been profitable. We funded it with royalties from my first book and with $20,000 investment, and by month two, we had already paid ourselves back.

We were profitable within the first year and so we didn't really need startup money, and we also didn't know we could get it. It wasn't even in our vernacular. About ten or twelve years in, we hit the $10 million annual revenue mark and that's really when we started getting calls.

There are two types of investors—high-growth company investors and startup investors, and we were well past the startup stage. Nobody came to us wanting to invest in us until we hit the high-growth stage number, which is $10 million. That is when investors started coming out of the woodwork. We were very confused about whether to accept an offer or not. They were trying to tempt us with money that we could take off the table for ourselves, so I think it was at that point that we courted an early investor. They thought we were worth $80 million and wanted to put $20 million in. They wanted $10 million of it to go to me and Bruce personally, and of course, we had never had $10 million, so that was a huge amount of money to us.

We thought about it and we thought, what do you trade for that $10 million? And what will we do with the other $10 million that we will put in the bank? Financially, we are fine. We have enough money to afford a nice car and have a nice home, and we don't really feel like we need that money in our life at this moment. It's not worth the trade-off of having someone counting down to when you're going to sell, or go public, or whatever you are going to do with your exit. You know, we really didn't build it to leave it. We built it as a lifestyle choice. This was our passion to teach these subjects, and to be sustainable and bring on other teachers. It felt really good doing that. So we said no.

One thing I didn't tell you about our business model, which I think is key, is not only did we charge a subscription service but we paid royalties, much like you would get with books. So a lot of our instructors were making more money with us than they were making writing books, or teaching, or speaking, or any other part of their career. So we started to get a lot of really loyal contributors to our subscription service. And, to this day, if you go on to Lynda.com, you'll see some of the teachers have taught hundreds of courses and those are the teachers you can guarantee are making their living doing that. So that makes me really proud because, and I don't mean to call out names, but The Huffington Post sold for, I think $150 million, and didn't pay a single contributor. So I'm really proud that we have always had this business model where everybody wins. Our customers would win, we would win, and our contributors would win—and I think that is the perfect business.

Newnham: Looking back, what were some of the highlights of building your business? What milestones particularly stood out?

Weinman: Well, in the beginning, we would have a cake every time we got one thousand extra subscribers, but then we started having too many cakes. Then at one hundred thousand, we took the entire company—and at that time, it was a couple of hundred people—to Disneyland with their families, and that was a really beautiful celebration. Every year we would have amazing parties. We were privately held so we really invested a lot back into our company.

But once we did take on an investor, it got more difficult because you're then being scrutinized for your bottom line. We were always profitable but we were also reinvesting our profits, and so that got a lot trickier once, eighteen years in, we took on investors. And that was really disheartening to Bruce and I because one of the joys of the business was that we could reward people. I used to always say, "If you don't reward people in good times, when are you going to reward them?"

We were very benevolent employers. We didn't offer options, like a lot of the dot-coms, but we offered great salaries and great benefits, and so employees truly were on board for the right reasons. They didn't need the options to buy into the mission and enjoy working for us. I would often hear, "If I won the lottery tomorrow, I would still want to come in and work here because I love working here." There was a period, probably the first fifteen or sixteen years, where I could count on one hand the number of people that had left voluntarily. It was usually because their spouse was moving or because they wanted to change careers. It was never because they were unhappy with the work environment. That is something to be very proud of. We built a company that treats its employees right and its customers right, and cares about its product.

Unfortunately, we are in this very capitalistic structure where all of the businesses that do go public or do have investors have to show growth. And if you don't grow the amount you say you are going to grow, you're penalized. It's all about the growth, growth, growth. But sometimes you have to invest in yourselves to grow. It's not just that you are showing profit, it's that you are putting your money where it needs to go to be proactive about a future. And that is something that unfortunately, most businesses, at least in the US, are very short-sighted about.

Newnham: So why did you take it on and what was the result of doing so?

Weinman: It was an interesting moment. We were virtually being ignored by the business press because they didn't know we existed. And while massive open online courses [MOOCs] were appearing on the cover of TIME magazine, what we were doing wasn't getting any attention at all. So partly, we were naïve because we thought that if we took on the money, then that would make news which would be good for us. It did make news, but it made the wrong kind of news in terms of increasing our subscriber base. It made the kind of news that raises all the investors' eyebrows and makes everyone want to invest in you, and scrutinize your performance. But it didn't have much impact on our subscription numbers.

Also, I think I was fifty-eight years old when I said to Bruce, "You know, by the time I am sixty-five, I would like to have another chapter." I felt like all the people who helped us build this are only going to be rewarded if we do have an exit. So this was another reason to take on investment. We knew the company was already more valuable than its revenue because that had been established a long time ago, so it was a way to reward all the people who helped build it, reward ourselves, and be able to have the next chapter. And we knew that we had the pick of the crop in terms of investors because people were just banging our door down by then. So that was the decision. And an exit ended up happening faster than we thought, as eighteen months later, LinkedIn offered to buy us.

The real challenge then came for us as founders because we had been in charge. We weren't just the lame-duck founders—we really were the vision of the company. And it wasn't really the investor who caused a shift in the way the company was being run to be honest, it was internal. We had people who were getting options—the new high-end executives that we had recruited because we had had investment. We had been able to get a really high-end chief technology officer, a really high-end financial officer, and a really high-end marketing officer. All of those people who were coming in were getting options, and they were all about the exit. They were not necessarily with our philosophy of investing in and treating people right, and the wonderful, loving, very family-orientated company we had built.

I think where they saw their responsibility was to the investors. And they saw their responsibility was to have as good an exit as we could possibly have, which we were not opposed to having but some executives wanted more autonomy. They didn't want to have to report in to the founders. They didn't want to have the rules that we had set in place or the values that we had set in place, and that was incredibly painful for us. It was naïve of us but we didn't expect it and we really felt pushed out.

Ultimately, it was a real slap in the face. And so the end of our time there wasn't very happy, but I think by the time LinkedIn offered to buy us, it was sort of a relief. "Okay, we don't have to be part of this whole political thing anymore." We didn't have MBAs and we didn't know how to get investors. We didn't know a lot of things, but we worked on our own nickel. And we learned through our own blood, sweat, and tears and built something we were really proud of, which I think is rare.

Newnham: I think it's also the reason you did so well. I have spoken to lots of entrepreneurs with similar experience, or who got bought out and then had to go work in the new company.

Weinman: Well, that was really a blessing because the deal was very clean. LinkedIn didn't want the founders. They didn't want any of the key executives. They wanted to put all their own executives in and they have a different vision for it which is their right because they purchased us.

And I have to say I am very proud of the dollar figure—one of forty-five unicorns last year, out of how many millions of businesses. So it's a big deal and probably one of the very few women-owned companies that was a unicorn. So I am happy about the financial outcome but I don't think, personally, that we had to get there the way we did. But that's my opinion. The reality is that it happened the way it happened. And there are probably some people that I am not ever looking forward to talking to again and other people that I am going to be lifelong friends with, and that's normal I think.

Newnham: Touching on what you just said about being a female-owned unicorn, how did you find being not only a woman in tech but a woman running a very successful business in tech? Did you ever feel overlooked?

Weinman: I think I was overlooked by the business press completely, but I was beloved by our employees, I know that. I feel their love to this minute. When I would speak at events, people definitely gave me a lot of respect. But I think the business press virtually ignored me. I mean, the sale wasn't even a big story, and to be honest, even LinkedIn didn't really consult with us. Very little interaction. They had their own idea, which I love, which I think is great. But I just question, if it were Mark Zuckerberg instead of me, would you not talk to Mark Zuckerberg?

So did I feel overlooked? Yes, I felt overlooked. I would like to have passed on to LinkedIn why I did things the way I did, and what I cared about and why, and some of the lessons we learned. If I were going to buy a company, I would want to know those things from the founders. Especially founders who were loved by their customers, staff, and contributors. That stung, but that's business sometimes. And to your point, a blessing to us in that it's hard to watch someone else run things and not have true control.

Newnham: In terms of the lack of press you received, were you selling in stories whilst running Lynda.com and you felt they ignored you?

Weinman: Absolutely. We went through marketing person after marketing person to try and get the stories told. And even the learning stories, which are beautiful stories such as the janitor who works at a school and the school gets a site-wide license so he teaches himself how to do web design and moves from being a janitor to being on their web design team. That's a great story.

I just don't think the press has respect for the fact that we have to show examples of female entrepreneurs. I mean, this is the reason I am speaking to you because I don't need fame and I don't need fortune. I don't have time. I have no platform at this point.

I am enjoying my moment of taking a break and I will come up with some more firm direction at some point, but there's no gun to my head to do anything. But I do feel it should have been more celebrated at the end and it should have been more celebrated along the way. Even the fact that our company had over a $100 million in revenue a year should have been celebrated—there are not a lot of companies that even have that kind of revenue, let alone which are women-led.

And like I said, at this point, it's not important to my ego. It was never actually important to my ego, but it is important because I think you do have to show examples. You can't expect change without celebrating the innovators.

Newnham: Lynda, this is the exact reason I am doing this book.

Weinman: I know.

Newnham: It always riles me that on International Women's Day, the press will all come out with their quotes from great women. But it can't just be one day, it needs to be all year round.

Weinman: Yes. I will tell you two nice things. Gloria Steinem wrote to me when I sold the company, because we know each other, and she said, "You know, Lynda. I have known a lot of successful women in my day but you achieved your success through not hurting the environment, not taking advantage of people, putting something positive into the world, and I have celebrated a lot of successes, but never with a b [billion] after it." And you know, I was really touched by that. And Sheryl Sandberg wrote to me.

Newnham: Looking back on your career, is there anything you would have done differently?

Weinman: I think one realization is that I didn't know enough about business. We hired a chief executive officer [CEO] about twelve years in, and he was so wonderful to us and such a great, amazing partner, and I loved working with him. But when the investors came in, our relationship changed. I think he felt beholden to the investors, not beholden to us, and that's when I realized that a CEO has more power than anyone else in the entire company when it comes to decision making. Had I gone to business school, I would have known that and I would never let anyone else have that position.

To me, the title didn't matter because I wasn't CEO for my ego. I just wanted to make a great company. Our CEO had so much more business experience than me and did such an amazing job, so I am really not trying to be disparaging about him whatsoever, but I think understanding that the CEO has more power than the majority shareholder, more power than the executive chair of the company, and more power than any investor, was news to me.

Newnham: Your courses allow people to find their passion. What's yours?

Weinman: I'm very passionate about the arts, education, film, women's rights, and feminism, so I am going to be doing something in one of those spaces.

Newnham: What advice do you have for female entrepreneurs today?

Weinman: I never thought of myself as a female entrepreneur specifically. I just thought of myself as an entrepreneur. I think I had some advantages, as a woman, and I think I had some disadvantages, but I think you should develop your own confidence. Mine grew and grew as I became more successful. I heard that saying, "Fake it until you make it" and I lived by that idea my entire career. I tried things that were uncomfortable and did things I didn't feel totally qualified to do, but I just acted like I did and that was key. And I would say that you don't take prisoners. You don't take no for an answer. You just do what it is you are supposed to do and figure out a way.

I have always been a problem solver and my husband is an incredible problem solver. When things don't work out, you find another way. So I would say that when you have something to say and something you want to do, don't let anybody stop you.

Also be realistic. I see a lot of people who just think that sheer force is going to put a square peg into a round hole. One of the real lessons from Lynda.com was to get market validation and know when you have a product that people want. It's not just your passion you're trying to push to other people but that you have something of value to others that they will respect and will want. And I think that applies to any entrepreneur—male or female.

Arlene Harris

Cofounder, Wrethink

*Known as the "First Lady of Wireless," **Arlene Harris** is a serial entrepreneur, advisor, investor, inventor, and wireless pioneer.*

Having been introduced to the wireless communications industry at the age of five, when she started helping in her father's mobile telephone company, Arlene officially joined the business at twelve, and over the following six decades, she has cofounded numerous businesses in this space, driving huge innovation in both mobile services and systems technologies. Arlene cofounded many of these ventures with her husband, Marty Cooper, the renowned "father of the cell phone." Their first venture was Cellular Business Systems, Inc. (CBSI) in 1983, which quickly dominated the cellular billing industry with 75 percent market share of the scrappy non-telephone company players. In 1986, CBSI was sold to Cincinnati Bell.

Arlene is a pioneer of early cellular standards and holds many wireless communications patents. Among her many accolades, Arlene was the first woman inducted into the Wireless Hall of Fame in 2007. She is also the business developer of the SOS phone service and the inventor of the award-winning Jitterbug phone; the latter was created for seniors and is sold by Samsung.

Arlene's latest venture is Wrethink, a multifunctional device that can scan and store documents, make video calls, and manage family activities.

Danielle Newnham: Can you tell me about your background and your introduction to tech?

© Danielle Newnham 2016
D. Newnham, *Female Innovators at Work*, DOI 10.1007/978-1-4842-2364-2_2

Arlene Harris: Well I grew up in Los Angeles. My father was an electrical contractor and some time when I was very young, he took an interest in radio communications with his trucks, and so that was really the beginning of my exposure to wireless communications. I was under five years old when he started that business. I had two older brothers and we all ended up working in the family business.

Newnham: Looking back, Was it obvious that you would end up running your own business?

Harris: What I would say was that it was obvious from a pretty young age that I had an interest or at least I had an ability to have some leadership skills. I don't know if they were natural. I had my first financial transaction, which might have led to me thinking I have an entrepreneurial edge, when I bought and sold my first car. I bought a car from a friend when I was fifteen—I had been working for money for my parents since I was twelve. I was actually working nights, weekends, and holidays. I bought a car for around $1,200 and sold it for around $1,500. So that was the first time I recall such a transaction.

My family was in and out of financial resources, so it was not a silver spoon upbringing for sure. My dad was a contractor. He was a real fighter and he had a really good strategic sense about how to invest in the future of technology. An example of that was in the 1950s. He made a move to put antennas way up on very high mountain tops around Los Angeles, which was a very visionary thing to do. It was very hard to get to the sites. He was very smart in doing that and doing the things that were hard to do but that gave us radio telephone coverage areas—this was way before cellular. It was around thirty years before cellular but by doing it, he gave us coverage areas that would allow him to give his customers a much bigger and better service.

But it was a rough upbringing. My brothers were tough, my father was tough, my mother was sweet, loving, and supportive, but it was a risk-reward loss environment. It was a pendulum that swung pretty far to the left and pretty far to the right from an economic standpoint.

Newnham: And then your family sold the business?

Harris: Yes, it was 1983, which was a really important year. It was the year of the first cellular system going live in the States. Chicago, which turned on in October of that year. We sold our business in January of 1983, and one of the reasons we sold it was because cellular was coming and was going to require really big risks to be taken. My father was already in his late sixties and the business had always been an environment that was fraught with argument and lots of conflict between my dad; not only as a business but with my brothers, which was not unusual for a family businesses. But when cellular came along, and we got a substantial offer... In fact, a couple of companies were trying to buy our positioning because the companies that were in a position to be licensees of cellular services primarily included the companies like my family's company. We not only had mobile telephone services from the 1950s but also paging services that were primarily started in the early 1970s.

The paging industry that pre-dated cellular had almost been a telescope to the future because of the nature of what was being managed and how the businesses were being executed. Paging companies were clearly preparing the industry and the area of communications that we were in—it wasn't called wireless then—to become the future cellular operators, which is what happened. That period in 1983, the first cellular systems went live. And for the next twenty years, there were cellular systems being built all over the United States, and of course, elsewhere that had similar characteristics to the paging and mobile telephone businesses that we had run before that. And all in competition with powerful telephone companies, by the way.

Newnham: I wanted to ask about when you met Marty and when you set up Cellular Business Systems. That was also in 1983, wasn't it?

Harris: Yes. So Metromedia bought our family business in LA and I had met Marty several years earlier when he was promoting cellular at Motorola. Then, right about the time that the industry got ready to launch, we sold our business and he left Motorola. So we joined together to start a cellular carrier management company, which was Cellular Business Systems. And we did that with another partner—a fellow by the name of Russ Shields. He had a software company and he wanted to join with us to create a new service bureau-type company that would serve wireless deployment to cellular. We sold that business to Cincinnati Bell in 1986.

Newnham: Was it always your plan to sell the business?

Harris: That's a good question. Probably not as soon as we did but there was a consolidation that went on. Cincinnati Bell had bought one of the other billing companies and we had had the most success at attracting what was called the non-wireline, or the companies that got cellular licenses that were not telephone companies. And so we were the most successful at signing them up for billing and customer service systems.

Cincinnati went on a buying plan that included us. And I would say that had we not sold, we would have probably done infinitely better than we did, but Marty and I decided that we were ready to make a change, so we did.

Newnham: The business was successful, but what were some of the obstacles that you faced?

Harris: Probably the biggest one was our financial partners. Financing in all of the businesses that I have been in has always been the most difficult issue. The banking industry was going through some really tough times in '83 and in '84 and '85. And our financial partner was a bank, so our methods of getting financing were such that it gave them a great amount of leverage. They then became unwilling to finance us and also unwilling to let us find finance elsewhere in order to grow properly, so we were really in trouble. You needed money to grow and to put down your roots in the business. And they just simply decided that—for regulatory issues and political reasons inside the company—they were pretty much unwilling to keep investing. They weren't going to let us find additional financing. So financing, in that case, was the biggest obstacle for us.

In fact, financing, in my view, throughout my entire career has always been the difficulty in the businesses that I have been involved with, and that's true up to what I am doing now. When you are doing things that have never been done before, it's hard to find financing. And back then, which is hard to imagine for someone young enough, but for these types of technological businesses, there was no such thing as real venture capital. You could get strategic investment but startups… When you talk about startups today, most people know the definition of a startup, but back then, most businesses went into business to stay in business, like my father when he started his. It's a family business. You start a business, you go to the bank, you borrow money, and you grow slowly.

Well, in the cellular world, you couldn't grow slowly, and you couldn't finance it yourself because there were millions and millions of dollars that had to be invested just to get things going before you could turn on the first customer. So all the businesses that were growing up around cellular, if they were going to scale rapidly, they couldn't be built like the family business is built. That's the way most businesses were built throughout history, but starting with the technological revolution, things changed. Now there were people starting to build businesses with the idea that they would sell them. Of course back then, the idea that you would sell usually meant, "We're going to build our business and take it public someday." It's going to get big enough to take public but the financing path to do that was very, very uncertain. You just didn't do that back then.

I mean, there were a few venture capital firms back then, but they were very wary that the dogs weren't going to eat the dog food. The projections for the number of cellular subscribers were certainly not what they eventually became, because consumerization of cellular didn't start until the 1990s. Prior to that, it was almost all commercial, so financing for doing anything new, even today, is still hard for companies who need to spend a lot more than they can spend just using friends' and family's money.

Newnham: Do you think that being a woman had any influence on how hard it was to raise money?

Harris: I believe that being a woman in any kind of business that requires competence that men aspire to is problematic. Today, that is still the case. You have to look at the field, whether it's automotive, or oil and gas, or technology. Any place where men aspire, it's very hard for women.

It's part of the reason it's been so important for me to make sure that I have gotten alignment on my vision with men, because today I still can sit in a room with someone who is calling on me and they will address the men in the room, rather than me. It's always been an issue.

Newnham: You recognized early on the importance of automation and computing. Did you realize how ahead of the times you were?

Harris: Thankfully, I had a stretch at an airline for about three or four years between two stints working at my family business. And when I was in that industry, I was right in the middle of a marketing job, and sales and so on, where we were scaling the airline for the wide-bodied airplanes. That meant there was an enormous amount of automation going on, so I got a really good education in the power of automation, computing, and organizing, and the rendering of the data and the methods by which computers can be used to streamline operation. So, when I went back to my folks' business, I really had that itch to make sure that if this wireless business was going to scale, that we were prepared for it and that we weren't going to end up having to hire a hundred people to do what computers could do far more efficiently and accurately, especially in terms of making sure that the customers were happy.

But, you know, it's real interesting looking back on how many things we were doing ahead of their time. I will give you an example—when I was commuting between Honolulu and Los Angeles, my roommate and I used a reservation system to do email. This was in 1969. It was all brand-new technology. Reservations were only a few years old. What they did was allow for the central deposit of reservation information in a computer system, and someone else at a CRT [cathode ray tube monitor] someplace else in the airline's system, totally geographically removed, could go in and withdraw that reservation and look at it. Well, in that reservation record, there was something called "remarks" and you could free-flow comments in remarks. So my roommate and I used to pick a reservation, such as Mr. Smith on the fifth of March, on flight so and so, six months out. And we'd book a reservation and then we'd use that reservation to write to each other instantly. Instant communication for messaging between us in a private system like that was unheard of. Well, we didn't know how profound that was.

Then in the early 1970s, we started having words show up in our vocabulary, like "word processing." A vendor would come to visit me to sell me office forms, contracts, and different types of forms that we used in our business, and all of a sudden, he started saying things like, "You can use it in your word processing system." Well, who the hell knew what a word processing system was? But of course, as time went on, we have learned all of this.

When Marty and I started CBSI [Cellular Business Systems Inc.] in 1983, people were barely faxing. You just had no easy way to communicate a document. When I worked for Air Canada briefly, I was still punching tape and mark-sensing

Hollerith cards to make reservations with a machine that you put this card in and it would go "kerchunk," and when you pulled it out, you could tell from what it had "kerchunked"—whether a reservation had been made.

So really, for me, it has been a life of technology moving forward.

Newnham: I wanted to move on to Subscriber Computing and talk about the billing system that you created.

Harris: Yes, when we had Cellular Business Systems, I hired my old engineer from my family's business to build a separate system called Switch Manager, but prior to that, I had put him in business to become a paging billing software company. And then we hired that company for Cellular Business Systems to build what's called "provisioning," which is the function that happens when you go into a phone store and they set you up in the store. Or configuring. They are all elements of provisioning a technological device. And so we built the system to do provisioning using, at that time, very advanced networking software. That system is still running. It's like in its eight-hundredth version, but it survived three or four acquisitions and it is now run by a company called Netcracker, which I believe now owns the residual of the assets that we built at Cellular Business Systems. But that provisioning system was required in order to be able to get throughput for the number of customers that wanted to sign up for cellular service; to properly start their billing, so it's a really important subsystem of the whole challenge of running a wireless network.

Newnham: And how did you come up with it? What led to its creation?

Harris: Well, I had already done that kind of a function in my family's business for provisioning pagers, so I already had that sensibility. When we started Cellular Business Systems, we were working on billing systems that were running on mainframe computers, about which I knew nothing. We ran our paging business on mini computers at my family's business, but the most important thing is not to think about the technology or the kind of computer that you are going to use, but the kind of problems you are trying to solve. And the real problem here was that you need to be able to activate and manage the customers that are coming on to your network.

After we started Cellular Business Systems, I said, "Look, I've got people who know how to do this from my old business, so I am going to go subcontract them to build a provisioning system." This was for cellular, not for paging. Each type of communication systems has a different language and different protocols. In paging, we called the technical address the "capcode," whereas in cellular you called it the ESN [electronic serial number], and to get it working, you had to provision or activate them correctly so they would work on the network. That's why we built Switch Manager.

We finally installed the system in New York at Metro One [Telecommunications Inc.] and they were able to activate cellular customers because we built it into the network, not simply as a separate function that only sat in the carrier switchroom. We built it so that it could be networked. As an example, back then, all the cellular customers who were signed up after their phones were installed in the cars. There were installation facilities all over the city to do that, so these installation facilities would be equipped with computer technology that would allow them to activate those phones from a distance. Well, it turns out the carriers wouldn't let other companies access the network directly but they did use Switch Manager so that they could process multiple simultaneous activations instead of one person in one office, doing one order at a time.

There were orders to activate, orders to cancel, orders for feature changes—a lot of orders going into the system to make it work the way the customers wanted it to work. We began the process that has led to the instant activations you enjoy today in phone stores. So that's what we built, and like I said, that system is still in existence.

Newnham: In the early stages of this technological revolution that you described, it must have been hard to know what customers wanted. How did you know what to work on?

Harris: Well, like so many things in technology, what you needed to understand was what you were connecting to and what the thing that you were connecting to did. You needed to know the capabilities of the devices that you were trying to manage. Once you knew what the capabilities were, then you had to apply business logic, which meant you needed to build a system flexible enough to allow you to set your practices and policies and procedures, which allowed you to manage that piece of equipment, and in Switch Manager's particular case, it was a cellular switch.

The thing that makes your cellular phone work is a big hunk of iron sitting in a switchroom, probably with air conditioning on raised floors with fire retardants, and wires and cables that go out to the outside and put a signal out to an antenna. Phone lines run all over the city bringing in information from a whole bunch of remote cell sites so that switch can actually properly process your transaction when you pick up your phone and make a call.

Whatever that switch is capable of doing, in terms of its functionality for subscriber management, we had to mirror that. We had to know what the commands were, and we had to expose that in another computer system that was hopefully easier to look at, had different, easier screens, and had logic that would allow it to do the things that needed to be done on this switch but doing it from the perspective of a customer service person. Somebody who has business rules to follow and so the systems that we built had to be able to manage the switch, technically, and expose the things that were being managed on the switch in a way that a human could more easily manage them.

And then, you can go on beyond that and you can start taking information from other systems and actually add value, and that progress has been happening for the last forty years.

You're using the information that you got from that system. You're combining it with stuff coming from other systems. Your systems are far more capable of making decisions about what can happen automatically and/or what should be exposed to a person for a person to make a decision. A good example of that is how prepaid works. Prepaid still works in the same way as when we innovated it in the late 1980s. You can mix systems up, and take information and combine it to come up with decisions that get executed by software or by people. For example if the systems didn't know how many minutes you were talking, they wouldn't know that they should turn you off because you just exceeded your credit limit.

The systems that also run prepay come out of that milieu I was just talking about, and billions of people today are using cellular phones because they can prepay for that service. Had we not implemented prepay, had that not been a way of protecting the carriers' revenue streams, the carriers would never have offered it.

The system that we built for provisioning and where we went on to do prepaid and budget management—those applications that sit around what you do when you manage a cellular subscriber do more than just making sure that they can make a call. Those systems sit at the core legacy of some of the important services that came later on. And a lot of that work we did gave me the courage to do workarounds and try and figure out how to solve problems in unique ways. And that's probably my greatest skill—to figure out how to grease the skids for trying to mitigate problems that we have either in the application of the technology or in the way we approach it both technically and as a business proposition.

Either from a political standpoint, or a business function standpoint, we needed to do things that are unique. So that one system that we did, which was provisioning, really was a formative piece of my career. And probably the most important aspect of that is that we unleashed services to billions of subscribers because we decided early on, again at Subscriber Computing, that we were going to allow customers to gas up. They have the ability to buy a phone and use it without having to pass credit screening. And at the time that we did this, credit screening was knocking out about fifty percent of the applicants, so that's probably what I would call the most formative thing that I have done. It set me up thinking, "You know, I know I can solve this problem that can open up opportunity for a lot of others".

The next company we worked on was called Cellular Pay Phone Inc. This is where we actually had Motorola and OKI Electronics build phones that were capable of managing billing by credit card. They actually had a credit card swipe on them. This was my first patent by the way. I should have had many patents throughout my earlier life but we were building systems for ourselves and never thought about intellectual property. But when I got hooked up with Marty as he came out of Motorola, he realized that I was really inventing things.

So my first patented invention was a cellular pay phone system. I got patents for it in the late 1980s, which was the very first over-the-air software-controlled cellular phone. Not one where you push buttons yourself, but where the phone is actually functioning itself to help you use it with your credit card, and again, that had an entire back-end system behind it. It wasn't just a phone. It was licensed to General Telephone [*General Telephone* & Electronics] in '88 or so, and they used it on oil rigs and rental cars, as well as public transport.

Newnham: How did that partnership work? Did you approach GTE?

Harris: No, we actually approached OKI and Motorola, who were friends, and they built the device and we built the systems. Again, it was about combining information that was coming from systems that allowed us to do this. Methods of communicating like TCP/IP [Transmission Control Protocol/Internet Protocol] were nascent or perhaps hadn't been invented yet. They certainly weren't in regular use. Everything that was developed that was communications-based was pretty much a custom. It was very fluid; like the Wild West.

Anyway, we got that done and we licensed it to GTE. The Subscriber Computing business was still going and we did some fraud management that was also switch related. We ended up selling that company to a small public company up in Silicon Valley. That was another case where my partners—the engineer and a fellow I had brought in from Cellular Business Systems to run it—decided that they would rather cash out than continue to try and execute the business because it needed capital. And again, it still wasn't really easy to get money to grow your business.

Newnham: Then a few years later, you came up with the idea for Jitterbug. Can you tell me more about it?

Harris: In the early 1990s, I was on the board of a call center that was doing dispatch. This is where you had an alphanumeric pager and you wanted to get phone calls from anybody, so you called into an operator and you left a message. It sounds a little archaic now, but back then, you didn't have a computer sitting on your desk that you could send a message from like you can today. So they had operators doing transcription. They became interested in trying to do a two-button phone and got into a project with General Motors, General Telephone, and Hughes Network, and so on. But that fell through and the system we worked on became OnStar, which is a big safety system that General Motors runs today where you have emergency service from your car. It's become more prevalent as the years have gone by, but they effectively used us and abused us, and dropped us and did it themselves.

But anyway, we were interested in this notion of safety and there had been a company up in Silicon Valley that tried to build a three-button service, but they ran into money problems and couldn't get financed, so I bought the assets of that company and I combined it with what the call center company was doing. We created something called SOS Wireless Communications—another one fraught with rocky roads. Getting into this wireless business was not for the faint of heart, at any time. We went through severe ups and downs, and finally we had to bankrupt the company in about 2001. Then in 2003 or 2004, I decided that it was time to resurrect it. Even though we had kept the customers on the air through bankruptcy, the company was not growing and we didn't have any product. But with phones getting smaller and smaller, and more featured, I realized that it was time to bring out a brand-new product, which became Jitterbug.

Then Marty had a meeting with the president of Samsung, a fellow by the name of K. T. Lee, who invited us to bring in my idea for a new service to Samsung and see what the phone looked like. They would then decide whether or not they would build it for us, and they did, which was almost a miracle.

Samsung was actually interested in Marty's company's technology. Marty was running a company called ArrayComm, which was doing very smart, advanced signal processing for cellular, so K. T. Lee's people were interested in that technology. The conversation started with that, but he got interested in what became Jitterbug when I told him that I had a business that had been serving senior citizens and that I owned a cellular carrier.

So, Jitterbug basically offered a simple cellular service, primarily targeting the senior population. And GreatCall is the company I started which produced Jitterbug. I had come up with a new design for the phone, new ideas for services that would make it unique, and it took about two years to develop it with Samsung. Then we put our systems in and we converted all of the SOS customers that we still had—we gained about 25,000 SOS customers in the mid-1990s and by the time we went live with GreatCall, I believe we had 6,000 left whom we converted to GreatCall customers.

The reason I bought the cellular carrier I mention was in order to avoid some of the pitfalls that SOS had gone through which included the manufacturer cancelling us when we were about ready to launch the product, four carriers throwing us off their network because they didn't want low-usage customers like ours, and IBM cancelling the chipset that our phones were built on. That's a little short list of the bigger problems that we faced at SOS.

We overcame a lot, but once the manufacturer stopped building our chips and the manufacturer stopped building the product, we pretty much stopped. When we lost a carrier, we found another carrier, and when we lost a manufacturer, we found another manufacturer. The manufacturer that designed our next phone started using a certain chipset, but in the same year, the chipset guy that we were using sold his business to IBM—and IBM decided not to build that chip anymore. So that was kind of the last straw. It was torture for about five years.

Newnham: What was the mission behind GreatCall?

Harris: Just like SOS, the mainstream cellular companies—whether it was Verizon, Sprint, ATT, Carphone, or Vodafone—are after high-volume, high-usage customers that pay them a lot per month, and what that does is eliminate or inhibit the ability of people who don't need a lot of service but need some. And furthermore, because of the way that manufacturers have implemented their devices, it makes it very hard for people who have various limitations—or just predilections for simplicity—to use those devices for safety, or to use those services if they were affordable and easy to adopt.

So the idea behind Jitterbug was to modernize what SOS had done and make it a full-functioning phone. The SOS phones did not take incoming calls, for instance. It was a phone that was only intended to be in your handbag, or in your pocket, or in your glovebox, and only used occasionally. And that's the way we priced it and that's the way we expected the customers to use it, so the average usage in the early days was only five minutes a month. So when we got to the early part of 2000s, and we see feature phones coming, with phones getting smaller and smaller, and with a display on them that a lot of people can't even see, there needed to be a new solution created to take advantage of the technology and to implement it in a way that was far more accessible.

Then you see what's happening with the adoption of more and more powerful handsets and the ability to use those handsets as a personal area network. Now you have the ability to help people do things like be independent, stay healthier, be safer, have more engagement with their families, and greater opportunity to share photos and the like, and again, you still have the same rendering problem. How do you get people who are really not going to be adept at doing those things have the technology implemented in such a way where they can enjoy it too? So there's a market there that really was more about safety and independence and the like. Now we are able to encourage further engagement and further satisfaction by the consumer than just the original purpose—voice calls.

But the real issue there is that your focus on the market has to be much more lifestyle-focused than it is feature functionality–focused, like do-it-yourself stuff. You really need to be able to support, understand, and curate a lifestyle that's going to improve people's lives by the fact that they have adopted your solution—and that's what my business is trying to do now.

Newnham: Before we talk about the new business. I wanted to stay in the 2000s for a minute. You saw huge changes during your time working in wireless, but when Steve Jobs brought out the iPhone in 2007, that was a game changer. Did you have sight of the way things were going?

Harris: I don't know that I was looking for a big touchscreen. I think that's the element of innovation that really changed the physical paradigm. But the aspect and the concept of the App Store, and the connection between the rendering on the device and what you have in your store, that was part of our mission before we even knew that Apple was bringing out an iPhone. And that wasn't so much our innovation. That was me looking at what Qualcomm was doing. Qualcomm had created something called Brew [Binary Runtime Environment for Wireless]. It offered a way for developers to build applications that could then be put on cell phones that carriers were selling. The problem with their method was not the technology itself. It was their business model. And Steve Jobs figured out that he could use their techniques and take cell phone services to the next level. And where the big jump came was in the implementation of the App Store.

The App Store allowed Apple to implement what Qualcomm had done, but while Qualcomm had done it for the carriers, Apple was doing it for Apple. So it was an execution and business strategy problem at Qualcomm that created the opening for Steve Jobs to do what he did. And at GreatCall, we had already adopted the notion that we were going to be providing features and functionality to our customers that were targeted to them using the Brew platform. And then Steve jobs comes out with his deal and the rest is history. So we were already ahead of Apple in that regard, but we weren't thinking about building the next coolest touchscreen phone—we were more focused on the lifestyle of our customers, using the technology that we could influence. Since we weren't the manufacturer, we had to influence Samsung to build for us what we thought our customer wanted—the Jitterbug—and we are still selling that phone with minor variations ten years later.

Newnham: Awesome. And on to the new business. What are you working on at the moment?

Harris: Right now, I am working on a home appliance and a whole new way to manage family dynamics. Again, that comes a little bit out of my experience at GreatCall. The biggest problem we face in the future as service users and as technology users is that it's getting too complicated and there's just too much to manage. So we've set up a roadmap that will lead to a lot less stress, a lot more adoptions, and more advantages for people that use technology compared with if you are left in a DIY environment. If you have to do it yourself, it's daunting. It's too daunting.

Newnham: What's the home appliance?

Harris: It will provide you with ways to communicate, share, manage, store, and tell stories. It's an integrated device with a variety of technological implementations. But it is a family device that gets used by the whole family, and we're very hopeful that we're going to be able to tell our story well enough that we can get this project financed fairly soon.

Newnham: What are some of the lessons that you have learned from the hard times that you're taking on to this latest venture?

Harris: I would say probably the most important lesson I've learned is that most of the bumps that I hit in the road come from people or companies who I have done business with changing their mind, or changing their strategy, or just changing. And so I would say that the most important lesson when entering into any deal with anybody is that you spend the time to make sure that you have alignment, and then, as best as you can, ensure that your alignment can't get disrupted. I think that's probably a really important element.

And you know that you just can't protect yourself, even with legal contracts, from the things that happen and can affect the people you rely on to help you execute, so making sure that you have alignment, as much as you can, with all of the players is critical. It's bewildering to get going down a path and have people who make up the companies that you relied on disrupt your plans because they've changed their minds.

Newnham: It's obvious that you have persisted where most may have given up. Where do you think your drive comes from?

Harris: I don't know. I guess you really have to decide whether or not your mission is still something that needs to be done. You see, I don't like to do things that people are already doing or that people have figured out how to do and I can just do it a little bit better. I like to do things that are really impactful.

So, for instance, with GreatCall, it is not executing today the way that I wanted it to execute. A lot of people have said, "Why don't you just go do something else and forget about it?" I can't do that because no one else is doing what GreatCall is now positioned to do. So I need to be continually working on trying to make sure that GreatCall does what I intended it to do, or at least that we have the elements of that wrapped into our new offering.

I think if there is something that you have seen that needs fixing or needs to be better, unless it gets better, it just stays there and continues to gnaw at you. So I think it's more about that than persistence necessarily. You just can't ignore that particular problem. It needs to get solved, and if I think I have an opportunity to solve it, then that's where I put my energy.

Judith Klein

Systems Architect and Fellow, Leidos

Judith Klein has spent the majority of her career building distributed, real-time systems of varying sizes, in different application domains, with a 25-year concentration on air traffic management at Leidos (formerly Lockheed Martin), a leading global aerospace, defense and security, and advanced technologies company.

Judith is a Fellow and her current role at the company is a certified systems architect in the Time Based Flow Management program, a long-term project for the Federal Aviation Administration to develop an advanced tool that helps to enhance existing capabilities to more accurately schedule arrivals and departures through all phases of flight.

Danielle Newnham: Judith, can you tell me about your background?

Judith Klein: I was born in Cluj, Romania, in 1954. Cluj [now Cluj-Napoca] is the largest city in Transylvania, which is a region of Romania. This region was part of Hungary at times [between 1940 and 1944], now part of Romania again. The population is majority ethnic Romanian [Romanian Orthodox Christians], followed by ethnic Hungarians [Catholics], and other minorities, such as Germans, Jews, and Turks.

Romanian was my mother tongue, my primary language, and I learned Hungarian from my Dad, from friends, and from neighbors. I had private lessons to learn how to read and write in Hungarian, which is a very difficult and rich language, part of the Uralic family of languages, like Finnish. The year I had to select a foreign language to study—in 5th grade—was the first year since communists took over that one could select a language other than Russian, and I selected English.

© Danielle Newnham 2016
D. Newnham, *Female Innovators at Work*, DOI 10.1007/978-1-4842-2364-2_3

Of course, there was no Internet in my childhood. We did not have a TV until I was in third grade, because that is when TVs made it to Cluj! I loved reading from first grade on. I walked to the local library and read to my heart's content.

I have a brother, Peter, who is six years my senior; other than our parents, we had no other family in Romania. The one grandfather who was still alive by the start of World War II was taken to Auschwitz in 1944, along with numerous aunts and uncles, as well as my mom and dad. Most perished there. Obviously, Mom and Dad survived [separately, they met after WWII], returned to Cluj, and eventually married. Two of my mom's sisters emigrated to the United States right after World War II. As you might expect, living through "the camps" had left a mark on my parents. As a child, I do not remember encountering anti-Semitism. I do know that, when I brought home my report card, even when I was doing very well, Dad would always say something along the lines of, "As a Jew, you must do even better than everyone else if you mean to get anywhere." If you ask any psychologist or psychiatrist today about a child of Holocaust survivors, they are likely to say that I am "damaged goods."

In school, I liked math and Romanian at first. Math was logical. Romanian grammar was also very logical, while literature was beautiful. Regretfully, I was not interested in geography or history. Music was somewhat fun. I had private piano lessons at home, but I did not excel at it. I stopped the piano lessons in fifth grade and joined a basketball team. In middle school, English became a hobby, not just another subject to study.

Outside of school hours and schoolwork, I spent a lot of time with the basketball team. Gradually, basketball took up more and more time, to the point of practicing six times a week, attending training camps several times a year, and travelling throughout Romania and other Eastern Bloc countries [Bulgaria, Hungary, Czechoslovakia, and East Germany]. I am left-handed and that was an asset to the team. I was not a particularly talented player, but I was determined to stay on the team so that I could travel with them. Traveling in those days was a lot more limited than it is today, so it felt like a special benefit.

The coach, I am sorry to say, was a very abusive person, verbally abusing all of us, yelling at the top of his lungs whenever we did not do exactly what he had hoped we would do on the court. Even in the middle of a game attended by many spectators, he would let out "Stupid girl!" or "Idiot girl!", and then administer punishment in the form of laps around the track, or knee bends. I had nightmares with this coach well into my twenties, yet I think I developed resilience and focus in the process.

As a side note, being left-handed was frowned upon in Romania of my childhood. Therefore, the art teacher took it upon herself to force me to write with my right hand. I now can write with my left hand still, although it looks like an elementary school child's writing. I am pretty much ambidextrous, which comes in handy.

In ninth grade there was a major decision to be made selecting the direction of study from there on: one could follow the humanities path or "real" sciences, the big difference being the level of math taught in the last three years of high school. There was no question that I was going to follow the sciences path, but there was an opportunity to be attempted in that, there were a few "magnet" schools with concentration in math, or in physics. Because the school hosting the math magnet was considerably farther from my house, I applied to the physics magnet instead. We knew that math would be rigorous there as well. I made the cut and I moved to the physics magnet school, which happened to be located across the street from my previous school. This move turned out to be a major change in my life, on multiple levels.

First, I moved from being the best in my grade for years on end, to a class filled with students who had each been the best somewhere. The level of study was much more rigorous in all subjects. I had a tough time keeping up. I felt discouraged. I felt that there was no way I could achieve on such a high level in all subjects.

Second, I had to give up the basketball team because the school principal did not allow me to miss school when the team had out-of-town games requiring some time away during school hours. Third, I made some of the best friendships of my life there. In particular, the four closest girlfriends I made are still my friends, over four decades later. Fourth and most important, I met my future husband when I was in tenth grade.

One year into the physics magnet, I retreated to one of the real sciences class outside where I focused on what I really enjoyed [math, Romanian literature and grammar, English] and, I take no pride in saying this, I neglected geography, history, anatomy. I made it to the mathematics olympics, a competitive "sport of the brain."

I prepared in earnest for the college entrance exam. My chosen major was mathematics. In Romania of those days, if you meant to have a good chance of making it into college, you had to study hard for roughly two years in preparation for the entrance exam. Those who did not make it on the first try, had a second chance in the fall, but they had to compete for leftover spots that hadn't been filled, spots that might be in a completely different field. For example, you might have wanted to go to medical school, where competition was fierce, failed to make it, and then you might have tried again at the engineering school and made it into civil engineering! I took weekly private lessons with a college professor of math to prepare for the rigorous entrance exam. At the same time, to earn some pocket money, I tutored younger students in math and in English.

Well, I made it into mathematics and that is what I attended for a year. It was towards the end of that first college year that my family and I secured approval to leave Romania and emigrate to the United States. While the family rejoiced, I was a bit sad and worried about leaving my then boyfriend behind, but I vowed to come back to marry him. Approximately nine months after leaving Romania, I did return and married Mike. A few months later we were together again in the US.

Newnham: Are there any particular incidents during your formative years that you feel influenced the person you grew to be or shaped the career path you ultimately took?

Klein: This is silly, but Mom repeatedly told me the story of my birth—of the doctor who delivered me declaring that my forehead looks like that of a mathematician—whatever that means?! The fact is that I enjoyed arithmetic from the start.

Several incidents and multiple people influenced me along the way, making minor adjustments in the way forward. At the same time, resisting influences is important as well. For example, I recall a conversation with Dad, after I had decided that I wanted to do mathematics at the university in my home town. I told him that I intended to follow the four years of pure theoretical math with a fifth year of computer science. This was, at the time, the way to get to work with computers. I have no idea what that meant to me at the time, since computers were practically non-existent then and there. The only computers were at the computing institute. Dad tried to suggest teaching math, but teaching positions had a high likelihood of being available in the countryside, not an attractive prospect to me, so I would not hear of it. As it turns out, I enjoy teaching, and I taught a few college courses as an adjunct professor at The John Hopkins University, but I very much wanted to live in the city, have access to arts and culture, so any teaching that was going to take me away from the city was unattractive.

I think the basketball years left me with determination, focus, and grit. Or did I have all those to make it through the basketball years? Who knows…?

Whether the year in the physics magnet or something else along the way made me a very industrious worker, I do not know for sure. I just know that I throw myself into assignments with dedication and determination to deliver a quality product, even at the expense of little sleep.

As far as career path is concerned, after graduation from college, I focused on getting a job, earning a living so my husband and I could be self-sufficient and start building a safety nest egg. Once I landed a job, I latched on to someone I admired, someone I could emulate. Over the years, all such people were technical rather than managers, making it clear to me that a technical path was right for me rather than a management path.

Newnham: And what was your first job?

Klein: My first job was as a programmer at the New York Telephone Company. The course that led to my job offer was a master's level course that I had permission to attend in my last semester at Carnegie Mellon University [CMU] in the undergraduate program. Professor Dan Siewiorek taught the course and he was the author of the textbook. I now know that this is not so unusual, but I did not know it at the time and I was very impressed by him and by the whole course.

I learned a lot in the two years at the first job. We were automating the generation of the phone books. I honed programming skills in a production environment that is much different from the classroom environment, of course. Those two years were a period of immersion into the American way of life. My husband and I were trying to take it all in. We found all kinds of fun things to do in and around New York City—free-of-charge or nearly free. Most important of all, our first son, Thomas, was born in the second year of my full-time employment. We decided to move back to Pittsburgh, Pennsylvania, so that we could be close to family.

The first job I accepted in Pittsburgh was at Compuguard, a company that was manufacturing programmable controllers. This experience was very different, much closer to the hardware aspect of things, programming microprocessors with very limited computing resources, specifically very limited memory. Performance monitoring and response times were much more important in this environment. The head of engineering, and my boss, had quit attending CMU so he could be part of the team that started the company. The idea of quitting college before graduation was a big surprise to me. We grew up placing a huge value on education. In Communist Romania, knowledge and the prestige of being a university professor, for example, were a lot more valuable than money because there were limited uses for the money. The differences between those who had little money or much money were not that visible.

Meanwhile, this "college dropout" was a very knowledgeable engineer and a very generous sharer of knowledge. This generosity is the most memorable aspect I retained from the whole time I worked there. A few key people from Compuguard left to form a new company, namely American Automatrix, and they invited me to join them. The new company was also doing programmable controllers for industrial buildings. Such devices are ubiquitous today. A simple example of such a device is the programmable thermostat present in most homes. My work in this new, small startup was very interesting. I wasn't just programming: I was participating in trade shows, presenting to potential customers; I helped set up the testing department, from scratch; we all had a chance to help name new products, write advertising brochures, etc., until we grew enough to hire specialized personnel for the various departments.

On one of our family vacations, we spent some time in Washington, DC, and fell in love with it. When the opportunity presented itself, we decided to move there. Having loved working in a small startup in Pittsburgh, I tried to find a small company in the Washington, DC, area. Alas, I ended up at Inco, a beltway bandit, meaning a US government contracting firm that was working on communications infrastructure for the military [think of email that is only used by the military, in the days before email was as ubiquitous as it is today]. The company was about five hundred people strong at the time I started working there. The work was interesting. The people were not as close as in the small startup. There were office politics and I quickly figured out that I am not interested in engaging with any such activities. I was interested in working hard, doing a good job, and having time left over to spend with my family. A few people made a memorable impression on me, including my team leader, who influenced me by example. He was attending classes toward a Master of Science degree while working full-time.

Our second son, David, born by then, kept us busy managing two sons and two jobs. Still, I was encouraged to look over the curriculum, find a class that sounded interesting to me, and attended that one class for one semester. Just in case I ended up continuing the studies, I thought I might as well apply for credit toward a master's degree. And that is how I earned my master's degree at The Johns Hopkins University, taking one interesting class each semester, until I had earned all the credits for graduation!

Next, my manager and soon-to-become friend, Bryan Wolf, was a big influence. Bryan passed away recently. We remain friends with his wife. Bryan and I communicated with ease and openly. His influence was more in the human aspects of the job. He taught me that each person is good at something. We need to find out what that something is and change assignments to draw out the best in each individual. Bryan taught me how to deal with people at all levels, even when he did not necessarily get the appreciation he sought from all levels. Bryan famously taught me metaphorically that cream rises.

McDonnell Douglas bought Inco. Then Boeing acquired McDonnell Douglas. That is how I ended up with a tiny pension from Boeing!

Newnham: You have now been working in aviation for over twenty-five years. Can you tell me about how you got started there and some of the earlier projects that you worked on?

Klein: Early in 1990, the project I had been working on was coming to an end. I had made excellent contacts and working relationships with employees of IBM who were in leadership positions, [IBM was the prime contractor to the US government. McDonnell Douglas was a subcontractor team hired by IBM.] I knew that my skills would be useful on another IBM project for the Federal Aviation Administration. I did not know anything about aviation, but my computer science skills and leadership skills were solid and varied. I applied for a position at IBM. By the time the offer was extended to me, I was working on the very project I had eyed before, having brought a team of McDonnell Douglas employees to work on the project.

At this point, with the successes I was having at McDonnell Douglas, I did not really need a new job, and the IBM offer meant a cut in pay, but I felt that the future possibilities as an IBM employee were worth the move. That is how

I became an IBM employee on December 26, 1990. A few years later, Loral bought IBM's Federal Systems Division, and a few years after that, Loral sold most of what they bought to Lockheed Martin Corporation. Recently, Leidos acquired the part of Lockheed Martin holding the aviation contracts with the FAA. The customer remained the Federal Aviation Administration, the project was the same. The company issuing the paycheck had changed.

My first assignment was leading a small team of software engineers. We were tasked with Risk Reduction Demonstrations of the fault-tolerant infrastructure. What does that mean? The system under development was a large system for air traffic management. In other words, the intended users of the system were air traffic controllers, people who look at computer screens to see where the airplanes are as they fly along [e.g., while they are at cruising altitude]. Air traffic controllers communicate with the pilots to guide them for safe and efficient operations [e.g., change the speed or altitude to maintain safe separation from other traffic or to fly around bad weather].

The system being developed was distributed [i.e., many computers were working together in a single geographical location, and computers in many such geographic locations exchange needed information to form a national system of systems]. Infrastructure software enables such cross-computer cooperation in support of the application software [the air traffic management software that calculates trajectories, detects violations of separation minima, displays the situation to controllers, and so on]. University professors such as Flaviu Cristian first published the algorithms employed by the infrastructure. For example, a team on our project coded the clock synchronization algorithm published by Cristian in 1989. My team had to demonstrate its correct operation. The work involved understanding the algorithm, understanding how to set up testing in the lab, eventually demonstrating to customer representatives after presenting the theoretical aspects.

In preparation for demonstrations, many software errors were uncovered and corrected. We even had the good fortune of finding a faulty hardware clock [operating out of its specification, similar to your watch being slow, forcing you to adjust it periodically]. Several other new algorithms were incorporated into the infrastructure to achieve the required fault tolerance [i.e., correct system operations in spite of failures of software and/or hardware components, each requiring demonstration of correctness]. We were working with a few professors who were consulting on the project, including Dr. Keith Marzullo, the inventor of Marzullo's algorithm, which is part of the basis of the Network Time Protocol. It was very interesting, intense, intellectually stimulating, time-consuming work—and I loved it!

Newnham: Technology has vastly changed in the last thirty years. How has your job evolved over that time?

Klein: Indeed, many things changed in computer science over the decades. Fundamental principles, logic, and methodologies evolved. Yet, "the more things change, the more they stay the same." The experience I gained is easily transferrable and applicable on subsequent projects. When I was developing software, I did have to learn new programming languages that had not even been invented when I first learned how to program. Better tools came along to help improve the quality and efficiency of software development. Think of how much easier it is to write an English essay with the help of a word processor, a spell-checker, and a grammar-checker.

As I progressed away from software development to software architecture, then systems architecture, I had to learn additional principles and approaches from college courses, from books, and from colleagues. Fortunately, I had excellent role models and mentors along the way. Some of them are still working and I still consult with them occasionally.

Large projects, such as the ones I work on, are team efforts. No single individual knows everything. We learn from each other, we help one another, we know whom to ask various classes of questions. We share the goal of delivering a quality product, together. There is no competition among us, not as far as I could notice. Individuals develop expertise in various areas and share the knowledge as needed. A new technology we choose to use on the program may be well understood by only a couple of individuals, and they lead a team who can learn and advance together. Rapid technology advances on many fronts are therefore tackled using a divide-and-conquer approach.

The preponderance of work I did and continue to do since 1990 is air traffic management–related, a multi-faceted problem domain. One could make a career out of problems related to departures and arrivals versus training air traffic controllers, versus ways of identifying software problems easily, and countless other aspects. Here is a specific example: say the pilot reports that the ride is bumpy due to clouds and requests to fly at a different altitude hoping to clear the clouds for a smoother passenger experience. The air traffic controller now uses a "what if" tool to determine whether any conflicts would develop if the altitude were increased by 1,000 feet or 2,000 feet. "Conflict" here means the violation of separation minima, not really an actual metal-to-metal accident.

The controller can ask the system to evaluate the situation if the speed, the altitude, or even the route were changed as specified by the controller. Based on displayed results, the controller can feel confident clearing the pilot to make a specific change. Such maneuvers are not new. The seasoned controllers were performing the calculations in their heads and kept larger distances between aircraft to allow for minor miscalculations. The fact that the system does these calculations continuously, and upon requested "what if" changes, helps improve operations, helps efficiency. I was the software architect during the couple of years we spent designing, implementing, testing, and deploying the user request and evaluation tool.

Aside from the multiple assignments related to air traffic management, I had occasional special assignments or side assignments. For example, at key points during the early development of a program, an external [to the project] team is brought in to assess whether the work products are far enough along and solid enough to progress to the next phase—design assessment is a specific example. The team doing the review listens to presentations given by key members of the program, reads available materials, asks pertinent questions, and comes up with an overall assessment along with a list of recommendations for improvement. I was at times a member of such teams or a leader of such teams. The application domain varied from national archives to collection of tollbooth fees. Reviews lasted between a day and a week. Each was an interesting field trip and the company benefitted by using my expertise where needed at the time, and I really appreciated a glimpse into other programs, an opportunity to learn new things.

For a number of years, I also was very involved in the Early Leadership Development Program. This is an internal program intended to identify individuals with high potential of excelling as a leader, a decision maker, and an influencer in the corporation. I helped interview applicants. They were new employees, with about one to three years of experience in the corporation, who showed enough potential to be recommended by their managers as candidates. I taught participants a seminar I developed to give them an introduction into the first course they would be attending on our campus. All participants were earning a master's degree while participating in the program. A few of the courses were taught on our campus and were approved by accredited universities towards degrees such as systems engineering.

Newnham: What has kept you working at essentially the same company for so long? Can you tell me what you value in the company and the culture?

Klein: I like the work. I like the customer. The company is large enough—even if I just look at the 1,500 or so people working in aviation, as opposed to the 33,000 or so working in Leidos—that I could move into various positions. I am satisfied with the recognition that I have received over my career, as well as with the overall benefits package. I wanted to learn, to feel like I am making incremental progress in advancing my career, and I achieved all that in this company—or succession of companies through the series of mergers and acquisitions. I appreciated having the opportunity to augment my full-time assignment with various side assignments, and the company has always appreciated my willingness to get involved.

Newnham: Your role has been multifaceted and included different disciplines. How does one master those skills? What approaches do you favor?

Klein: The main message that I retained from my Johns Hopkins University master's degree in technical management is "pick good people and do so early." The corporate processes document—capture, synthesize—experience and lessons learned. Individuals working on programs improve the documented processes as the need arises. The business development team scouts projects coming up for bids years in advance. Solutions are sometimes sketched out or even prototyped long in advance of the solicitation for bids. Carefully selected teams work on the proposal. Key personnel working on the proposal work on it following contract award. I had the privilege of working on the winning proposal for a $1.1 billion program awarded in 2003. I was the software architect on the program from contract award until deployment to the field. I then worked as a system architect on some follow-on enhancements. Members of such project teams have different expertise and lean on each other to propel the result forward.

The approach I favor and I advised my interns to follow is: do what you like, do it well, volunteer to pitch-in with expertise where you have it so that you can pick up extra knowledge in the process. Become the go-to person based on strength of knowledge. Don't wait for power to be appointed to you, usurp it!

Newnham: I liked that you included a timeline of your personal life in the CV that you shared with me, including marriage, and the birth of children and grandchildren. Family clearly means a lot to you. How have you managed a busy career with family life?

Klein: Yes, family is very important to me. I grew up with both parents employed. My brother and I could walk everywhere we needed to go. Nobody had to chauffer us around and it was safe. This is what I thought was "normal." I liked it. I had no desire to be a stay-at-home mom.

Also, my husband and I are a good team. We share responsibilities and we make decisions together. Our first son spent full days in excellent schools, including after-school care. Around the time our second son was one year old, my father-in-law and his wife moved in with us. By the time my father-in-law passed away, our first son was married and our second son was in college. Life was at times very stressful. We had a lot of youthful energy and we made it work. My husband earned his master's degree while working full-time, as did I. This meant that we stayed up late doing homework after others were asleep.

There were nights and weekends when I had to work or my husband had to work. There is no way to know whether this was the best for our sons. There is no going back and trying it another way. We attended school concerts, sporting events. We were involved in the boys' activities. And now we try to be involved in the lives of our three grandkids.

Newnham: You have been awarded the Lockheed Martin Fellowship four times. What does that kind of recognition mean to you?

Klein: You may have heard of the quote from Napoleon Bonaparte: "A soldier will fight long and hard for a bit of colored ribbon." I tended to find some "colored ribbon" that I treated as a motivator to reach the next thing. When

I first learned about the possibility of reaching certification as a systems architect, I looked into the requirements by reading the application. I concluded that it is achievable, over time. I treated that application as a list of items to achieve, one by one, culminating in certification. My end-of-year resolution included, for many years, "Make progress toward achieving certification as a systems architect." And so, like the tortoise in the fable, slowly and steadily I won that race.

Not long thereafter, Lockheed Martin introduced the Fellows program and I was interested right away. I obtained a copy of the application so I could determine whether there was any hope of achieving it. The application was rather intimidating but rather than give up, I went to talk to my mentor, my guiding light, Jon Dehn. He was very encouraging and explained that the application had many options, many paths toward certification. One did not have to achieve each and every one of the items in the application, only a significant amount of the items on the checklist. And so, I embarked on the new "slow and steady wins the race" list.

I first achieved the Lockheed Martin Fellows award in 2006. It is awarded for a three-year term. I since renewed successfully in 2009, 2012, and in 2015. Like with many other things, the first time is the most exciting and rewarding. I received a statue I keep on my desk and being a Fellow gives me the occasional opportunity to go on a field trip, participate in a proposal review, participate in an awards ceremony, participate in some technical panel—and so it is a fun privilege.

Newnham: Who have you learned most from in your career? Did you have mentors?

Klein: Yes, I had mentors, although none formally declared. I latched on to people I admired, asked them for guidance, informally emulated them, and followed their example. Jon Dehn, a senior Lockheed Martin Fellow has been someone I admired since I met him in 1991. He has helped me quietly, gently, expertly. He is apolitical, an honest, hard-working individual, a very intelligent and modest man. He is the one who first suggested that I become a software architect. He is the one who helped me through the process of becoming a certified systems architect. He is the one who helped me through the process of becoming a Lockheed Martin Fellow. He is the one who inspired me to get involved with the Early Leadership Development Program, with teaching interns as well as people starting out in their careers. I learned from many people, including those I was mentoring, and from summer interns I hired.

Newnham: Where do you think the future of aviation lies?

Klein: There has been a lot of talk lately about self-driving cars. There are many safety concerns leaping to cars without any humans in the loop. Incremental improvements are evident [think of seat belts, airbags, cruise control, various mirrors for much increased situational awareness].

In aviation, the problems are somewhat similar. There should come a day when the destination is provided to the onboard automation and the system cooperates with various other systems to get to the destination with practically no intervention. Today, there are very many people in the loop, planning time slots, providing permission to take off, adjusting speeds along the way, vectoring to get around bad weather or to avoid a traffic jam at major intersections and so on, all the way to the gate. The skies over the East Coast—around New York, Philadelphia, Washington, DC, can get extremely crowded at times.

Who knows? We may yet get to where The Jetsons' individual flying machines are ubiquitous.

Newnham: What ambitions do you feel that you have yet to fulfill?

Klein: I have an ever-growing bucket list that I am adding to faster than we are able to check things off it. But I would not necessarily call these ambitions.

Professionally, I have gradually removed items from my list of extracurricular activities. I seldom volunteer for assignments outside of my direct position as system architect on Time Based Flow Management. I strive to achieve a life-work balance, to spend time with my retired husband, with my three grandkids, and enjoy the arts.

Newnham: What are you most proud of in your life and career, and why?

Klein: Given the definitions…

"The Lockheed Martin Fellows Program is established to recognize and encourage the highest levels of accomplishment in the individual technical contributor fields, with a mission to connect the best technical talent in the Corporation to our most difficult technical challenges."

"The mission of Lockheed Martin Engineering—Joint Architect Working Group [JAWG] is to provide Lockheed Martin technical leadership by developing a resource of 21st Century Systems and Software Architects committed to advancing their profession, continuous learning, process improvement and collaboration internally and externally to meet our customers' challenges today and in the future."

I should be proudest for being a certified systems architect and a Fellow, yet I am proudest when the customer calls me fair, when a colleague thanks me for all I taught him or her, and when an intern I took under my wing thanks me for the guidance I provided.

Newnham: Finally, what advice would you pass on to others looking to follow a similar career path?

Klein: Do what you like and like what you do. Work hard. Be fair. Be nice. Help others—superiors, peers, and subordinates alike. Be patient. And finally, find balance in your life. Don't just live to work but work hard for self-respect, self-satisfaction, and to support the lifestyle that you appreciate.

Holly Liu

Cofounder, Kabam

Holly Liu *is cofounder and chief development officer at AAA mobile gaming company, Kabam, formerly Watercooler, Inc., which she started in 2006 with Kevin Chou, Michael Li, and Wayne Chan. The business has undergone several pivots, from starting as a corporate social network, to Facebook communities for sports and TV brands, to Facebook games—on which Holly led the design of the award-winning Kingdoms of Camelot franchise, which grossed over $250 million—and finally, to mobile games today.*

Previously, Holly held the position of chief of staff, leading Kabam's HR efforts for more than 700 employees, spanning six offices in the United States, China, Germany, and Canada. Under Holly's leadership, the company has experienced rapid growth, including staff numbers increasing 500 percent in three years.

Before cofounding Kabam, Holly was senior user interface designer for AOL, where she led the design of community web products. Holly has a master's degree in information management and systems from UC Berkeley and a bachelor's degree in mass communications from UCLA.

Danielle Newnham: What is your background?

Holly Liu: I grew up in the United States and my first job was in a very conservative field, working for an accounting firm. At college, I had felt everything was very egalitarian between men and women, but as soon as I started work, that changed, and I was very surprised. Men began treating me differently,

© Danielle Newnham 2016
D. Newnham, *Female Innovators at Work*, DOI 10.1007/978-1-4842-2364-2_4

sometimes nicely like letting me out of the elevator first and other times asking me to do menial tasks. I began to notice some of the more egregious things, such as colleagues telling stories that made me uncomfortable. And me having to say, "No, I don't want to go to Hooters again."

Newnham: Is this what accountants do?

Liu: Yeah, in my experience, because you would go out with clients or be away at the client's site with a team of mostly men versus women. Sometimes I ended up at Hooters and thought, "I don't really want to be here," but there wasn't much choice. I was really junior then, so I just worked really hard. I was naïve but I soon realized that this environment wasn't for me. So I went back to school—to UC Berkeley—to get my master's degree in information management and systems. I fell in love with human computer interaction, which is really user interface design, or even product design. It's that layer between the user and the actual application. It's that experience of "When I tap over here, what does it do? After I swipe, what shows on the screen?" All of those things, to me, are how someone experiences your product. That's your gateway. That's your view.

So I pretty much fell in love with it and stayed in the Bay Area because I fell in love with tech. I did a short stint back in consulting before getting a lot of my product design chops at AOL, where I worked on community products, which included blogs, forums, media and entertainment, and safety and security. The one I enjoyed the most, though, was community products, because it was basically using that user interface [UI] experience to meld it all together. And it was at that point at AOL that I realized I had found my stride.

So I really enjoyed my time at AOL. I was there for three years and one of the things I learned as a designer there was that my job depends a lot on feedback. I design for a purpose. But with designing products at a company the size of AOL, a lot of initiatives start and stop and unfortunately during my time there, a lot of my products never went to market. They got to beta stage, which was great, but then something would happen, or our chief technology officer [CTO] would change, or there would be a reorganization. It was just very unfulfilling to be a designer and not know the impact of your design.

So that was one of the major reasons for leaving and wanting to start my own business. And I am sure when anyone starts their business and launches their product, they have all these visions of grandeur about how everyone is going to come and use it. And that you will get a lot of feedback… but you usually just hear crickets.

The thing that was really nice though was that my product was out there, so at least I could iterate. Otherwise, it becomes like a religious war internally, about what the engineer thinks, about what the product team thinks. Ultimately, it should all be about the user. And if you are not getting users, then you work with the marketing team and find out how to get more users. So that was one of the reasons why I left.

The second reason why I left to start a business was because we thought it was a good time. It was 2005, 2006—the height of Web 2.0. We were right down the street from a company called Meebo, an instant messenger application powered by AJAX, which made everything super responsive. In some ways, it was prepping us for the touchscreen phone—so really pioneering. YouTube had also just sold for over a billion dollars and there was this thought of "If you build it, they will come." So, secondly, we started the company because the timing felt right.

Newnham: Can you tell me more about that initial business; how you chose your founding team?

Liu: It was kind of a crazy time back in 2006. So we decided to start our chops in corporate social networking, which was almost like a Jive or Yammer—a Facebook within companies because Facebook and social networks were new and growing fast at the time. It was me and three other founders who started the company. I am the only female.

I think what is interesting today is that twenty-five percent of the team at Kabam are women. Often, when I talk to other female leaders, I find that the percentage of women in a company is usually a reflection of senior management. So if there is a woman CEO, the company is much more gender diverse. Take Marissa Mayer, for example. The first thing she did when she got to Yahoo! was to stack it with women. So, in the context for us—me being a female on the founding team means I do see it bearing some fruit today in terms of the gender makeup.

In terms of the skillsets of the founding team, I am a huge fan of having complimentary skillsets. Back in the day, because it was the web, you pretty much needed somebody to be on the business side and someone who could build product. I know I am generalizing two big groups here but when you first startup, everyone is a generalist. I often refer to it as a rowboat—you are all in the same boat and you can feel every single move made by each person. So it was all on us four to move this thing forward.

It was also clear from the get-go that we all had our roles. We had business—the CEO, design—me, and we had engineering, with two cofounders being engineers—backend and frontend. And even though now there is so much more research done on this, in 2006, there were no incubators that we knew of. There was no place for a startup like ours to learn what to do as first-time founders or to hack our way past all of these things, so we just got on with it. And I know this doesn't sound exciting, but I think we are one of the more boring cofounding teams because we all knew each other's role. There was a fundamental respect for each other on that side. For example, fundraising fell to the CEO, so sometimes he'd consult with us on it, but ultimately, it was his decision. And even in my role as product designer, it was very easy for people to say they could do it too, but it's not easy to be good. So similarly, I would gather opinions but it was ultimately left to me to decide stuff.

We also all knew each other well. When I talk to students, I always say look to your left and right for cofounders, because it is better to start a company with people you have already worked with or on projects with. So among our founding team, I grew up with the CEO. He was always more business orientated. We were also at Berkeley together too, so we really got to know each other a lot more there. Business wasn't my strong suit at the time because I cared more about fixing problems and I was more focused on product. Even growing up, I used to keep a bug list to make note of all the things in the world that I thought could be designed better. Then we hired the frontend developer from AOL. The backend guy—he and I met at another job and had worked on a project together. So like I said, I think working together helps reduce a lot of the risk when you go into business together.

I think it also helps if you are all at the same stage of life, because you spend a lot of time together. I was the older one—literally the mom of the group. I was the first one to get married and have kids. And all the management books on gender talk about this personal aspect, because I think it's something women deal with a lot more than men. I even tried to hide my second pregnancy for as long as possible. Our COO has kids around the same age as mine. He puts up pictures of his kids at work, but I don't do that. It's funny because I am the cofounder of the company, but I know I will get judged twice as hard. I do wonder if I would care so much about things like that if I were the CEO. I would probably think, "Screw it," especially if the company was doing really well. The demands of motherhood are really hard, especially if you are nursing early on. And if you aren't, there are other things you have to combat, so it is a bit of a losing proposition either way.

So that's how I met my other cofounders. We followed conventional wisdom before it was the conventional wisdom of knowing your founders before you start up. So that worked really well; we didn't really fight. And in fact, I heard our CEO say this other day, "The market is hard enough to fight, a team shouldn't be fighting each other." And that helped so much because the market is incredibly difficult, you need every single bit of will going outward and moving you forward. It is incredibly hard to have a successful product and then a successful company. There are more than twenty thousand things that need to go right in order for it to happen. It's actually amazing that startups happen – just like the miracle of birth. Maybe because it is so hard, fewer people go into it. Some people who are successful say, "I just kept at it." And there is an element of that because a lot do drop out. You just don't need self-induced pain from infighting, because being a startup is painful enough.

I would also say you need to be aligned around your vision and your values. But the funny thing is, when you are very small, it is hard to be clear about those. It's like a small family. You don't write down your values, but you are all on the same page. It's only when you hit some differences or as you get bigger that they become more apparent. So for us, when it came to decisions, we would say, "OK, go big or go home!" And that's actually morphed into one of our values of going all in today. If we make a decision, we commit and we go all in. No looking back. And that's been a little bit of our history, because we didn't believe in split focus. Our CEO was always saying, "Let's focus, let's focus, let's focus."

Newnham: Talking of focus, at what point did you pivot and become Kabam?

Liu: So we did several pivots. We did the corporate social network, which was the business that we presented to investors when raising money. And, at that time, it was hard for first time founders to raise money. There were no accelerators like YC or 500 startups at that time. We raised it from a firm called Canaan, who incubated us. We were probably one of their first seed investments. We raised money on just a PowerPoint and no product. Then once we had released a product, it was crickets. It is always the reverse of your dreams when you release a product. It was so hard to get users, so we changed our product several times. We were actually almost at the end of our runway. We were talking about whether we should return the money to the investors, or have a fire sale, or just go find other jobs.

And then, at the time, Facebook opened up their platform to any developer, which became a pretty big deal. Literally, companies were created in a weekend, and they were getting billions of page views, and there would be like two developers making a fortune off of ads. So we thought, "Go where the users are." Distribution is so hard. I thought, "What is the point of me doing design work if no one sees it?" So we decided to go where the users were.

The first thing we looked at was market conditions. The second thing we looked at was team capabilities and finally, people's passion points. We looked at how we started the company, because we were excited about Web 2.0, the democratization of the web, and how we felt the first business could help the workplace. But we realized really quickly that our team's capabilities were all consumer based. If you have a B2B business, you need a sales team and probably four middle-aged Caucasian men. I hate to say it, but we were four young Chinese Americans, so we just didn't think we could sell to companies as easily at that time. And it wasn't something that we were passionate about either.

We went into a room and brainstormed. We talked about Facebook and how we didn't have to do what we were originally doing. And the thing we landed on was TV shows, because at the time, shows didn't have good access to the fan groups and fans wanted more access to the shows, so it was like the most perfect marketplace. So we started building community platforms for TV shows and sports teams. We ended up growing them to be some of the largest Facebook communities. In fact, by the beginning of 2008, we were the largest and had over sixty million registered users. This was when we were called Watercooler.

So we ended up moving into the entertainment space, which was much better for us because we were consumers and passionate. I was also used to designing for consumers and not used to designing for B2B. And it took off partly because the platform was so amazing, and partly because there were several features that we did that were very sticky for our users. But 2008 was another turning point for us because Facebook started building Fan Pages. A lot of the features we had were built into Facebook for brands, so folks like the television network ABC, or even an entertainment company, could now go straight to Facebook and really do things they had originally been doing with our fan communities. So there were changes in Facebook but there were also changes in the overall macro economy, particularly a recession in the US. And once again, it killed us because it killed our ad-based revenue, which was our main revenue stream. So it was another turning point where we took another look at whether we wanted to shut it down or do something else.

Also, at the time, we were trying to raise our hardest round, which was our Series B. In terms of raising money, up until the point Lehman Brothers were going under, people were still pretty interested. We even had a signed term sheet from a VC at a well-respected company. But the day they were supposed to wire the money across was when Lehman Brothers crashed. And then we never heard from them. A week went by and we were wondering what was going on. Then a week later, they said it wasn't going to happen. We had been really dependent on that, so it was probably one of the hardest times for the company.

Again, we looked at three things. One was market conditions, which were pretty bad. We looked at other companies, such as Zynga, who did **FarmVille** and who were still blowing up, so we knew that games were recession-proof. And most of all, our team loved playing games.

The second thing was that it was still blowing up on Facebook, so we looked again at team capabilities. We were now a B2C company and we knew we knew how to build Facebook applications. Between all of us, our team had over a hundred years' worth of building Facebook applications. This was really important, because a lot of people tried doing these things, and they should have succeeded, but they didn't because they just didn't know it as intuitively as we did.

Then, finally, we looked again at passion points. Our CEO, in particular, was a huge gamer who would download a client just to play a game. So the game we ended up building, **Kingdoms of Camelot**, was a lot like the games he was used to. He came to me to help design it for Facebook. We needed to make the entry points as casual as possible because it was a very deep and mid-core game. We also still had some commits on the sports side of the business, so we wound down TV. Then in 2009, we put as much as we could into the **Kingdoms of Camelot**.

We actually started with a two-person team. They built it in around four to five months. We had no idea that it would be so successful. In fact, we had never seen anything like our game on Facebook. We didn't have a lot of money, we decided to call on our friends and family, bribe them with pizza and beer to get them to play with it and give us feedback. I've done a lot of user testing in the past, and I can tell you, this was the worst one I've ever sat through. You'd think your friends and family would be nice and hold back punches, so you're a little worried all the time about including them on this. But oh my goodness, they were so mean! My brother-in-law ripped it apart. And all of our friends said, "This is horrible." Watching them was just the most painful experience I had ever seen, I would have rather been waiting in line at the DMV. But, we fixed what we could and then we were all in: "Go big or go home." And then we launched.

We did a few things with the game that were quite innovative. It was the first time this type of game was on Facebook. We also enabled chat so that players could talk to other players in real time. Chat wasn't live during the user testing because they would have only been able to talk to others in the same room, which isn't that compelling. But once we turned it on and we were able to connect people by their interests—that was quite compelling for people. Being able to communicate and connect is part of what made it so social. That had never been seen or done on Facebook before. Prior to that, you could only chat with your friends or gift only to your friends, so you were strengthening bonds within friends versus "meeting" other people.

Another thing was the game play innovation, which was the ability to attack someone on a map where they owned those coordinates. So it was all mapped to some real life and real things, which I know sounds super geeky but it was quite a complex, deep game that allowed a whole virtual world in many respects. And it allowed you to connect with people who weren't necessarily your friends but had this same deep interest. And that is a little bit of what the whole Internet has been about. It's what got Google to its rise. It was like, "OK, now I can find somebody who might be in another state but loves Beanie Babies that are only purple from 1992." And that's the beauty of the original thesis of the Internet. Now everybody's on it. So at one point, we were saying, "Let's shrink this world and get trusted recommendations."

So that was our second pivot. And our third was moving into mobile.

Newnham: Yes, tell me about Kabam and what pushed you into mobile.

Liu: Honestly, the largest push came because of a tax imposed by Facebook. There were a lot of other reasons to expand beyond Facebook, but that was a big one.

Interestingly, we never grew as big as *FarmVille*, but we had some of the best monetization metrics. We were this small kind of niche thing. To drive users, we got good at buying traffic, what we call UA—user acquisition. We got really good at it on Facebook. We knew exactly how much revenue we would get for every dollar spent. Also, for some time, our CEO had wanted to get onto mobile. Mobile had been around for a while, but this was 2012 and it felt like the right time. So we launched on mobile and it got to number-one top-grossing game. I think this was the first time a freemium model had hit top-grossing. Now all the top-grossing games are freemium, as everyone realized that this model is a much better way for both business and users.

In terms of games in the West, there had only been one business model in gaming, which was you pay to play. That meant users relied on marketing material and trusted recommendations before they bought, much like the movies. But this freemium model was different. I could build a relationship with the customer and I work for every dollar. I know the gaming space has taken a lot of heat for this, and I can understand that, but the reason we went with the freemium model was because it was something closer to our DNA.

With a freemium model, you have to think of your product as a service. It's games as a service, and so you think about the end user a lot more. For us, it was in our DNA because we came from the web. If there is something wrong, I can update it on the backend and I can fix it for you right there, instead of having to fix something in the sequel. And also the main model on Facebook was freemium, and because we started on Facebook, nobody would pay to download. There was no way to do that. And as the model was already part of our company DNA, to do something different didn't make sense to us.

Also, this model had been around for years in Asia, particularly China. It does super well, partly because console was banned for some time there, so the gaming market grew very differently. But now everyone in the West is on board and they all make games with the freemium model.

Newnham: So you start to build on mobile. Did you find success straight away?

Liu: Yes, very quickly. It sounds like a Cinderella story, but it's like what the **Pokémon Go** founder says, "**Pokémon Go** was the overnight sensation that took twenty years to build." It was down to timing for us, but we also had built layers upon layers of foundation. We had already built **Kingdoms of Camelot** and had all these pivots—so it was actually six years in the making. We had so many lessons learned from all the twists and turns of the business. So yes, it was successful straight away, but only because of the lessons we learned. And people were ready for a game like that on mobile.

Newnham: Due to success and acquisitions, you have grown into a massive organization spanning several countries and cultures. How do you retain your company culture when that happens?

Liu: Well, I am one of the few cofounders who has worn so many hats. My hats have been very different, including HR. I have stayed on the people side of things. I think there is some stuff that is still us, including our values, which don't change over time and they shouldn't change over time. They will evolve for sure and we have worked to make that happen.

When you are smaller, there are things that are common for everyone, but as you get bigger, it's more about how you do things that affect the culture. And that really is culture, to be honest. So I always say, "Culture is caught, not taught." It's really about behaviors, and for us, how it has changed a little bit over time has come down to the different stages of our company that impacted how we needed to operate. And even how you operate is how you behave toward one another. So, to me, there were three stages in our company. There was the founding stage, the growth stage, and what I call the "scale stage."

The founding stage is obviously dependent on employee size because people equal culture. So if you are up to thirty people, you are probably all in the same room, and at that stage, culture is very similar across the board. They probably hang out at lunch time, they have a Foosball or a ping pong table, and it's very similar. And at that size, I don't think you need to write down your values or mission because everyone knows them and everyone is on the same page. But if I could do this time again, I would probably have pushed harder to qualify the seeds of our values. But then again, we pivoted three times, so I think it's just that we were scared to write something down— in case it changed. We wanted to be adaptable in some ways, which is so much a part of our culture.

The growth phase is when a lot of CEOs think about culture, but when you get to that stage, it's a little bit too late. I think with a CEO's job, you can never overdo trying to align people as much as possible—from their gut to their everyday thinking. I can't imagine why a CEO wouldn't want to invest in that. So the growth stage is when you bring in a whole load of people, depending on how you grow. We grew really fast. In 2011, we went from one hundred and fifty people to four hundred and fifty by the end of that year.

What's really interesting with our business model is that it has allowed us to buy studios. And they can be on their own if they want—with their own P&L too. They are their own little fiefdom. On the one hand, that's great because they have a lot of pride and stick together. But then on the other hand, it is hard to integrate. For a while, we had quite a sales-based culture, and because it was a growing market, the thought was to spend money on users. Spend money to make money. Grow, grow, grow, grow! And with the growth culture, you collect debt. We have collected a ton of debt around many different aspects, but it enabled us to get where we are today.

Things are different now. We only release two to three games a year, whereas before, we would release one every quarter. Each one takes fifteen to twenty-four months to build, whereas it used to take us around three months on Facebook. But it is not the same anymore because it is now so incredibly expensive. This is for different reasons, including retention. We want long-term users. That's what we care about, so we're not going to build a game that is super shallow. We are going to build one that's deep.

Then there is the phase where you have several offices. When doing operations that way, you need someone who's really good at communicating. We're at a funny phase where a lot of our senior executives are still hands-on—partly because we don't have as many games coming out. So they are very hands-on and know the games really well. And they know the people very well and keep them on track with goals and OKRs [objectives and key results].

So our culture has changed a bit over time but our values have been very consistent. They have evolved through each phase to get us where we are today.

Newnham: How have you found being a female entrepreneur? What advice do you have for other women starting out?

Liu: The first bit of advice is to just go and do it. The second is to be ready for a ton of No's. In other words, make sure that what you are doing is something you believe—wholeheartedly enough to get you past those No's. That's what you need. A lot of entrepreneurs say that part of the reason they were successful is because they never gave up. They just kept going. And I think that's true. Success is relative. You might just be the last one standing. Every single startup has their "Oh shit!" moments, but you just have to get through it. And as a woman, I think you have so much more fortitude. You just don't realize it. It just doesn't look like the same fortitude that men have. Just the fact that we have to work twice as hard to get half as far makes me a well-built machine!

I am Chinese American and we are only 5.6 percent of the population in the U.S. I remember my dad used to say to me, "You have to work twice as hard Holly. Partly because people look at you differently and they are going to judge you differently. You are different."

And, for women, it's not a level playing field. I used to think it was, but as I got further up the chain, I saw how gender makes a huge difference. To me, it feels like I have been doing the 400-meter hurdle race. But there are no hurdles on the guys' side. And I've been shot in the leg. And I've been told I have to get to the finish line.

But it's so worth it, so go for it.

Anisha Singh

Founder and CEO, mydala

Anisha Singh is Founder and CEO of mydala, which she founded in 2009 with Arjun Basu and Ashish Bhatnagar. As India's largest mobile coupon provider, mydala has 30 million registered users and operates across 209 cities in India.

Anisha began her career with the Clinton administration on Capitol Hill, where she helped women entrepreneurs raise funding. She then moved on to Centra Software in Boston, where she set up e-learning systems for Fortune 500 companies and higher-education institutions. After returning to India in 2004, Anisha launched her first company, Kinis Software, which provides digital solutions for real estate firms.

Anisha graduated from the College of Art, Delhi, holds a master's degree in political communication, and has an MBA in information systems from American University in Washington, DC.

Danielle Newnham: What is your background and when did you get first excited about tech?

Anisha Singh: I was actually the most uninspired child growing up—one that you would probably ignore in a room. I wasn't a star. I wasn't the kid you looked at and said, look she's so cute or so talented at this. So I grew up being ignored and as a result, I ignored the world, fearing doing anything that would draw too much attention because the possibility was that I wouldn't be good at it.

© Danielle Newnham 2016
D. Newnham, *Female Innovators at Work*, DOI 10.1007/978-1-4842-2364-2_5

I realized some years later that fear can actually be a good thing if channeled. Fear can drive you to strive to achieve things that never seemed imaginable. A chance application took me to grad school in the United States and it just so happened that I got a class with a professor who saw some potential in me, pushing me to speak up. It was a class in information systems and I loved it. It gave me a rush, and after that, technology was something I started looking at very seriously.

I went to intern for a fabulous woman named Julie Holdren, who ran a company called Olympus Group out of Washington DC. I saw this woman and all I wanted was to be her. She could do thirty push-ups and she was running this company with three hundred people. She had twins and I was like, how fabulous is this woman? I want to be her. So that was it. I went from being the person voted most likely to get married straight after grad school with no real ambition to being this person who had found this spark and who ran with it. The timely combination of meeting my professor and interning have made me realize that mentors and role models in whatever shape and form can go a long way in helping you choose the route you end up following.

So after that, I ended up working with the Clinton administration, helping women entrepreneurs to raise funding on an initiative called Springboard Enterprises, which I thought was a fabulous, fabulous initiative. I met a lot of really cool entrepreneurs who had no backing, no funding—single mothers who were doing phenomenal stuff. And seeing all this, I think it was an amalgamation of everything that came together, but it literally set me on the path of where I am now.

Also, it's interesting because my father is a very successful entrepreneur now but, growing up, we had a really hard time. I swore to myself then that I would never be an entrepreneur. I just wanted a regular paycheck because I didn't want to be scared that we wouldn't be able to pay school fees for my kids. And now I tell people, "Never say never" because you never know what is going to happen.

Newnham: What did you do after the Clinton administration?

Singh: The Clinton administration was only part-time because we were doing Springboard. Once Springboard was done, I needed a real job that paid, so I moved to Boston with a company called Centra Software, which was in the e-learning space. I had job offers in DC, but I had heard the CEO of Blackbird speak at my school and something he said really stuck with me, which was that you should always do something you fear because if you stop, it means you are not growing. I was in my comfort zone in DC. So I picked the job offer in Boston, where I didn't know anybody. They were really nice to me and I believed I was going to change the world. I was going to bring learning to India.

I set up a lot of e-learning systems for Fortune 500 companies as well as higher education institutions and worked there for about five years, and then I was done. I knew it was my time to move on because I was too comfortable there and I had clients calling and saying, "Why aren't you doing this in India?" So I moved back to India thinking again, very naïvely, that I would set up my very own company. I would set off on my goal of taking e-learning to India but I was too ahead of the time and realization soon dawned that the dream of a quick-growth company needed to be tucked away. That was the harshest thing I think a new entrepreneur faces when reality trumps expectation.

I started my first company, Kinis Software, in 2004. I remember three months post setting up, sitting curled up on the couch, thinking "Shit, I am never going to be able to pay salaries. This is the worst decision of my life." But fortunately by then I was ingrained with a belief that if you keep pushing forward you will make headway. You might have to change your route a bit but it will happen. Plus the beauty of being in India where failure is frowned upon actually turned out to be a blessing. The thought of an aunt telling my parents "I told you so" kept me going. As I mentioned, fear can be a wonderful driver. We changed the course of Kinis to do digital content across the board and soon the bills were getting paid and the team grew. It is now a profitable self-sustaining company that has little use for the likes of me.

Newnham: So how did you come up with the idea of mydala?

Singh: For someone who didn't want to be an entrepreneur isn't it ironic that when the entrepreneurial bug bit me, it bit me hard? I had moved back to the US. My first company kind of became a joint venture with another company there, so I was moving back and forth, which was excellent because I got the best of both worlds. Then I got married and settled in New York City, but there came a point when I had to be truthful to myself, that I was in the same comfort state that I loathed. Then there was just this point where I knew I needed to do something else, so I started looking at ideas and I saw this Chinese couponing system, which was basically people getting together offline and getting discounts. The only e-commerce ventures that I had taken off in India at that particular point in time were in the travel industry, which I believed was because you bought your ticket online, but you had an offline experience. So I thought, this might just work.

Right about the same time, Groupon was taking off in the US, so I took that model and came back to India. I actually just packed a bag and said, "I'm going to go back. Bye husband. I'll see how it goes. I'll email you." I moved back and started the company when I was three months pregnant and so the joke is that I had two babies in one go, which is true. And mydala just took off. We even got our angel funding really quickly, without even asking.

Newnham: I was going to ask about the funding process.

Singh: Our angel funding came easy because the idea was different. Then we focused on growth and soon had three term sheets. So, we knew a lot of people from New York and I approached some of them with the idea. What ended up happening was one connected me to another and they connected to me to a late-stage fund in Delhi, and these partners invested in their personal capacity. So that worked out really well for us and we went from being a three-person outfit to a forty-person outfit very quickly. Then reality hit because we were the Groupon clone, so we had three term sheets and we didn't act fast enough. We were thinking our way through, and at the same time, we were trying to focus on the product. We knew we had a good business idea but we went with the wrong set of investors, and they yanked the term sheets from us on the day of signing without a solid explanation.

Newnham: How was that for you? Here you are thinking you've got this investment and everything is about to happen…

Singh: Devastating. I mean, we put all our savings into it and at that point, my husband had joined us as well as the CFO. We had expanded and were about seventy people, and had opened virtual offices in different places around India. It was truly devastating. All our savings were in this and I had just given birth as well, so it was just insanity. And then there was no money. We had fifty-two competitors in India. Seven were more heavily funded, each north of $20 million. But, we still knew we had a sustainable business model.

Newnham: Did you feel like giving up?

Singh: Of course. You know, anybody that tells you they have never had that thought is talking a lot of shit because every entrepreneur has that thought. I think that's what separates the successful or what I call the 'crazy breed' of entrepreneurs… it's at that point when you should quit but you don't. I tell people now, "Your company can't have a plan B" and it's the truth. You can't have a plan B. You just suck it up, deal with it, and keep moving. I'm glad that's what we did.

We had buyout offers at that point, but truthfully they were worth peanuts and we knew we had a good business model because what mydala was doing was really different. We weren't a discount site. We knew there was a pain point we were solving, which was local businesses in India had no way of getting online. They would see brands were on Facebook but they didn't know how to get there.

These term sheets, valuations and raising money were new to me but felt like it was what internet companies did so we did it. Once the term sheets went away, we sat down and looked really hard at the business. My other company, which had never gotten any funding but was a profitable model, seemed to stand out so I told my cofounders, "Here's an idea, why don't we run this like a real business? Focus on making money instead of raising money." So we got back in the trenches and set mydala on the path that would take us beyond the scale that even we had imagined.

On the user side, we did three things. We knew the users liked something as basic as ABC—astrology, Bollywood, and cricket, so we decided to leverage these three areas. We did astro deals and we tied up with Bollywood. We're the only company that has every A-list Bollywood star, such as Shahrukh Khan and we started giving deals on all the cricket matches.

Newnham: How did that work out for you?

Singh: The ABC leverage mixed with actually understanding what our users wanted led us to tweak our model. We went mobile first because we saw users were logging on from their mobile devices. We realized that users didn't want to pay the entire amount up front but were okay with an option value, so we modified the model to charge the user a basic marketing fee and pay the rest at the time of redemption at the merchant.

This also led us to think through payments. In India at that point there were only 30 million credit card users but a billion plus in the population. Clearly, if we wanted scale we needed to innovate on payments—something that would allow the user to do a micro payment in seconds.

We started talking to the telecom operators and launched with Vodafone in 2012. All these things changed the graph of mydala. The downward U curve suddenly turned to a sharp upward J curve. We expanded to 98 cities in India almost overnight. Well, that's a bit of an exaggeration but time was moving insanely fast. And it was fun because we were now racing against time to capture a pan-Indian audience. We now work with all telco carriers for billing and have a registered user base of 38 million users across India.

Newnham: How do you make money? Do you take a commission from the user?

Singh: Yes, usually we charge the user an option value, there are businesses that pay us to showcase them. We do things differently. We knew that we were going to be their marketing partner, so local businesses such as restaurants, dental clinics, and so on will give us a discount or a package—most prefer not giving heavy discounts but are okay with giving twenty-five percent off—and we pass it to the user. These deals are showcased to the users based on the user's buying patterns—so habits, location, mobile balance. So users see discounts tailored to them of things around them.

Newnham: What were some of the earlier obstacles you faced, other than the funding issues you mentioned?

Singh: There were plenty of obstacles, but I think that's true for all entrepreneurs. It definitely isn't easy doing business in India and I hate bringing up the woman angle but the fact is that it was and is even now tougher for women.

It wasn't easy trying to convince talented people to join the team of a newbie internet company, even when Internet wasn't a buzzword. It didn't help that I was pregnant. It took some really forward thinking believers to believe and stick with a pregnant CEO with her non-funded startup. I am forever grateful to my cofounders Arjun and Ashish who were, and still are, my pillars of strength and had insurmountable belief in me, even when investors would question me on whether I would even return post baby.

Newnham: You scaled up when you thought funding was imminent. Did you have to scale back down?

Singh: No, we didn't scale back down. I hate firing people—that is my weakness. I used to see it as a strength but realize now that in some cases it is a weakness. I didn't have to fire at that time because we were losing people in any case. The people who didn't leave us in fear of no clear path got poached by better funded competitors.

If we were paying someone 30,000 rupees, they would offer 90,000, and we just couldn't match that. If I had to look at the upside, the founding team remained intact and that team is still with us and we know that we are all in this together.

Newnham: Can you tell me about some of the earlier milestones of the company?

Singh: Well, I remember we would sit by Google Analytics. And you know how you have the real-time data? We'd be so excited. And watching the meter go up to close to 940—I still remember that day. I was like, "Everyone turn on a PC right now and get on mydala!" because we needed to get to 1,000. That was our big thing, getting to 1,000. Now, we get fifteen million visitors every month so the scale has become slightly different.

I also remember when we did our first big deals. So we sold out 1,000 vouchers in two hours, which for us was a very, very big deal because we thought we had hit our high point. But now we do about 220,000 to 250,000 coupons on a daily basis. So if you would have asked me if I thought that we would get to this scale… No. We were not looking that far.

What is also interesting about milestones is that we always hear in India that the potential here isn't the main eight Tier-1 cities but the buying power outside of those cities instead, and everyone is trying to get there. That is the holy grail. We never thought that we wanted to go there but now we get forty-five percent of our transactions from non–Tier-1 cities. It is a big market and growing rapidly.

Newnham: And what's happened to your competitors?

Singh: Building an offline to online business isn't easy in any country but in a country like India it's exceptionally hard because the infrastructure is grossly underdeveloped. To crack that and get to the masses especially outside the major metropolitan cities is hard. We were fortunate to have understood mobile and ridden the mobile wave when no one had thought of it. Plus we had morphed into a local merchant marketing platform. I think our competitors found it hard to scale or maybe didn't understand that an Indian model worked better than a Groupon model. There is only a handful left and they operate out of a handful of cities that we are in. Groupon recently exited—they sold their business to Sequoia, who relabeled it Nearbuy. There are a couple of other smaller ones in smaller pockets. There are different online cashback sites, but nobody is really trying to understand the user in their entirety. For us, it is about understanding and personalizing everything for the user.

Newnham: In addition to personalizing offers to users, is it seasonal and around specific events also?

Singh: It is a mix of both. It depends on the marketing needs and the kind of business it is. Some business use mydala through the year for all their marketing. Some use us seasonally during festive months. We cater to a wide range of businesses and close to 150,000 merchants. These include everything from large movie or coffee chains to small mom and pop shops that ramp up their business only during festive months.

Newnham: What's next for mydala? What are your goals for the business?

Singh: I don't know. I tell investors that too. Our ultimate goal is to build a solid business. But I will tell you this: I want to have a profitable business that makes all stakeholders a lot of money and one that brings value. I want to leave a legacy making my parents, in-laws, husband, co-founders, and all those who supported me proud.

I think you get to the stage where you question your purpose. This is not on a business level but on a personal level for me, and I've started wondering where I am making an impact and going beyond making an impact just in terms of merchants. I feel like mydala now has to have a bigger impact, so we are looking at what we are going to do on a social level as well. I am a big believer that if you get, you have to give back so, on a personal level, I am toying with some women mentorships, similar to Springboard. I don't know what we will do in terms of mydala. We still have to make money, otherwise the investors will be very upset, but there's got to be a bigger impact that we are making.

Newnham: And users know that they are having their information accessed?

Singh: This is a misunderstood statement we're talking about reaching users on USSD. There is no accessing information there. Users come to mydala WAP and personalize their own feeds—that is the information we tap into.

Newnham: What are you most proud of in your career thus far?

Singh: I am proud to be making a dent in the universe in some shape or form. It might be the tiniest dent but it is there. More than proud, I am at a point where I am happy. It's not like I'm satisfied and I am done. But I am at a point where I am happy with the impact we make. With the businesses we help market and grow. None of this would have been possible if we decided to shut shop the numerous times we should have.

It is why I tell my older daughter, "You can't quit. No matter what you do, baby, you've got to keep going. It is the only way you are going to win. It's okay if you don't want to do it anymore, but if you are going to do something, you've got to work really hard at it." That is what I have learned and what I pass on.

Newnham: What are some of the traits you think you possess that make you a strong leader?

Singh: More than anything, perseverance. You can be an introvert and be a great leader. You can be an extrovert and be a great leader. But you have to have perseverance. I have taught myself to be an extrovert, but I think perseverance above all will take you so far in life. It will get you through a lot.

Newnham: How do you think we get more women into tech?

Singh: I feel you get to a point when it is your moral responsibility to give back. I mean this even as women entrepreneurs. We need to mentor others and I don't just mean women mentoring women. My initial mentor wasn't a woman, it was my male professor. I feel mentors are so important and they change things, especially for women, who have a lot of doubt compared to men.

People laugh when I say this, but I was really shy when I was younger and I wouldn't speak up. But I've become very vocal about this subject now that I have daughters, because I feel that there are not enough role models and female entrepreneurs. Female entrepreneurs and women in tech should be the norm, not the exception.

Women are the same all over the globe. We all have the self-doubt and are queens of guilt. But I like what is happening now in India. There is a real change happening. It's like the tipping point. I'm seeing a lot more confident women who are trying to do things on their own, especially around tech entrepreneurship. And it's great. For the first time the proverbial glass ceiling is cracking at different places because there are phenomenal women all around the world chipping away at it.

Newnham: What are some of the most important lessons that you have learned in your career?

Singh: First, you can't have a plan B and you can't quit. If you have decided that you are going to take the plunge, then you take the plunge.

At the end of the day, as long as you stay in the game, you have probably won half the battle and you don't even know it. I joke about it now but I have been an overnight success for seven years.

Second, you'd better be solving a problem. I have so many entrepreneurs who come to me now and their business model is that they want to raise money. That's not a business model and that cannot be the end goal.

Judith Owigar

Cofounder, JuaKali Workforce

Judith Owigar is the founder of JuaKali Workforce, an online micro-jobs platform that links employers with skilled manual laborers in Kenya's informal sector.

In 2010, Judith cofounded AkiraChix, alongside Angela O. Lungati, Linda Kamau, and Marie Githinji. A not-for-profit organization on a mission to inspire and develop women in technology to become leaders, AkiraChix runs a year-long program that includes training, outreach, and mentorship for women in technology.

Judith was a recipient of the Anita Borg Change Agent Award in 2011. She was also awarded the Unsung Heroes Award from the US Embassy in Kenya.

Judith has a degree in computer science and a master's degree in applied computing from the University of Nairobi.

Danielle Newnham: What is your background?

Judith Owigar: I was always very adventurous and playful and did lots of extracurricular activities in school. I was in the school choir, played netball, and did swimming and debates. I always got involved in many different things. I was lucky because it never affected my school work, which I was good at.

Surprisingly, I didn't do computer lessons in high school because I found them pretty boring but I used to hang around the computer club, so that is really how I developed my interest in tech. I was more interested in the math area so I just wanted to find college courses with math in them. Computer science was one of those courses, so that's pretty much how I ended up on the course.

© Danielle Newnham 2016

D. Newnham, *Female Innovators at Work*, DOI 10.1007/978-1-4842-2364-2_6

I guess growing up, I did not really know what I wanted to become, I just knew what I didn't want to become. So this is pretty much how I selected my career, a process of elimination.

Newnham: What didn't you want to become?

Owigar: I knew I didn't want to become a lawyer, a doctor, or a teacher, so when it came to choosing my career, I just did an elimination of what I didn't want and what was remaining was engineering and computer science. My brother had also told me that I could make money after two years and that was enough to convince me. And so that's how I ended up in the tech industry.

Newnham: How soon after graduating did you start your first business?

Owigar: Well, I started a mobile business right after graduation. Myself and a group of friends from my computer science class came together to start it and were talking to the UN about becoming a client, but working with organizations like the UN is a long process and we all needed to earn a proper living at this stage. The business focused on mobile technology, which at that point was pretty new, and all of us had done previous projects using mobile applications. So we planned to build a mobile communications system for the UN because they have so many people in the field who use mobile devices, including in remote areas. We were going to build an app for them that would collect data and track people, but since the deal didn't go through quickly enough, we got jobs and stopped working on it. That would have been at the end of 2007.

Newnham: So what led to AkiraChix?

Owigar: AkiraChix was started in 2010 after I met two of my cofounders at my second job. We were in a tech company with five developers. Four of us were women, but what we would find is that people would still question who was coding in the company, despite the fact we were eighty percent representation. So we felt that women in tech were invisible and that people probably don't even recognize our contributions. We felt the tech industry wasn't a good or comfortable place for women to work in at the time. There was a high dropout rate of women in the industry, which was due to them not being visible or recognized for their work.

So we decided to start AkiraChix to build a community of women in technology, where we could encourage each other and build each other up so that we could become really good at what we did and progress in our careers. Whilst setting this up, we also realized that there were very few female role models who we could identify with, and look up to in Kenya, and so one of the gaps we wanted to fill was to become role models for other young girls entering the field of technology.

Newnham: And what was the tech startup scene like in Kenya back then?

Owigar: It was very young. The first generation of tech entrepreneurs were just starting businesses. We didn't have a lot of visibility, and at that point, we only had a mailing list, called skunkworks, to connect people in the tech industry. And this mailing list is where tech people used to talk about different things. It was like our virtual meeting place. And then I think a year or two later, we had the first meetup, a barcamp, which was the first time that tech people were coming together in the same place to discuss issues. So it was pretty young. It was something new. There wasn't a lot of glory or press, so it was more an industry for the curious, the adventurous, and the nerds.

Newnham: How has the startup scene and AkiraChix evolved since then?

Owigar: I would say that Kenya's startup scene is in the teenage phase now. In the teenager phase, there are a lot of changes. There is a lot of conflict, a lot of confusion, and if you actually look at the tech industry, that is exactly what is going on here now. We are going through the growth spurts and the growing pains, which means there is a lot of misunderstanding and questioning going on. Some people might think we have lost direction, but I feel like this is actually a part of its growth and it will help us mature. But we are not mature right now, not even our technologies. We are just moving on from copy and paste, to innovating, to our own specific problems, and finding our own specific solutions.

In terms of women, I must say that when we first started AkiraChix, there were very few visible women in tech here and very few occupied leadership positions in the tech industry, so that was definitely the number-one problem we had identified. And even when we were participating in tech events, there were very few women. Usually, my friends and I were the only group of women, but now, we can identify far more women leaders in the tech industry. And there are others working on the issue now, so it is not just our issue anymore. Other clubs, and hubs, and universities here are consciously trying to increase the number of women in the tech industry now, which is great.

In terms of mentoring, we have a mentorship program that is part of our training program. Our training program targets young women from underprivileged backgrounds who have finished high school. We take them through a one-year program in mobile and web development, graphic design, and entrepreneurship. One of the reasons we introduced our mentorship program was because we realized that some girls would drop out and we wouldn't know the reasons why until after they left, so we introduced mentorship as a way for older women to walk our students through the entire AkiraChix journey with them.

We also realized that many times when the girls dropped out, it wasn't really a technical or an education issue—it was usually a social issue. So the mentorship program is also there to identify any problems early on and so the girls can have someone to talk to when they have issues while in the program, but also someone who can help them prepare for the world of work. We cover how to present themselves, how to communicate, what is expected, how to balance career and family. All of these things help them stay in the program and continue in tech.

Newnham: And what other reasons do you think contribute to women leaving tech?

Owigar: In the earlier days, when I was talking to women who left the industry, it was because there were so many men. And it was like you had to fight for your place in the industry or to be recognized as a woman in tech. So many of the women who were leaving would just choose another industry that was more welcoming, where they didn't have to do as much proving of themselves, or where they didn't have to hide their femininity to succeed.

I think the second reason is that there is indeed a glass ceiling. Even if you do progress, you don't have people who can show you opportunities. Or you realize that as you go up in your career, many career mentors or career sponsors are often men. And then there is the situation where a man is mentoring a woman's career and the woman is married, and that can create a really uncomfortable environment in her family if her husband is not supportive. So I think this is where the place for peer mentorship comes in. Of course, there are some men who will mentor women who are completely comfortable, but just looking at how society has been shaped here in Kenya, it is a tricky road to be on, so that itself limits career development for many women.

One of the ways we can accommodate this is to have peer mentorship where women can mentor each other and support each other, even as they are going up the ranks.

Newnham: What do you hope to achieve as a result of AkiraChix?

Owigar: Really, my vision for AkiraChix is equal representation of men and women in the tech industry. I would like to see more women, not just using technology but building technology, too, to meet their own needs. I would like the tech creators to look like the tech users. Right now, most people look at women as consumers of technology, but I would like to see more women creators because I think that will influence the kind of businesses that are built and the kind of solutions that are created. So that is my vision for AkiraChix. But I would also like to take the program to other towns in Kenya, and even to scale it to other countries in Africa.

Newnham: Can you tell me how JuaKali started and what your mission is?

Owigar: So JuaKali is a mobile application and web site that links workers in the informal sector to markets and people who need their services. I got the idea for it when I was helping a lecturer at the University of Nairobi who was doing research into how workers in the informal sector use technology. I used to handle the focus groups for him here in Kenya. The thing that surprised me was when we went to the street where the JuaKali workers are. It is a street that I used to pass a lot, but I had never seen them before. They had been invisible to me every time I used to pass there. So I asked myself, "How many people don't even know that these guys are here? How many people pass here every day and don't even see them?" So it was the first time I had the idea of how to make them more visible.

Interestingly, there was a time that I needed a plumber in my house and I didn't know where I could get one, so the only thing I could refer to was these workers, who I knew now. I asked myself, "How do other girls in my situation figure it out?" Usually what people do actually is call the building caretaker, or call a friend, or ask on social media. That's how most people get plumbers or even carpenters and electricians. But one of the challenges these workers face is that people do not believe in the quality of their work. Some of the workers are really good but because many of them have not gone to school or have acquired their skills through apprenticeships they are not trusted. It should be noted that there are a large number of them who don't do good work. In fact, the word itself, Jua Kali, now has another meaning, which is when someone says someone has done a "Jua Kali job," it means they have done a substandard job, so Jua Kali workers are basically perceived as substandard workers.

So what I was creating with the system in JuaKali was a way for these workers to be able to market their skills but also a platform for them to build references that would help them get more work. I want to build a reference system for Jua Kali workers so that if a worker goes for a job, he can actually go on the site and say, "These are the jobs I have done and these are the customers I have worked with." That is my number-one vision for it because references will ensure more work for them.

Another thing I realized whilst interacting with the workers was that because other people view their work as substandard, they also look down on themselves. So I guess something else I would like to work on in the future is to help them see themselves as contributors to the community and to society. Because you know most of the people that do Jua Kali work, they do it because they have no other employment option. They are seen as people who failed exams and all they could do is Jua Kali work, so my other vision is to also give them pride and dignity in their work.

And my big pie-in-the-sky vision is that if we can improve the situation for workers in the informal sector, we can actually improve the economy, because workers in the informal sector make up eighty percent of the workforce in this country. So if you improve life for them, you improve life for the country.

Newnham: What are some of the biggest obstacles you have faced with JuaKali and also with AkiraChix?

Owigar: I think the greatest challenge for anyone starting anything here in Kenya is definitely access to funding, especially seed capital, so what most people resort to is bootstrapping. With AkiraChix, we got a lot of personal donations to fund the organization. We got a lot of volunteers in and we got a lot of free space, so that's how we moved it forward in the beginning. For JuaKali, it started with my own personal funding, and then I got a small grant that pushed it further, so I definitely think seed funding is one of the greatest challenges for entrepreneurs in this space.

Another challenge that entrepreneurs face is identifying partners and people who they can work with. I guess this goes hand in hand with knowing your market. It depends on what your business is, and also knowing and understanding which market to target, and who is willing to pay for your product or service. In the non-profit world, it could be identifying who the best funder is, who believes in what you are doing, and who is going to partner with you and help you build what you are doing.

The third challenge is mainly legal—so how startups should organize themselves legally. It can be as simple as how to register your business, because many people make the mistake when it comes to assigning the right entity, and if you don't get a good lawyer or someone to advise you, then you have to pay for that much later on.

Newnham: And how have you gone about overcoming some of those obstacles?

Owigar: I think it has been a lot of trial and error. And we have had a lot of bangs along the way and learnt from our mistakes, as well as other people's. I think the point is to talk to people a lot and get yourself a board or people who can advise you, preferably with strengths that you don't have. And people with knowledge of the industry that you are going to work in has also proved to be very important.

Newnham: You mentioned the issues with seed funding. How has that improved since you set up your first business, considering the Kenyan startup scene is evolving at quite a pace? Are you seeing more funding coming in from outside now?

Owigar: Most of the help with seed funding has come from outside Kenya. I think it is much harder to fundraise in Kenya than to fundraise out of the country. So at least there has been more interest from funding organizations and VC funds coming into the country, which has definitely been an improvement. But the problem with that is a lot of these funders want to put in from $100,000 all the way up to $2.5 million, which means it's much easier for people or companies that have at least a proof of concept, or some revenue to get that money. But for most people looking for amounts up to $50,000 to get the ball rolling, it's really hard for them to get what they need.

A lot of people look to the friends, family, and fools route for support. But I don't think that is applicable to a place like here in Kenya, because it comes from the presumption that your friends, family, and fools have this disposable income which they can invest in your company, which most people here don't have. And even when you look at many of these families, even with a growing middle class that we have here in Africa, many are a generation or two away from poverty, which means either you grew up poor, or your parents grew up poor, or your grandparents were poor. So the idea of giving money to a business and you are not sure it is going to actually come back to you, or you are supposed to get money back after five years—it's too risky for most people to do this. And even banks are not willing to give credit to small companies that are starting out. So, that is where the challenge is.

Newnham: Are there crowdfunding platforms in Kenya?

Owigar: Yes, in Kenya we have our informal crowdfunding and we call it harambee. This is a culture we have always had. It is when people come together and contribute toward something, but usually the nature of harambees are for medical bills or when a child is going to study abroad or if something happened in the country, like a disaster, and people need to come together. That is when crowdfunding works, but crowdfunding for business is not something we have actually done here. People have tried it and it has failed. I really don't know why it has failed, but it has.

Another challenge I see with funding is definitely that funders will often give money to people who look like them. I guess it is a bias because they don't intentionally do it, but it just happens like this and so that affects who gets money here.

I also think another issue for female founders that I specifically deal with is the confidence gap. There are many women who will take a lot of convincing to build their business or sell their products, or even if they are making sales, they don't see that their business could scale. So I don't think they are as confident in themselves and in their abilities as men might be, and I think that actually limits their businesses because of it. And we need to change that.

Newnham: Both your business and non-profit have a strong social mission. What drives you?

Owigar: I realized early on that I am mainly driven by having a social mission. Even in my previous job, whenever I was given a project, I always wanted to know whose project it was. I didn't want to just code the software, I wanted to know the story behind what we were building and how somebody was going to benefit from it. Because money was never enough for me. So, in time, I realized that since I want to work on projects with a social mission, if I am to start a business, then it just has to have that or I will lose the energy required to work on it.

With JuaKali, the social mission developed later, but when I discovered it, that was what drove me. It is the same with AkiraChix. Just knowing I am creating a better world, not just for myself, but for other people, that is what gives me energy to do these things.

Newnham: What advice would you offer other young women who want to enter the tech field?

Owigar: The first one I would say is to be adventurous. The reason I say that is because the tech industry has so many facets and it changes so fast that it requires you to change with the times. Also, be curious about what is happening, because when you change with the times, you become relevant because you are constantly learning.

Also, surround yourself with people who want to encourage you to be the best version of yourself, because what I have realized is that the people around you are the ones who influence where your career is going to go. Whether you start a business with them, or they challenge you to become better, or they could pull you down. Either way, they are very important, so choose carefully.

Newnham: Finally, what are you most proud and why?

Owigar: I think I am most proud of the first accolade I got, which was actually when I was a student at the University of Nairobi. I entered a competition at The Institute of Electrical and Electronic Engineers Student exhibition and I won the best female engineer. That recognition meant so much, especially because, at that time, my family was going through a really hard time. I decided to go to the event just to see if there was anything out there for me. And then I won and it changed my view on life.

At the time, I had nearly given up. I didn't really know if I would be able to succeed in this life or contribute anything, and then I entered this competition and people recognized my work, and they thought it was good, and they thought I could make a difference. And that made me think, okay, I actually can make a difference. I shall always go on knowing I can make a difference, irrespective of what is going on in my life.

Brenda Romero

Cofounder, Loot Drop

Brenda Romero *is a multi-award-winning game designer, artist, writer, creative director, Fulbright Scholar, and the cofounder of Romero Games and Loot Drop, which she founded with husband John Romero.*

Starting her career at Sir-Tech Software in 1981, Brenda remained with the games developer and publisher for almost 20 years before moving on to work at Atari and Cyberlore Studios. Brenda's 30 years of experience in the games industry includes work on the hugely successful Wizardry, Jagged Alliance, Dungeons & Dragons and Ghost Recon franchises. Brenda has also worked as program director of the UC Santa Cruz Masters in Games and Playable Media Program, and was chair of the Savannah College of Art and Design's Interactive Design and Game Development department. She is presently course director for the MSc in Game Design and Development program at University of Limerick.

A stalwart of the video games industry, Brenda also created a series of analog games entitled The Mechanic Is the Message, which she began in 2008. The series is composed of six separate non-digital games that include Train and Síochán Leat (The Irish Game), which is currently on exhibit at The Strong National Museum of Play in New York.

Among many awards for her contributions to the industry, Brenda was awarded the Game Developers Choice Ambassador award in 2015.

Danielle Newnham: Can you tell me a little about your background?

© Danielle Newnham 2016
D. Newnham, *Female Innovators at Work*, DOI 10.1007/978-1-4842-2364-2_7

Brenda Romero: My mother would have described me as a friendly kid who was almost always happy. I was a bit of a loner, but not a sad loner. I enjoyed being myself and playing by myself. I also remember that I just loved writing. I still do. So basically, my childhood was about making up stories and making up worlds. I also loved playing with Legos because I liked building things—again, specifically building imaginary worlds.

It's interesting because I think if you had interviewed me at different times of my life, I would have something different to say about this, but there was a particularly transformative event that shaped me. I look back on it now and think it's pretty great that sometimes the fissures that happen in our lives can seem absolutely horrible at the time, but they can also end up being these amazing catalysts for other things.

So when I was thirteen, I lost all of my friends—not for dumb reasons, but I guess their parents probably thought I wasn't the best kid to hang out with. Somebody suggested when I was about ten years old that what would make me cool was if I swore—and God knows why I listened to that, but I did. And I am sure I didn't know exciting words at that time. I wasn't dropping f-bombs at ten, for sure. But then I remember discovering cigarettes. I wasn't really smoking, but we thought, "Could we get a pack of these things?" Anyway, looking back now, I think other parents—and being a parent now myself, I think the other parents made a valid parenting call. The parents and other kids obviously thought I was going on a rougher path. And two friends, specifically, even said "We don't want to hang around you anymore," which was tough.

I should also say that another catalyst was that one of those girls had also stolen liquor from her parents and blamed it on me. I don't think that if I had been an all-round wholesome kid the blame would have stuck, but it did. In any case, the end result was that I was thirteen at the time and at that age, there are probably fewer things worse than losing your friends. It was a pretty significant piece of social damage I guess, but what it also did was absolutely cemented in me the idea that I was going to be somebody. I was not going to be who you said I was. I was going to be somebody. And no matter where I was and no matter what I was doing, my whole goal was to be one better. Whatever you did, I was going to be one better. Whatever position you were in, I was going to be one position above it.

So I was always looking at where the next step was. What is the path? And I think some kids come by that via a role model, so they see somebody ahead of them doing that, but I grew up in a pretty poor farming community where there were not a lot of those kinds of people for me to take those steps, so I wouldn't have seen it. So for me, it wasn't revenge. I didn't feel any hatred, interestingly enough. I was just adamant that I was going to be somebody.

I first started designing games and got into the games industry when I was fifteen. My mother, amazingly, thought that was just the greatest thing. She was always incredibly proud of me, so that was also a factor. I never heard "Oh, that's a ridiculous job." Never. She thought I was at the forefront of technology and always supported me.

Other significant events occurred during this time. My dad passed away when I was four. My sister, who is nineteen years older than I am, was a super-feminist. This was, of course, during the time of women's rights. And so, what I was seeing in front of me was my mother—who was literally the mother who can do it all—and my sister. So I never grew up with any sense that my gender was limiting at all. In fact, until people started interviewing me and talking about my gender, which happened I think in the late '90s, it had never really even occurred to me. I mean, obviously I am surrounded by guys, but unless someone actually points that out to you, you don't necessarily notice it.

Newnham: You got into games early. What were some of your gaming influences growing up?

Romero: When I first started getting into games, we didn't have any money. It was just me and my mom. I think her total income was around $7,000 a year, so we didn't have anything. What we would do, however, is we would go to yard sales, which were really popular when I was growing up, and I would get something small for like a quarter or a dime, at every yard sale we went to. I would then buy cheap board games that didn't have all the pieces, and I would make my own games with all the pieces.

Then when I was around eleven, I encountered the original Dungeons & Dragons, and to me, that was absolutely magical. Not only did it lay the groundwork for all the role-playing games that I would later work on, but it also allowed me to create interactive stories, which was one step further than just plain old writing, which I had enjoyed so much.

Then at some point, my mother managed to get the Commodore VIC-20 at the house. I loved coding. I loved typing in things from magazines and seeing what happened. But with the VIC-20, there was a cassette tape, which was incredibly limited. So for me, where things really became amazing was at high school, where we originally started out with a TRS-80, but then these were replaced by very early PCs. And man, I fell so in love with coding then. I would stay at school late. Every single study hall, I would try to get a pass to go and code. For me, it was like building with these digital Legos that I could do anything with.

Then at fifteen, I was approached by Linda Sirotek [now Linda Currie], who was also fifteen. She and her brothers and father had this game company called Sir-Tech, where they were working on a game called Wizardry. So, we were in the girl's bathroom at school and she was looking for a non-menthol cigarette. She was asking a bunch of people, so I gave her one. And to be polite, she struck up a conversation with me where she asked if I had a job. "No." Had I heard of Sir-Tech? Also "No," And had I heard about Wizardry? "No." But had I ever heard of Dungeons & Dragons? Yes, I had. I had played it. So that was pretty much all it took for me to join the company. That was more or less my interview.

So I showed up at her house. I think it was October 6, 1981. That was the first time I got to play Wizardry. It was just incredible. If you took my passion for programming, my passion for Dungeons & Dragons, and that I just loved computers because I could build anything with them—seeing Wizardry for the first time was mind-blowingly amazing. Seeing Wizardry for the first time had a huge effect on me because I had never seen anything like it before. The equivalent for my kids today would be if they saw a car levitating down the street. It would probably have a similar effect on them, as seeing Wizardry for the first time did for me.

So I got lucky. If I had answered that question wrong, "Have you got a job?" "Yup,"—my whole future would be changed. Also, I remember that just before that interview at Sir-Tech, I had interviewed for another job where my friend was a waitress. I went in, unbeknownst to me, with a lower button on my blouse undone, which I couldn't have seen looking down. Anyway, the wife of the restaurant owner was there and thought I was trying to hit on him, so I didn't get the job because of that.

Newnham: Thanks goodness.

Romero: Yeah, no kidding, right? You know, I am thankful to that blouse for the rest of my life. Although it would be a really stupid way to hit on somebody.

Newnham: So you were fifteen when you joined Sir-Tech. Were you still at high school?

Romero: Yes, I was still at high school. At Sir-Tech, they had what was called a Wizardry hotline. It was open every day from 4 to 8 pm, Monday through Friday, so I would go there after school. I would even do the 2 to 10 pm on the weekends, if I could. It just turned into an all-out overwhelming love affair.

Newnham: And was this hotline for players having trouble playing the game?

Romero: Yeah. So a classic question that we got was, "I can't find the wizard on the tenth level. How do I get to the tenth level?" And so I would say, "Well first of all you have to find the elevator in the dark area on level one, take the elevator to level four, and get the blue ribbon. The blue ribbon will gain you access to a private elevator that will take you to level nine. From level nine, when you walk out of the elevator, take the door on your left, and in the far left corner of that room, there is a teleporter that will take you down to the tenth level, which is a series of seven rooms. And after those seven rooms, you encounter Werdna, defeat him and finally win the game." As you can tell, whole tracks of my brain are still devoted to remembering all the facts that you could ever need to know about the Wizardry games. I was basically a living hint book.

Then I moved on from that job. I basically did a bit of everything—from packing boxes to customer services if something went wrong with the game, to public relations, to product development, to development management, to game design, to traveling to trade shows. If someone needed something done for the game, I would volunteer. "Hey, I could do it!" So it took from writing the manuals and all the documentation around the game, which I did for years to, "Hey, could you do some research on monsters or weapons?" To designing some levels, to then eventually being a designer on the series.

Newnham: You stayed at Sir-Tech for almost twenty years. What led to you deciding to leave and start a new challenge?

Romero: I would say I actually stayed far too long—not that it was a horrible place. Look, it's easier to look back in hindsight and say, "These ten things could have been better," or to be surprised that these three things happened, right? I think that's easy in hindsight but when you grow up in an industry and at a company, which I quite literally did, you don't really see those things until later. And that's the good and the not-so-good things.

But, by not leaving earlier, I missed the opportunity to learn from other people. I think if a company is dynamic and changing, and it's working on different types of games and different platforms, then you are still learning, right? But with Sir-Tech, I feel like I got as high as I was going to get and I was not financially vested in the company. I mean it was twenty years, man, so I felt like I had learned everything I could learn about an RPG [role-playing game] as Sir-tech made them. And I was more or less learning from the same individuals.

So what led me to leave, really, was boredom. And I don't mean there wasn't always something to do, but in 2001, I just knew I couldn't make something with a sword again, at least not right away. I had made games and swords for twenty years. And it was not that I didn't love the Wizardry series and that I didn't love the games that we worked on, but I just needed something with a gun or something that wasn't in that time period. So, anyway, I contacted them, because I was just coming back from maternity leave, and before I could even say "You know, I think I'm going to be looking for another gig," I found out the company planned to close after it shipped Wizardry 8. So, it was a done deal regardless. And ridiculously, I ended up going from there to working at Atari on Dungeons & Dragons, where there were no guns either, but that was the IP that started them all, so it felt like a good idea to do that at the time.

I then stayed at Atari for two and a half years, which was this interesting thing because they were quite obviously shutting down that studio. Well, it was quite obvious to me. I don't think it was quite obvious to many other people, so I left there to join Cyberlore as soon as the game was done. And they did indeed close that studio very shortly after.

Newnham: And when did you decide to set up on your own?

Romero: So, even though I think I am very driven and very self-motivated, you know, my problem isn't how to work eight hours today, it's how not to work twelve or more. Especially in Ireland, where I live now and where it stays light until nearly eleven o'clock at night in the summer. Last night, I walked home at what I thought was a totally reasonable hour of around seven. And I then noticed that the grocery store was closing and realized that it was ten.

So the answer to the question is that I had been working at a company called Lolapps. Up to this point in my career, I had no exposure to the business workings of how a company stayed afloat—what it takes and so forth, I just had no idea. I mean, maybe I could have looked, but I was far more interested in how systems in games worked. I was the creative director at Lolapps. They had two games that they were trying to get out the door, so I said, "I'll tell you what. I can take one and let me call in a friend of mine, as he's got some extra cycles, and see what he can do with the other—if you guys are okay with it?" They were. And game one was already out the door.

Game two—the one John, my husband, was on—eventually turned into Ravenwood Fair, which was a massive success. It made them millions of dollars. And that's not to say I haven't worked on projects that haven't made lots of money for companies before, because I have, but what was unique about this project was that it didn't make me feel as if I were a part of the company.

They had a different set of ideals from what mine are. They came from the web apps space, which was sort of fail fast, just get it out the door, go-go-go, and I came from the "let's try and polish the hell out of this thing and get it out there." And they would also crunch for the months of January and February. And I am no stranger to crunch. I think my longest crunch was nine months. Crunch is usually twelve-hour days, five days a week or six days a week. And a death march in game development is every day, every hour you can put in. Those are my definitions but they're also common game industry terms.

So I had certainly been in crunches and death marches but this specific one was, "Well, we're going to tell people we need them to crunch through January and February." And my thought was why? We are not off on our milestones, so what was the reasoning behind it? And the reasoning behind it was that, "Well, we get a lot of work done if we do it like this." But these guys had just crunched to get Ravenwood Fair out and so there is really no reason to do this other than to get double the time out of people. And you know, if you have reason to do it, my experience is that the whole team will be behind it, but this was unnecessary. And they wanted John to do a new game for them. So we ended up leaving.

Also, I was really fortunate because John really ended up being my mentor for starting my own business. He had founded his first startup when he was fourteen—Capitol Ideas Software. And he first started coding at eleven, so he had started at a very early age too. And then he went on to found a whole bunch of companies—many that are still around. So there was sort of the notion that, well, we could make another game for Lolapps and make them lots of money, and have people work in ways that we wouldn't have them work, or we could just go do it ourselves. And why wouldn't we want to do that? So, for me, that's how I stepped out into being a founder.

Having not seen other people do that, and not having been in that startup ecosystem, it was more like: other people have companies and I just work for them. But as soon as somebody starts questioning why you don't do it yourself, you think, 'You're right. Why don't I?'" An example of this is our eleven year old. When he was nine, he came up with his own company, Tiger Scratch Studios. For him, if you want to make games, you'd obviously start your own company, because that's what he sees right in front of him. Whereas I grew up in an egregiously blue-collar community and if you wanted to work, you worked for someone else.

So that was my step out into founder land.

Newnham: What were some of the surprises that you found from running your own studio? Some of the lessons that you learned early on?

Romero: Well, the hardest lesson, absolutely without a doubt, was that not everyone is going to like you. And sometimes you can't necessarily tell people everything, which is actually something I started to learn even working at the C-level. For instance, I can remember one of the most difficult things that I had to do. There was this guy who was one of the friendliest people you could ever meet. I never knew him to not be positive and I was just thrilled that he was working in the games industry. He was such a nice guy. I walked by him on my way to get coffee and he said, "Hey Brenda." And I said, "Hey Darren." But I knew when I said that that he was going to be laid off in an hour. And you know it's like, oh my God. So the people decisions you have to make—those are just gut-wrenching. I hate letting people go to this day. I hate doing layoffs. Those are horrible—especially when you are genuinely deeply affecting the lives of other people. I hate that but there are just no two ways about it. And I know that if I ever get to the point when I don't hate it, then I have lost some piece of my humanity.

But as I said, some of the hardest lessons as a founder are that people aren't always going to like you. Another example is when one of our projects was cancelled by a publisher, so we had to lay the team off. We didn't really have a choice. We couldn't fund the team because we were funding other projects at the time, so we had to lay them off. And one of the team members walked over and quite literally dropped the laptop in front of me so that it hit the ground really hard. And I can infer, based on that, that the guy didn't like me anymore.

But, as a business owner, you're not always going to make decisions that are popular. In fact, you're not always going to be right either. You might be doing the right thing the wrong way or the wrong thing the right way. Or, I'm sure, the wrong thing the wrong way. So being human and being prone to error and things like that are going to happen as well. And people are not going to like your decisions.

Another big piece of learning for me over the last few years has been really making sure that I set budget aside, in every project, for things that are just good for employees and not just good for the project specifically. Nearly always things that are good for employees are also good for the project in the long run.

For instance, let's just say whatever the project is, five percent of the project is set aside for bonuses, for surprising employees, for having cool things in the office, for training, and so on. When it is allocated like that at the beginning, even if you are a super penny-pincher, you know that that budget is specifically set aside to do things for people and it can't be spent on anything else. And I think, honest to goodness, it is such a trivial thing really, but mentally, it's a big thing because then you are not worrying, "Oh well, if we do this for them, what will we do if we need it for the game later?" It is already allocated for the team and that is where it will be spent, so we incorporate this into our costs from the start.

It's interesting what you learn in a seemingly short period of time—although it's been six years since I started my own company, which is not that short. The things that would have crazy terrified me when I started the company no longer terrify me. For instance, if it seemed like a key programmer was unbelievably upset and angry and potentially going to quit for whatever reason, that could cause me to drop everything and do everything I needed to not let it happen. But nowadays I have a much more holistic look. "Well, you know what, if he wants to leave, and that's also causing issues with other people on the team, then we should let him go." You have to know that, truly, everyone has to be replaceable because if they are not, you are in trouble.

Also, I have learned to be smarter about budgeting and smarter about planning. I'm not someone who has a poker face, so if I feel stressed out that something is going to happen, anybody around me would also know that I'm stressed out about things. So it takes way more to get me concerned right now than it ever did before. And that is a good thing.

Newnham: Can you tell me about the design process? What it's like at the beginning and as it evolves?

Romero: So usually the design process for me begins when I become fascinated with a topic. It's not because I am looking to make a game necessarily, but I just become fascinated with certain topics. For instance, I am currently fascinated with the Sinaloa Cartel and the whole system that's around that. So look at El Chapo—he was, and I believe still is—illiterate. He was born into abject poverty but nonetheless he creates an entire empire with an illegal product, and becomes one of the most successful men in the world while people are trying to kill him. So, I am not saying he hasn't done many abhorrent things on his rise to fame, but it's a fascinating system and it's fascinating how he has mobilized people in Sinaloa. They view him as a Robin Hood of sorts.

So that's super-fascinating to me. And what I think is common with a lot of game designers is that I will just read obsessively about these things. Every news article I can get my hands on. I have probably been finished with the Sinaloa Cartel and El Chapo at least three times. And then they will find him or he escapes, and I will go into the wilderness reading about this stuff again. So I know that obsession, at some point in time, will find its way into a game. I don't know where but I know I've learned enough about it that my head is ready to use it.

So, for most of my games, it starts with an obsession. Having worked on RPGs, I tend to stick to historical subjects. And since they are based in history, I am fortunate that I can just study history, which shows you what systems were already there. How did a historical event happen? What are the systems that allowed it to happen? What skills did people have? It's all there. So once I make a decision about that, I will do one of two things, but both work simultaneously usually. As I am researching stuff, I start working with a programmer to make a prototype just to test out some design ideas. And the prototype may not look anything like how the game is going to look but it's letting me find out how if what I see in my head is plausible, fun, and interesting. What can be done to make it more plausible, fun, and interesting?

And once I have a good idea that this is something that will fly, it then turns into something very much like the movie process. So for bigger games, which we are not able to fund ourselves, I write a pitch document, which is usually twenty pages. And along with the pitch document are an art bible and art moods, so people can see what it looks like, and a company summary. And then that goes to our agents and our agents pitch it to publishers. A publisher expresses interest in a game and then they fund the game in exchange for a big chunk of the revenue.

Newnham: I know all games are different, but on average, how long does it take to get from concept stage to release?

Romero: Probably three and a half years. There's other games where we have a quick concept and we try to slam it out as quickly as we can. Certainly when we were working in the mobile and web space our products were... Man, Ravenwood Fair was two and a half months from concept to completion. It was two and a half months of calendar time but probably actually four months, which is still ridiculous.

Newnham: And what has been one of your favorite games to work on and why?

Romero: I think probably Gunman Taco Truck. The reason why is because everyone who is working on the game are all people I genuinely love being with, and genuinely enjoy hanging out with. The game is funny. It's a labor of love. It was an idea my eleven-year-old kid had and all the family has been involved with it in some way, shape, or form. And it got picked up by Adult Swim, so we're not too far from finishing it and it will come out on Steam and mobile soon enough, hopefully. It's just been a blast to work on.

And then I would say for big games, I am really enjoying the pre-production stuff on John's latest shooter. It's a great learning curve for me. Obviously, I've played shooters a lot and I know quite a bit about shooters, but it's a great opportunity to be able to learn from somebody who literally pioneered the genre. And I don't know how else you'd get that opportunity, so I'm asking him questions, watching what he's doing, challenging some of the stuff he's thinking about design-wise, and you know, having a back and forth with him, even if it's a disagreement. It's obviously his game, so it doesn't really matter what I think, but having the opportunity to butt heads with him and see where he's really digging in is good because he will only dig in if it's right, which is hugely educational, and this is an education you simply cannot get any other way.

When you reach a certain point as a game designer, the only way you get an education is by working with people who are better than you. So in this case, I am fortunate to work with somebody who has triple the output of games that I do. He hasn't made an RPG yet, but maybe we'll do that at some point.

Newnham: How would you say the gaming landscape has changed since you started out?

Romero: In some sense, everything has changed. And in other ways, very little has changed. It is still, "I am trying to create an experience for you. That experience will be conveyed to you either on a table top, or an iPhone, or on a console, or an Apple II." So there's going to be some kind of machine or platform that we will use to transfer this game from me to you in some set of rules. So all of that has stayed the same. The things I find fascinating—all the areas that I like to explore in making a game—has stayed the same.

But the biggest changes have been the speed of game development, which has changed radically. It's funny because as much as I want to say that, maybe we've actually just gone back, because in the early days, taking a year to make a game was like "Whoa. What the hell are you doing?" Then as games' graphical fidelity got better, production took longer because production values take time. But probably the biggest change—besides obviously hardware changes, which goes without saying—has been our ability to communicate directly with players and players' ability to have a direct say about what they like and don't like about the game. For instance, recently I was debating playing one of two games. I put it on Twitter and got answers back very quickly. And that also extends to our ability to disseminate design information between one another. Recently, I was giving a talk on "what [game development] teams need to know," and as part of that talk, I was curious about what advice should you give to a team. If you could give a team any advice, what would it be? And I got back dozens of answers from people in the games industry, so the ability to reach out very quickly and to have this network of people that can rally behind a single tweet to give you great advice is unbelievably valuable.

Saying that, at the same time, this easy access to game developers has created some crazy things, right? Like No Man's Sky. They delayed the game and got death threats for it! So there is certainly a price in being super available. I mean, I have been called pretty much every name in the book. So there's a price for it but you have the ability to have very quick dissemination of design information. You know having GDC [Game Developers Conference] talks online on YouTube that you can watch… Having this sort of worldwide development community and ability to share information back and forth is incredibly valuable.

Newnham: And when you get feedback on a game by using Twitter, for example, do you feedback that information to your team?

Romero: Yes, absolutely. Like when we were setting up here, it was a time when we were able to say, "Okay, we are starting from scratch again. What would we like to do?" What if you wanted to set up a really great company and you didn't want to just rest on your laurels and say, "Hopefully, people will want to come and work with me." I mean, John has been very fortunate because there are a lot of great programmers that want to come and work with him, so hiring programmers has never been an issue for us, but what if you just wanted to do something you think would be really cool for people? So I thought about a company that I knew people consistently say that they love to work at. It was Insomniac. So I contacted Mike Acton and asked him what his secret was. He said, "Here you go." So once we get the ball rolling, all that stuff will exist and is already accounted for in the funding.

Newnham: When you talk about funding, are you talking about taking on investment or the games getting funded?

Romero: When the games get funded. We've never taken on investment.

Newnham: You've addressed several issues in gaming, such as being a woman. What do you see as some of the biggest issues today that you think gaming can tackle?

Romero: I think representation in games. I am going to argue both sides of this. On the one hand, I think it's really important if your game allows character customization, to really think that through. So for instance, I know that in some games, I can adjust the glabella of my character. And the only reason I even know what a glabella is, by the way, is because of a game. And in that very same game, if I wanted to make a character that was brown skinned, I had a hair choice between cornrows or an afro, as if that was the only type of hair you could have as a brown-skinned person. Whereas if I wanted to have a character that was a color other than brown, I had tons of different hairstyles that you would consider to be traditionally white.

So, anyway, there is this lack of representation in games and I think it's important that if you do a lot of character customization, that you account for those things. You account for the ability to pick male, female, or gender-binary characters, and that we don't make assumptions if the game involves having love interests and we let players choose—we don't make gendered choices for them. So I think all of that stuff is important, and as development teams become more diverse, I believe that the content of games will themselves become more diverse. It's not a chicken-and-egg dilemma, as some people say, because more diverse teams make more diverse games. It's a fact.

On the flipside, however, I think you should also be able to make your character precisely who you want your character to be because the exact moment I give you control over who that lead character is, I remove my ability to control your story and some part of the experience. So you surrender a bit of your storytelling ability when you do that.

Newnham: And what would you like your legacy to be?

Romero: You know, I am going to go with the very first thing in my head: I think it would be great to make a game with my daughter. When she was pretty young, she said she wanted to make a game with me. I am hoping that we get to start that this year. And if it means I leave a second generation of female game developers, I think that will be pretty great too. To leave the game industry a little bit better than I found it.

Carol Reiley

Cofounder and President, Drive.ai

Carol Reiley *is the cofounder and President of Drive.ai, which is creating AI software for autonomous vehicles. Formed out of Stanford University's Artificial Intelligence Lab, Drive.ai is creating what's next after the automobile.*

Carol spent 15 years researching various applications of robotics, including underwater, land, space, and surgical. She also founded TinkerBelle Labs, which focused on addressing global problems through the design of innovative technical solutions.

Previously, Carol worked at Intuitive Surgical, which manufactures robotic surgical systems, including the daVinci Surgical System.

Carol has authored two children's books—Ada Beta, an interactive book about programming, technology, and robots, and Making a Splash: A Growth Mindset Children's Book (Go Brain, 2015).

Carol is on leave from a PhD in computer science, holds a master's degree in computer science from John Hopkins University, and has a bachelor's degree in computer engineering from Santa Clara University.

Newnham: Can you tell me about your background?

Reiley: I was born in Michigan and I grew up in the Pacific Northwest because we moved there when I was five. My dad is an engineer, and my mom is a flight attendant, who was a stay-at-home mom until my younger brother went to kindergarten. I think it gave us a dual perspective because my dad is very logical and a builder/DIY person, and loves to jump into things. He always dragged us around and asked us to think about physical things and how do you fix this?

© Danielle Newnham 2016
D. Newnham, *Female Innovators at Work*, DOI 10.1007/978-1-4842-2364-2_8

He is a problem solver so we would really geek out with my dad. My mom really thinks about humanity and people, and asks how whatever I am doing impact the world? So whatever I was interested in, she would always bring it back to how is this important? Growing up, it was a really nice balance to have these two sides.

They were also both really encouraging of whatever career I picked. I think they were a little shocked that I went into engineering because they were probably expecting my younger brother to be an engineer—which he is—but I also ended up majoring in engineering.

Growing up, I did very well in school and was well-rounded. In math, science, sports, and English as well. I liked writing—it wasn't like I knew I wanted to be engineer. My personality is very quirky and I liked to try a lot of different things, which I guess I still do.

Newnham: And who were some of your earlier influences? Was it your dad who encouraged you to go into engineering?

Reiley: Not at all actually. He taught us how to do basic programming but in the same way that he also taught us how to play basketball so I don't think he was pushing us into a certain direction. I had great teachers who would pull me aside and encourage me in certain areas. In junior high and high school, I had thought I might want to become a doctor because I had really wanted to help people.

I even spent four years volunteering at the hospital, doing different tasks like the emergency room where I would file and pass out coffee or the gift shop where I would deliver flowers to the maternity ward, and I just thought it was such an interesting place that you got to see the whole lifecycle from birth to death. And I really thought I might want to become a doctor but then I learned about the pacemaker. I thought about how doctors who work so tirelessly, helping patients one at a time, but had the insight that with the invention of something like the pacemaker, you could actually impact millions of lives at a time. My 16-year-old mind was blown.

And around then, you would hear about Bill Gates, who is also from Washington State, and Steve Jobs, and about the dot-com. And that was all around the same time I went to college, in 2000. It was at the peak of the dot-com era when I applied for colleges. I had picked different majors for different schools. For the Silicon Valley schools, I had selected computer science because it seemed the most promising.

Newnham: So did you have your sights set on Silicon Valley even then?

Reiley: I was interested in either Washington State or California. I wasn't thinking super-long-term. The biggest thing was that I had not formally programmed before. My first real programming class was freshman class of college and it was tremendously hard and scary because you are pitted against people who have been coding since they were ten. So it felt like a completely unfair advantage and it made me feel very dumb, and I almost quit several times.

Newnham: What kept you going?

Reiley: When I was picking schools, one factor was the major. I picked engineering and went to Santa Clara because they gave me a full scholarship tied to the fact that I would stay an engineer for four years. It came with a Research Fellowship which meant I had to pick a project in a research lab for four years. If I had gone to UC Berkeley however, where I had originally planned to go, I would have been a business major and not an engineering major. But my dad had gone to UC Berkeley and was telling me horror stories about how competitive it was. So I chose Santa Clara because it seemed more of a level playing field, where there were a lot of other beginners who were taking their first coding class. And, even though engineering was very hard anywhere, it felt a little more fair than it might have been at other schools.

Then I got into robotics because of this research fellowship. It was a tremendous lab lead by an amazing teacher named Dr. Chris Kitts who was a mechanical engineering professor. I had knocked on his door and said, "I know I am a CS major but I have a fellowship. And I know you don't take CS students, but can I work with you?"

I picked robotics as the field of study because it sounded really awesome. It was a hybrid of computer science, electrical engineering, and mechanical engineering. I also learned that engineering is about teamwork and solving problems, which hadn't been fully clear to me until the application of the research project. My first project was to build an underwater robot that swam around a swimming pool, a shallow water one. I did everything from the soldering of the electrical boards, to the teleoperated controls and assembly of that first iteration. I later even got my scuba diving license when in subsequent years we built serious underwater systems that went to the bottom of Lake Tahoe or Monterey.

Newnham: And did you know what you wanted to do after the four years?

Reiley: I knew I wanted to get my engineering degree. And I had always wanted to do business and entrepreneurship. My dad is also a small business owner, so on that side, I had always known that I wanted to open my own business or build something on my own. I didn't know much about tech entrepreneurship, but I had strong leadership skills.

Also, in my junior year as an undergrad, one of my female professors called me into her office after our first or second midterm. And I thought, "Oh no. I must have bombed that midterm and I am getting kicked out of the class." But she called me in and said, "Carol, I think you are one of the top students in this class and I would really recommend that you apply for a summer internship with the Computer Research Association. And I would be happy to write you a letter of recommendation." I thought she had the wrong person, but because of her support and Chris Kitts', I went off and won the research fellowship. At the time, I didn't know what a PhD was or why people got one. But the more I learned about a PhD, the more it became clear that's what I wanted to do. Besides enlightenment of solving core research questions, I wanted to be a professor to have an impact on student's lives like my professors had on me.

Newnham: So after Santa Clara, you go to John Hopkins to do your master's and PhD in computer science. But you also taught some classes there, didn't you?

Reiley: I did, yes. I put together two new classes while I was a grad student. I love sharing whatever I'm learning or obsessing about. I always find the best way to learn something is to teach it. I was getting my masters at the time of my first course on the area of haptic feedback. Haptics relates to the sense of touch, which creates the sense of touch by applying forces, vibrations, or motions to the user. So I had this class on how important haptic feedback—as one of our five senses—impacts our interaction with technology both in virtual reality or physical devices.

My PhD was on AI and computer vision. While doing that, I got a chance to tag along with my PhD advisor who was on sabbatical at Stanford in 2008. Interestingly in a self-driving car AI lab. The seed was probably planted there. More on that later. While I was back in the Bay area, I saw the whole mobile app and platform revolution happening. When I returned to Hopkins and said we need to be a part of this. I ended up co-teaching an app development course for the Facebook platform (since we didn't have a budget for everyone to do iOS development on iPhones).

During my time as a grad student, I felt a weird disconnect between the academic world, where we had the fortune of working on a $1.2 million robot, the da Vinci System, and a world of low-cost tech, the maker movement. So I really wanted to bridge high-tech with low-tech to make it accessible to everyone. I started Tinkerbelle labs because of that. I had this entrepreneurial bug that told me I would be most useful not in a research lab, but to build a product that solved a real problem and that people loved.

Newnham: So what led to Drive.ai?

Reiley: I had started working at Intuitive Surgical for a few years, and I had my dream job. I was developing a new novel, snakelike surgical platform that could enter through a natural orifice and not make any visible incision on the body. What drives me is how to help humanity at scale. I started thinking about how to prevent people from needing surgery. Would it be diagnostics? Preventative medicine? Surprisingly and non-intuitively, that led to self-driving cars. Building self-driving cars could have the biggest impact on healthcare.

People are terrible drivers. The shocking fact is that car accidents are the number one cause of death for young adults. And 1.2 million people die every year from them. And yet we tolerate it on the road, and we're numb to this.

Seeing this big, big problem that—if we could help solve, could stop people from even entering the operating room. It's almost looking at preventative cases. So my personal reasons for wanting to start a company and join Drive.ai was about saving lives. And my mission in life is to save the world—one robot at a time. And the self-driving car is the first robot that most people will have.

In terms of the team and cofounders, I met up with the Stanford Artificial Intelligence lab and we all have a background in robotics or deep learning. Deep learning is the most advanced algorithm we have today for artificial intelligence and it has broken all the benchmarks. They're the gold dust of Silicon Valley. This is one of the teams who pioneered a lot of the work in both autonomous driving and artificial intelligence. And my background is also in AI and computer vision, so we joined together and started Drive.ai in April 2015.

On a side note, I was due to get married but had decided that instead of having a big wedding, we would save the money we would have spent on it and instead put it towards a startup. A year later, I was doing this startup and seed funded it with my wedding fund. I joke that instead of calling florists and negotiating vendors, I was calling VCs and negotiating term sheets. I also managed to get us free office space to build our tech and MVP. It was a parallel track of what could have been if I had planned my wedding but was actually building my startup instead. The money we saved paid for our initial equipment and paid the engineer's salaries before we raised our Series A.

Newnham: So when did you have to raise more money?

Reiley: The seed funding we had gave a buffer for the team so we could start building a prototype and start exploring the market as well as looking at what we actually wanted to do as a company. What is our mission and what do we care about? And how are we going to impact the world?

We started fundraising after about nine months and the fundraising took a few months, and was an interesting experience. It's always one of those things where you are extremely excited to do it and then after a while, you just want to get it done. You are taking this little kernel of an idea, your baby and trying to sell this amazing vision. It's a lot of polite rejection. VCs don't always give you clear answers, so it's always like this ongoing thing. It's kind of like dating I guess and if there is a fit, there is a fit. It's a trying experience but exciting and makes you appreciate how to refine your idea and gain clarity and then how to market and sell the idea that has been stuck in your head and that you want to have people believe in.

Newnham: Was there much skepticism from investors around your competition?

Reiley: Oh yes, there was so much skepticism. I think, in general, the automotive industry is a very, very tough one. You know, Tesla is the first auto company that has cracked into becoming a real one in the last fifty years. There are long cycles and the auto industry is so cost-sensitive. So it is incredibly hard but because I come from the medical robotics world which is longer cycles, we anticipated it. I think actually a lot of the VCs were going on their past experience where they had taken a lot of knocks in this area. There was for instance, Fisker and Better Place, where some VCs had invested large and lost out.

With self-driving cars, there is a hardware software component so this is definitely not an app company. This is not Snapchat where you can iterate every week and put out a buggy release. Because with self-driving cars, crashes are real. There is a lot of technical risk and business risk and a lot of obstacles like regulation in our way and all the things we are going to have to face moving forward so it's not a quick turnaround company where something comes out in a few weeks or a few months.

So yes, there is tremendous skepticism about how we will crack into this industry. Also, for me while pitching, I did not encounter one woman in all the meetings that we had.

Newnham: Can you explain a little more about the tech involved in Drive.ai?

Reiley: Sure, we are really interested in building software for self-driving cars. We are focused on building the brain of the self-driving car so it starts with what sensors go on there. How do you get the car to see the objects around it? How does it make decisions based on what it sees? And how do you actually execute the control on the car so that it follows the path you want it to follow, and handle all these dynamics scenes, such as a small dog running out. We're using AI to power everything—from the sensors to the perception to the decision making. Even the communication inside and outside the car.

I guess, on its highest level, AI is one of the hardest areas of computer science. You wouldn't take it as a freshman for sure. It was one of the hardest techs to exist and so the amount of females is much lower in this area than it was in computer science. I think the numbers for computer science are around eighteen percent that graduate with a degree, thirteen percent are in the workforce to start with, and then they drop out like flies.

I think people are also really confused about what AI is. I have been trying to think through a definition because it is so broad. For me, artificial intelligence is anything that an algorithm can do to have a system behave like a human does. So it could be embodied in a computer, it could be in a self-driving car, it could be the spam filter on your Gmail. It is anything that is perceived to make a decision. So data as input and a decision being made as output.

Newnham: And approximately how many sensors are needed to track all this? How autonomous will a car using your software be?

Reiley: What Drive.ai is trying to do is make a more low-cost solution to self-driving cars. To be clear, we're not building our own car. If you look at the Google self-driving car it costs, I think, over $500,000 to make, so that's just not affordable for a lot of consumer cars but what we believe is the hardware is at a stage where it is really good and what is missing is these algorithms that can really empower the hardware. So cameras, for instance, is one technology that we believe deep learning can really impact. Right now in your car, you have a camera, rear-facing, and when you back up, it beeps at you. What we would love is to have these cameras be smarter and recognize objects to give you context.

As a human, we drive with our eyes really but it is extremely scary for me when we speak about how a human drives. I recorded myself driving for two weeks and it revealed how limited we are. There's this belief in the self-driving space that we need to have a detailed map but humans drive around without really having a detailed map in their heads. You kind of know where you are going to go and you can drive there but we want to utilize the low-cost sensors such as cameras ultrasonic LIDARs [Light Detection and Ranging], radars and so on. We don't know what the final set is but we are going to drive down costs and make the sensors that we use smarter so that they are available for everyone to have.

In terms of autonomy, it will be Level 4. [In the United States, this means that "the vehicle performs all safety-critical functions for the entire trip, with the driver not expected to control the vehicle at any time. As this vehicle would control all functions from start to stop, including all parking functions, it could include unoccupied cars." —National Highway Traffic Safety Administration's proposed automated vehicle classification.] So we are doing full autonomous driving which means there is no asking a human to intervene. I think it is the only way to do it safely because I ran all these studies about pilots in the cockpit where the autopilot tells the pilot, in case of an emergency, to switch back control to the pilot and given those signals, people are so panicked in that state and not able to comprehend what's happening.

Newnham: What other obstacles are you facing, either internal or external?

Reiley: We like to go after hard problems because it is the only way you can make an impact. So, on the technology side, there is hiring amazing talent. In the Valley, deep learning talent is such a scarce resource right now because the top ones are going to Google and Facebook. We were lucky because we started off with an amazing core team with eight founders, all whom have tremendous technical backgrounds so I couldn't have asked for a better technical team to start with. But, now we are expanding the team and hiring equally talented people to get us where we need to go.

It's also a hard tech problem. Autonomous driving hasn't been solved by anyone yet. Google has been working on this problem for about twelve years and has done it really well which has paved the road for us, and really pushed this technology along.

There is also legislation such as California law which still requires a person to be in the car but we believe the value comes when people are actually out of the car, i.e. not driving. So other cities and countries might be taking the lead like London, Singapore, Australia… because there are legislation issues over here and working with the government to change infrastructure on the roads and to change the laws per state is a huge barrier. There is also the high cost of doing a hardware and software project. To collect and scale the data with fleets of cars driving around and so on.

Another key issue is business strategy. How do you build something that solves a pain point? Who do you sell it to? How do people use it? How do you not become a liability if there is an accident? And for me, it is also how do I build something that impacts people?

Newnham: You have been granted a license to test your software in a vehicle, something not many have achieved. In terms of a milestone, how did it feel?

Reiley: It was such a relief, because at that point, our seed funding had run out and all of our cofounders had deferred their pay for several weeks while we were trying to close this deal. So it was a huge relief that we survived and we could finally start building a company as opposed to being so scrappy. It was also a very exciting time to be able to change modes.

Also, testing and getting the license was important for us to get early on because you can build things in simulation or you can do closed course testing, but at some point, you have to grow up and get real-world data from real-world testing. Our team had been testing internally for quite some time but we wanted to release our testing on the road and figure out where this technology would be valuable. So when we did that, we were one of three startups in that space. I also feel that a lot of the automakers aren't taking this exploration very seriously because they got the license but from data as of March 2016, we are in the top five most vehicles on the road doing autonomous testing and that doesn't seem right. We have less than a dozen cars and ten drivers which have been granted a license to be tested as autonomous but we have other cars in our fleet. I would have thought the bigger companies would have had more than us testing but there you go.

Newnham: What are the benefits of having autonomous vehicles on our roads?

Reiley: There are so many but if you think of it from a really high level point of view, it could completely change the infrastructure of cities. Around sixty percent of the time in San Francisco, people are just circling around trying to find parking spaces which is ridiculous, and that just adds to the traffic because there are never any spaces.

We will also see vehicle-to-vehicle communication and vehicle-to–stop signs, so in a perfect world, where all cars are autonomous, it's going to be so efficient that you won't even need stop lights. And everything will go so smoothly. I think we have a lot of challenges ahead, especially when we go from zero percent to one percent autonomous cars, and then also, one percent to mainstream. It's definitely a long road but we are extremely excited about how to craft that zero to one percent autonomous car experience.

Another benefit is it's going to change how people commute because it will be easier to commute down to LA, so you no longer need a house. I think your car will be your third living space in the sense that your car is probably the only place right now where you are not connected to your computer and the web, and so it is one of the few times you are currently isolated from that. And I think a lot of ad agencies—and I am sure Google and Facebook, and especially Apple—will be extremely interested in capturing those last few hours that the average person commutes.

On a different vertical, when I think about an autonomous car, I don't think about it like a slight improvement to what we have currently but I see it as such a big transportation change. It's the horse and carriage to a car change. This is now a computer on wheels and you are going to be living and breathing in your computer. It's going to be mainly software based so the possibilities of that, as a software engineer, are tremendously exciting. How your experience can change as you interact with the inside cabin of the car and the outside world will be very different. It is a completely new agent.

I consider a self-driving car a robot but I don't think most people do because they are used to seeing it as a humanoid. It really is going to be a computer on wheels and because of that people are going to find ways to have your car over communicate so there needs to be new standards and lights. In some point in history when you switched over from the horse and carriage to the Model T, someone had to put in indicator lights and this was some time later so, for a while, there were no indicator lights or break lights.

So with Drive.ai, we want to take the lead in creating the new standards on how this non-verbal robot will communicate with me while I cross the street. The car might know what it's going to do, but I have no idea what it is going to do. And I can't make eye contact with the driver. So how does my car communicate with people and other cars? That's an extremely interesting and exciting problem for me.

Newnham: Have you ever felt discouraged during the process of building Drive.ai?

Reiley: Yes, there are certainly times when I have felt discouraged and stressed. And you wonder if you are doing the right thing. How can I help my team work more efficiently, be better? I think in those moments, you have to go back to the basic principles of why you are doing what you are doing and how do you get back up again. A lot of times when I feel stuck, I just need to find a new approach or talk to people. I need to find time to unwind and go in reverse.

I know this because it happened during my PhD. I was extremely discouraged and for months was depressed. There are lots of times when you feel that maybe it's not the right road, but that's when being honest and being authentic is so important. Am I working on the right thing? Is this a problem I even need to solve? And I think this is the reason talking to people can help a lot because it brings that clarity.

Newnham: You are obviously attracted to big problems, but what does success then look like to you?

Reiley: I think as humans, we never feel satisfied so if we get to the next step, then there will be even more exciting challenges for us to go to. All I do is pick things that have the most growth potential and I always try and work on interesting problems. I optimize for learning so that is how I view life. As long as I'm learning, and not stagnant, that seems like success to me.

Newnham: Where do you see the future of AI?

Reiley: Well this is something my husband [Andrew Ng] and I talk about a lot. He's actually one of the world's foremost experts in artificial intelligence and I think he puts it in a really good way. People wonder how AI is useful. We were at the Microsoft CEO Summit and had learned about how back in history, companies would hire a "VP of electricity" because electricity was this brand-new concept and everyone was really excited about it. But people also wondered how electricity would impact the world. And we see AI in the same way—in that it is going to change everything and anything. It's going to be everywhere and impact every industry. So we view AI as the new electricity in the sense that if anything can be smarter, it will get smarter.

And I don't fear robots like some do. I think it's a US cultural thing. Japan has a much healthier outlook to robots. It will change and there will be jobs that no longer exist, but it is similar to the computer because people used to fear that too. I believe there is just a fundamental fear of the unknown so when you don't know, you project fears on to it. Andrew and Elon Musk have been going back and forth on this but when Elon was talking about his fear of artificial intelligence, honestly, that is really the same as thinking about the fear of overpopulation on Mars. We have to get Mars first. And we are so far from that and there are many other issues with it. So I think that's the analogy there.

Going back to people fearing robots taking jobs, they did. They took some but they also created more. They took secretarial typing jobs for instance but it also empowered us and freed us to do more important tasks. Like think about your laundry machine—it is a robot and it took away a job. But I don't know if you feel bad about that. So there is concern about some jobs being taken but I hope that people are then able to free up their time to being more impactful so I don't worry about the rise of the robots. We are also still a long way off from AI doing anything realistically human.

Newnham: You are a great advocate for women in tech. What changes do you think need to be made to encourage more women into the field?

Reiley: I do think there are a lot of different issues at different stages of keeping women in tech. But starting with the pipeline problem, I wish I had learned how cool and exciting technology was when I was younger, because I would probably have started earlier. I loved writing—and I think coding is the twenty-first century equivalent. I am fascinated how creative it is. But just like writing, there is a lot of upfront effort, right? When you are learning your ABCs, it seems boring. But once you learn it, it then starts becoming this really creative world where you can go anywhere and make anything you imagine through stories. Well, coding is a lot like poetry. In fact, the first computer scientist was Ada Lovelace, a female, and her father was the poet Lord Byron, so she came from that mix. That's who my children's book series is inspired by, and how I created Ada Beta.

So I think a lot of how free, creative, and beautiful coding and being an engineer is—it is lost on young girls today. And it's one of the reasons I am working on children's books—so that early on, the perception that it is just for geeky guys is removed. When I ask a lot of male friends how they got into engineering, they circle it back to gaming, so I think we just need to reframe it to show that coding is fun and creative—and then girls will be interested.

Right now it is interesting because Stanford's number-one class for women is computer science. Berkeley has changed the name of their class to The Beauty and Joy of Computing—and that alone has impacted who takes the class. So a lot of this is just being mindful of that so yes, pipeline is an issue and my solution is to work with girls on that side.

In terms of retention, I think it is the responsibility of a cofounder to get more diversity in the group. Not just women but different ages, different races, and different experiences—so it's not just people from an Ivy League school for example. It is a hard, hard problem and I am sad to say we have not hired another female engineer on to our team yet, so one of the first things we are doing is putting together goals for hiring. Numbers for a startup are extremely important and you only improve what you measure so we need to be tracking diversity. I also need to make it clear that it is important and that we have a goal attached to it, which will be tracked.

Newnham: What would you say is the most important lesson you have learned in your career thus far?

Reiley: Just do it. If you have an idea, just make that first step and go for it. I have a lot of girlfriends who say, "I wish I could…." And I say—just do it! So I think that is my most important lesson and piece of advice.

I see so many people holding themselves back and I know this is really trite but if you take that first step, and know where you want to go, then that is the most important thing. Even if it's crazy, people need to take that first step. Know where you want to go then go for it because I would rather see you fail and get up, than talk about the what ifs. I don't care if I look stupid, I just throw myself into these different things and that's what my Making a Splash book was about. I know nothing about children's books. Andrew and I don't have children yet. And I am not a psychology major. But Carol Dweck's book on mindsets is one of my top books and I wanted to write it for children.

So, in summary, the first step to getting the things you want out of life is this: decide what you want. Then go for it.

Newnham: You have talked about the importance of stating goals. What goals have you set for yourself over the next few years?

Reiley: I started making a goals list in eighth grade after an inspirational speaker came in and said that you are X amount more likely to stick to your goals if you actually write them down. So since then, I have got this list that has everything I have accomplished on the left and everything on the right is anything you dream of doing in your life. So I have a binder full of these goals which is fun because you can go back and see what eighth-grade Carol wanted to do back then. There are a lot of goals.

Newnham: And if you achieve your goals. What do you wish your legacy to be?

Reiley: I just want to be remembered for being a good person and to be of use, whatever that takes me towards.

Cathy Edwards

Cofounder and CTO, Chomp

Cathy Edwards cofounded and was chief technology officer of app search engine Chomp, which she started with Ben Keighran in 2009. After raising just over $2.5 million, Chomp was acquired by Apple for a reported $50 million in 2012.

At Apple, Cathy was the Head of Search for iTunes, the App Store and Maps, before becoming Director of Evaluation for Maps.

Cathy previously worked as senior mobile product manager at social networking web site Friendster, as product manager for messaging startup 3jam, and in strategy and research roles at telecommunications company Telstra in her native Australia.

Cathy left Apple in 2014 and founded a new stealth startup in 2015 with some ex-Chomp colleagues.

Cathy has a degree in linguistics, computer science, and pure mathematics from the University of Western Australia.

Danielle Newnham: What were you like as a kid and when did you first show an interest in math?

Cathy Edwards: When I was nine I was lucky enough to go to a school that had a mandatory weekly programming class through year 10. I also really enjoyed math classes and my teachers encouraged me to participate in a variety of extension activities like national and international math competitions. I am grateful to this day for that exposure; it was rare for a school—let alone an all-girls school—to have such a strong computing focus back them. I think without it I probably wouldn't be where I am today.

© Danielle Newnham 2016
D. Newnham, *Female Innovators at Work*, DOI 10.1007/978-1-4842-2364-2_9

At university, I deliberately picked a degree structure that was very flexible and allowed me to take a broad range of subjects from different departments. I knew I wanted to major in pure math because I'd always loved it, and I figured computer science would be both fun and useful. I added the linguistics major later, after I took some first-year courses and fell in love with it.

There were a fair number of women in the linguistics classes, but we were a definite minority in the math classes. However computer science had by far the smallest percentage of women out of all the subjects.

Newnham: Whilst studying, you started working for Telstra. Can you tell me about your work there?

Edwards: In my third year of university, I received a national scholarship from Telstra which also included the option to intern in their research lab for the summer. I prototyped the hardware and software for a wearable device that allowed you to text surreptitiously. After my internship, they offered me a permanent role in their Artificial Intelligence research group. We did large-scale machine learning [like predicting which customers would be likely to commit fraud], natural language processing, and voice recognition work.

After the research labs were shuttered in 2005, I moved into a new role in the newly created chief technology office and managed a team of developers and designers to build prototypes of future mobile products. This was pre-iPhone, but we presented concepts like Internet radio and music streaming and an app store.

Newnham: You then moved to United States for 3jam. How did that come about and what did you do there?

Edwards: I was in Australia and wanted to make a career change but I was young and inexperienced so I didn't know how to make that happen. A mentor of mine at the time said I should go and get an MBA because that's a great way to catalyze a move. So I applied to INSEAD in France and was accepted.

I had given my notice in at work and was probably two months away from leaving and moving to France to study when I had this moment of uncertainty. A sort of quarter-life crisis where I thought, "What do I actually want to do with my life?" And I saw this pathway ahead of me where I would get my MBA, then I'd be in debt, and then the conservative thing would be to go to another big company or be a management consultant, and be hired by someone who would pay off that debt, and I would be right back where I started. And I thought, no, that is not what I want to be doing with my career.

What I realized was that I wanted to start and run a tech company. And although an MBA might have helped me with that, I thought I could just skip the debt part and get the same experience working for a startup or two in Silicon Valley first. It was a tough decision but I decided to drop out of the MBA program before I'd even begun it, and starting trying to find someone to employ me in San Francisco, despite the fact that I'd never been there before.

So I was in Melbourne, applying for jobs on Craigslist and interviewing over Skype, and trying to make the whole thing happen. And I was lucky because at that particular time, talent was very scarce on the ground here in Silicon Valley so people were willing to take some risks and hire me without ever having met me in person. I literally showed up in SF for the first time ever two days before I started my first job at 3jam, which is kind of crazy.

Newnham: And going back to you wanting to start a company. What made you feel this way? It's not for everyone.

Edwards: Well, in a way, it's surprising that it took me until I was twenty-five to figure this out. My parents are entrepreneurs with multiple different businesses in Australia, albeit not technology businesses. I am the oldest child, and on weekends my siblings and I would often be at our parents' office doing whatever job needed doing at the time. So I grew up from a very young age understanding what it took to build a business: it's all hands-on deck and you do whatever needs to be done. And I brought that ethos to every job that I did.

And the thing is that if you actually have that entrepreneurial mindset but you are in a small role at a big company, it can actually be not a great thing because you're looking strategically at all these areas of the business that have nothing to do with you and you're thinking, "We've got to fix this and we've got to fix that." And that can be quite disruptive because you don't actually have the authority to do anything about them, but you go and try to fix them anyway. So, I needed to be in a bigger role where I could focus on all of these strategic problems that I was thinking about, and obviously founding a company is a pretty natural fit with that. It had been in my bones all along but it just took me a little while to realize it.

Newnham: And what was Silicon Valley like back then? How has startup culture changed since you arrived nine years ago?

Edwards: I think in many ways, it is still the same. There is still this phenomenal optimism. I liken it to a modern day Florence during the Medici period. People are going to look back on Silicon Valley and say more things got created in a shorter period of time than any other time in history. And I am not just talking about this year—I'm talking about over this hundred-year period. If you look at it from a historical perspective, it is such a groundbreaking time in terms of technological advances, and in terms of development, and it's amazing to be surrounded by that level of opportunity and growth.

So I think in that way it's been the same for the last nine years, although maybe we are a little more aware of some of the challenges facing women and minorities. We still have a very long way to go to fix these systemic issues but I'm encouraged that the conversation is happening more visibly now. That core opportunity to change though-that has stayed at the same high level over the past decade.

Newnham: After 3jam, you get a job at Friendster. Can you tell me more about some of the obstacles that you faced there in terms of the mobile space?

Edwards: I arrived maybe six months after the iPhone launched and I think it is hard to overstate the way the iPhone launch changed the mobile ecosystem. 3jam was founded in the era prior to that, when carriers had all the power. Literally, carriers would dictate to the handset manufacturers: "This is exactly what phone we want. This is how we want the hardware to be. This is the software we want running on the phone." And yet, the type of companies carriers were… they were largely ex-government bureaucracies because most countries had already or were in the process of privatizing their mobile carriers from what had traditionally been a government utility. And so they weren't necessarily the sort of places where things like design and product management were deeply understood.

The other thing that was really pervasive was the fragmentation in the market. The reason that apps became such a thing after the iPhone launched was not purely because of its design and that sort of thing, but it was just so difficult to be a third-party developer prior to iOS and prior to Android. The code running on each phone was subtly different, so you literally had to build a different version of your application for each phone, which then meant, of course, that you had to own every single phone out there so you could test your application and make sure it worked. So the overhead of development and testing was extremely expensive and time-consuming.

And then, on top of that, there was no App Store, so people couldn't even find your application easily. You were dealing with a limited market of people who were tech-savvy enough to know how to find your app and install it. And so the costs were higher, the market was smaller, and it was generally just a very difficult time to be in the mobile business. And Apple, and Google with Android, really changed that.

At the time that I joined, Friendster was hugely popular in Southeast Asia— the Philippines, Malaysia, Singapore, Indonesia. And that culture was an interesting environment for a set of mobile products for a couple of reasons. First is that people were primarily using mobile devices to connect to the Internet; and, secondly, they have an economic style that is sometimes described as a sachet economy, which basically means that people think it's better value to buy exactly what you need right now rather than to buy in bulk and then have to store it. It's sort of the opposite of the US in that sense. So people would rather go and buy a single sachet of laundry detergent for today's wash than buy a big bottle of it. And so what we were able to do was take advantage of these two facts to monetize a social network in a way that hadn't been done at the time, which was to sell Friendster-only data packs and SMS packs via the carriers and do a revenue share with them. This was pretty groundbreaking back in the day. And I worked with the carriers there to launch this novel revenue sharing data and SMS packs for mobiles in that region.

Newnham: So what led to you starting Chomp?

Edwards: I'd worked for a year and a half in Silicon Valley at this point so I had found my feet and felt ready to start something myself. And the timing happened to be right both with the industry and finding a cofounder.

My cofounder Ben and I had been friends for a while at that point. He is Australian as well and had also been in the mobile industry for many years, and we had initially met because of that. We had become close, though, because his wife and I used to work out together; sometimes afterward, we'd have breakfast and Ben would come along. He was looking to start a company too, and we had good chemistry and complementary skills, so that had fallen into place. Finding a cofounder can be tricky and relies on a bit of luck that you're both ready to do it at the same time. In terms of dividing up the work, he focused on distribution, marketing and business development, and I led engineering and design, and we were able to collaborate deeply on product.

Because we both had backgrounds in mobile, we really understood the changes happening in the ecosystem with the launch of iPhone and Android. In 2009 apps had reached this tipping point where there were so many that you couldn't expect to find the one you wanted by just browsing the top charts anymore, so search was becoming more important. So there was huge potential for an app discovery business. And that's what really led us to start Chomp together and start thinking intensely about those problems.

Newnham: When you started Chomp in 2009, it was the middle of a global recession. How did you find starting your own business in this climate? And what other challenges did you face?

Edwards: I was not particularly concerned about the global fiscal climate. Ben and I saw the app business taking off and were confident there was an opportunity for a great company helping app developers and app consumers find each other. We did hundreds of user interviews to really understand consumers' app discovery behavior before launching Chomp. I think our detailed understanding of user behavior and how users responded to the app helped us be successful in the early days.

Creating differentiated technology was critically important to Chomp's business. There are several unique technical challenges in the app search domain that we identified and solved by bringing together a new machine learning technique called topic modeling with traditional informational retrieval methodologies. Our search needed to be drastically more relevant for users than either Apple's App Store search or Google Play's search, and we achieved that with our patented technology.

Being a female CTO was less common back then than it is now—and it's still not very common—and there were definitely some challenges that came along with that. Many candidates for engineering positions used to avoid going into detail when I asked them technical interview questions because they had never interviewed with a technical woman before and didn't believe I could possibly understand their answers. This was despite me being introduced as the CTO of the company! However, I think having a female leader helped us hire a strong diverse team. We were thirty percent women, plus greater than population representation for African Americans and Latinos, so we built a strong culture of inclusion.

Growth was also the number-one challenge as it is for any startup company. We utilized every technique available to us—from traditional PR to social media marketing to SEO to building viral loops into our product to business development deals. And our business development lead, Taylor Cascino, was sensational and drove pulling all these deals together. Chomp powered search for the Verizon app store, Best Buy in the UK, Blekko, DuckDuckGo, and many others which all helped.

Newnham: Can you remember specific days where you felt everything was going great versus if there were days when you wanted to give up?

Edwards: My memories of Chomp are so positive, so overwhelmingly awesome, so there weren't any times when I thought about quitting. I really feel very grateful for that time in my life. Running your own business always has its ups and downs, but I would much prefer to have those problems than be frustrated in a smaller role. Every day at Chomp was a privilege and I never felt like giving up. We had an amazing team and I loved working with everyone.

I also really enjoyed working with our technical advisors David Blei and Don Metzler. Dave is a machine learning guru who created the topic modeling algorithm that we were working with. Don has years of expertise in the information retrieval field, so it was a privilege to work with two technical luminaries.

But on the flipside, fundraising was a challenge. It's always hard, but I think there were some particular challenges in our case because of my background. Chomp was creating new intellectual property around information retrieval, which is a deeply technical problem. I think the venture capitalists that we talked to were largely expecting to see someone who looked very different from me, and someone who had a very different background. Being an immigrant, and thus not having been to a brand-name American university, also didn't help. Overcoming that was frustrating because you're working against a bunch of assumptions that weren't being spoken out loud. No one's going to say, "Oh, I don't think you can create this technology because you're a woman." They're not even necessarily consciously thinking that, but it came out in more subtle ways. And I think that was probably the biggest struggle of the entire experience. But we ended up finding a wonderful investment team who were incredibly supportive, including John Malloy at Blue Run Ventures, who was on our board, and SV Angel.

Newnham: You released Chomp Search Ads. When did you see the importance of creating such a product and what was the process like from ideation to execution?

Edwards: An app developer friend of mine had an app about World War II. Every day you opened the app, it would tell you what happened on that day during World War II. It was a great app, but didn't exactly have mass market appeal. He was never going to be able to acquire users in a cost-effective way using the standard techniques at the time, like buying app installs from games or TV advertising. So it was a no-brainer to me that he would benefit from being able to market his app to users that were already expressing interest in World War II through their search queries. Ben and I were convinced that this would change the game for app discovery. Sadly, we were only able to launch in private beta before the acquisition happened, but I am glad to see that this is now being embraced by both Apple and Google.

Newnham: I know you signed a confidentiality agreement with Apple that prevents you from saying too much, but what did the deal mean to you and what were your roles there?

Edwards: Obviously, we were extremely pleased with the exit. It was a fitting end for the company to be able to work on the problem of app discovery within the platform itself at Apple. It allowed us to instantly make a much bigger impact than we were able to at Chomp.

I had a few different roles at Apple. I was initially running search engineering for their various stores, so the App Store, iTunes store, iBooks store, podcasts, iTunes U, etc. After the launch of Apple Maps, I also took over local search. I then took on a role focused on ensuring that Apple builds quality algorithms and services, which included everything from building and managing A/B testing frameworks and analytics systems, to determining statistical quality, to automation and performance testing, to driving roads in countries all around the world to ensure that the map is correct.

I had a really great time there and learned a lot. But, I was excited to start my next company and that's why I ultimately left. I'm now in the early stages of building my next company. We're not currently disclosing what we're working on, but I'm very excited about it.

Newnham: As an expert in several areas of tech, which areas are you most excited about now?

Edwards: I continue to be really excited about the potential for machine learning and natural language processing to create more intelligent products. However, those algorithms are often opaque and complex. I believe we are going to see more challenges ensuring that those algorithms do not contain implicit bias or discriminate against certain user groups. I'm excited to see how the machine learning community deals with these problems.

Newnham: What advice do you have for women looking to start a career in tech?

Edwards: It is really important to read as much as you can about subconscious bias and some of the challenges that you will face. Not to discourage you but to arm yourself with tools to know how to overcome some of those challenges. I see lots of women get disheartened because they come into tech expecting a pure meritocracy and then start to believe that they're not capable because they have some bad experiences, even though those experiences are more due to systemic issues than their actual skills. I think it's extremely important to be able to evaluate yourself accurately against your peers. I know far too many women who believe they are at best middling—and at worst failing—when they're actually near the top.

Newnham: What is the most important lesson that you have learned in your career so far?

Edwards: I think it's critical to become aware of power dynamics in the workplace and how they influence how people see you. They're incredibly important, and some people have an innate sense of how they work, but most people don't. Study the interactions in meetings that you're a part of and see who interrupts who, who everyone looks at, and who spends the most time talking. Pay attention to emails you receive: who can be direct in their requests and who uses lots of extra words to explain and downplay their requests. Look at body language and listen to tone of voice as well as what's being said. And then make sure your communication matches the image that you're trying to project. People respond so powerfully to these subtle behaviors and it can really change how much people respect you and their perception of your seniority.

Dame Stephanie Shirley

Founder, FI Group

Dame Stephanie Shirley *is a pioneering technology entrepreneur turned ardent philanthropist. She arrived in Britain as a five-year-old unaccompanied child refugee in 1939. In 1962, Dame Stephanie founded the FI Group, a revolutionary tech company that employed a team of predominantly female freelance software engineers, many of whom were mothers. Dame Stephanie remained the company's chief executive for 25 years. The business floated on the London Stock Exchange in 1996, making Dame Stephanie and many of its staff multimillionaires.*

Since retiring, Dame Stephanie has focused her efforts on her philanthropic work. She has donated more than half her fortune to charities connected to technology and autism, both of which have had a profound impact on her life: technology because she devoted her career to it; autism because her late son Giles was autistic.

Dame Stephanie has served on several company boards, including Tandem Computers Inc., the John Lewis Partnership Plc, and AEA Technology plc, previously known as the Atomic Energy Authority.

Dame Stephanie was appointed Officer of the Order of the British Empire (OBE) in the 1980 Queen's Birthday Honours, for services to industry. She was promoted to Dame Commander (DBE) in the Millennium Honours in 2000 for services to information technology.

© Danielle Newnham 2016

D. Newnham, *Female Innovators at Work*, DOI 10.1007/978-1-4842-2364-2_10

Dame Stephanie's memoir, Let IT Go (AUK Authors, 2012), is planned to be made into a film.

Danielle Newnham: Can you tell me about your background and your journey over to the United Kingdom?

Dame Stephanie Shirley: What I can really remember are the childish things. Not the historic event of ten thousand unaccompanied child refugees, the largest ever migration of children, but it was me leaving home, losing my doll, being intrigued by a little boy who kept getting sick. So it was very much childish memories of trauma… I mean, people were crying on the platform as they waved goodbye. Adults and children cried, but I did not. I am very disciplined, but there were lots of children screaming and crying. Each of the ten trains in the Kindertransport had about one thousand children, aged five to sixteen, with just two adults. So, although it was well organized and we had numbers around our necks, it was still a lot of children, largely unsupervised, and a pretty horrendous but very important part of my life.

I think it was that Kindertransport experience that has really driven my life, partly because it was such a big change in my life. No other change will faze me anymore. I've actually learned to like change, and in a high-tech career, that has become quite useful. I also realized that, very early on, I wanted my life to be one that was worth saving. You know, if you say to a five, six, seven year-old, "Aren't you lucky to be saved?" I soon got that message that I was extremely lucky to have been saved. So it made me determined that my life would be one that was worth saving. Very dutiful I am, so I try not to fritter it away. So, in my eighties, I still effectively work full time and I enjoy it. I'm grateful to have something to get up for each morning.

Newnham: Once at school in England, you showed an interest in mathematics. Do you remember the first time you got excited about it?

Shirley: Yes, I can. My foster parents had sent me to a Roman Catholic convent, taught by old-school nuns in black habits and white wimples. They were sufficiently professional enough to say to my foster parents, "This child is gifted in mathematics and she needs to go elsewhere." I was about thirteen, and since in those days, secondary education was not free, I had to sit for scholarship exams. So I knew fairly early on that that's what excited me. Later on when I was in a secondary school, I wanted to go on studying mathematics but it was a girls' school and the only science that was considered respectable for girls was botany. Plants and things like that. So I really had to battle that, and eventually, they realized that I was a bit of a special case and allowed me to go to and from the boys' school, which really was an eye-opener for the sexism that I was going to meet later on.

Newnham: And when did you discover the world of computing?

Shirley: I was taking my honors math degree at evening classes and a fellow student there was working at a corporation that had got one of the earliest computers. He said, "You would find this interesting. Come along and have a look." So I took holiday and I spent a week, or it might have been a fortnight, in his laboratory, basically making myself useful and learning the very rudiments of how you make this machine do whatever you want it to do. And, it was like falling in love again. It was really exciting and demanding. You knew somehow that it was going to be so important for the future.

At the time, most people were concentrating on the hardware, but I was entirely focused on the software, which at that time, was given away free with the hardware. So I was a bit out of step already because I was saying that the software was important, but it was an early start. I would have been in my early twenties. This was at the laboratory of a fellow student's employer. I was still working at Dollis Hill Post Office Research Station and taking the evening classes at the same time.

Newnham: Can you tell me about the work you did at the post office?

Shirley: I would describe my work as a junior mathematical clerk. I was working on one of those electric comptometers, developing graphs, doing some statistical work, working on something called "waveguides." But the things I remember most are the transatlantic cables—lots, because there were so many of them. And lots of calculations on the very first telephone exchange, which was at Highgate Woods in England, and working on the Premium Bond computer, ERNIE [Electronic Random Number Indicator Equipment], where I was one on a team of two responsible for checking the randomness of that lottery system.

Newnham: And then you decided to set up on your own. Can you tell me about what led to you leaving Dollis Hill and setting up your own business?

Shirley: *I left Dollis Hill on marriage because I married a physicist whom I met there, on the so-called "waveguides." And although it wasn't essential for me to leave, I felt it was better that we pursued our own careers because there were very few women in research at that time anyway. So I moved to a little computer company and again basically hit that glass ceiling. It was an excellent company, about thirty strong. I was doing very innovative work there and managing a small team for the first time, but again, I felt blocked.*

Pretty well overnight something happened, where I was told, "It has nothing to do with you." So I decided to set up a company to develop software where there would be no glass ceiling, because I was going to slant it the other way and predominantly employ women, like me, with a young family—planned or in existence. So the very first minute in the annals of the company talked about, "The employment policy will be jobs for women with children." And then as I realized the importance of training, that changed to "Careers for women with children." And then there were a lot of women looking after disabled partners or elder care, and so it eventually changed to "Careers for women with dependents."

And then, in 1975, Equal Opportunities legislation came in, which made it illegal to have our pro-female policies. I mean, I didn't go into business to make money. I went into business to have an interest, sure, but mainly to provide a route for women to lead our own lives. And that crusade for women really drove us for many years. Suddenly, we, the women's company, had to let the men in. It was great fun.

Newnham: I can imagine. So, you have talked about this glass ceiling. Did you find it almost essential to set up your own business to provide yourself and other women with work? And how does it compare to today?

Shirley: Well, I had been with two organizations—one large, one small—both of them excellent organizations, but where I had felt blocked. In my first job, there was a salary scale for men and a salary scale for women, which was very much lower. And one was meeting this overt discrimination. There were certain things you could not do. I couldn't work on the Stock Exchange. Part of my work should have taken me onto a ship, but I wasn't allowed to do that because, "We don't have women on ships." You couldn't drive a bus or an airplane. It was illegal for women to do these things, so those things are easier to break down than some of the covert issues of discrimination today, now that all those legal barriers have fallen away.

Newnham: I liked this anecdote in your book when you talk about how you employed not just women, but mothers, and that when somebody called, you would play some audio with someone typing furiously in the background to disguise the sound of a baby crying. Do you feel we have moved on from that time? Is it easier now for women to have it all?

Shirley: In some ways, it has changed beyond all recognition, but in others, I still hear women talking about the discrimination they feel, whether it's real or imagined. But what's important now is that as women we have a choice. Very few women choose to work as I do. Many employers now allow people to work flexibly and I'm conscious that I opened those doors for women and others because we were so flexible about what we did. You know, part-time, full-time, flexi-time we started— home-working, hot-desking. We even had a cafeteria of benefits so people could choose how they wanted to get paid. Whether they wanted more salary, or more holiday and less salary, this sort of thing. So we were really breaking new ground all the time. And when you look at the analysis of what women today want, two things come out very clearly. It is always an emphasis on flexibility, and secondly, work-life balance. Those things are available to women, but you have to maneuver your way around to get them.

My work-life balance was zilch. Zero. I just didn't have any. The only time I forgot my learning disabled son, Giles, was when I was working. I didn't have holiday. It sounds ridiculous, but when you are building up a company, you've got to give it your all and I hadn't quite got my all because I did have family. And they were difficult years, which honed me into the tough cookie you see today.

Newnham: What was the landscape back then in terms of women in tech? And when do you feel women started to step out of the software pool?

Shirley: Programming actually started as a female job. It was part of the clerical industry. We had the coders at Bletchley Park, so it started off very feminine. And then I think what happened is that men started to realize how important this work was and how well paid it was. I could not believe I should be paid so much for doing something that was such fun— so the men started to come in and basically elbowed us out.

In the early days, one did need mathematics to work in computing, so that took some people away. Now, I cannot understand why there aren't more women. Nothing could be more flexible, more fun, or more international. It doesn't matter how strong you are or the timbre of your voice, you can write software if you want and it is very stimulating and fun. But women in Britain are now starting to be taught coding again, which is an improvement.

Newnham: We know sexism exists in nearly all industries. Can you talk us through some of the sexism that you experienced and how you dealt with it?

Shirley: Partly, certain courses of action were actually closed to us. The others were just made very difficult. And whatever you were doing, you seemed to be a second-class citizen and viewed as a sex object in the work place. If you travelled on the underground tube system in the rush hour when it was busy, you would often find a pair of hands come around your body. I mean, it was impossible.

You would be trying to sell some significant piece of software to a government department, for example, and a senior guy there would be pinching your bottom, and you had to learn to deal with this. I think my company learned really to dress in a very unprovocative way. We didn't wear trousers for a long time because that was considered unfeminine. I was not a feminist but we really had to struggle to be accepted as whole human beings.

Newnham: Can you talk me through some of the bigger or most memorable projects that you worked on?

Shirley: We used to actually measure scale in terms of the number of women employed because it was a social business, that's how I saw it. And we got up to teams of hundreds of women on one project. The largest project that I was ever associated with was costed at half a billion pounds, so that was over many years. But when a project was in and out in six months, they were much more exciting because we did things like underwater weapons research. And the black box flight recorder for the supersonic Concorde, which was quite a sophisticated software because we were taking readings from about forty analog instruments, including the height, the acceleration, and the cockpit noises, and putting them into a really safe, best-protected black box—as they were called, which I can assure you are not black. They are bright yellow.

Newnham: I know you viewed your business very much as a crusade. Can you tell me more about the mission behind it?

Shirley: It started off very selfishly. I wanted to be employed myself, in a job that appealed to me. And then I realized that there were so many other women with similar requirements.

Social changes happen by example and as soon as somebody saw me working on a freelance basis, they realized, "Oh, perhaps I could." And I never had to advertise for staff in the early days because the tiniest little mention in the press and I'd get a flood of quality applicants. "I've got a PhD in computer science,"—though they didn't call it call it that in those days. "I've worked for five years with General Electric Corporation. Can I come and do some coding for you?" And so it was a very enthusiastic workforce, especially when, later on, they were given shares in the company. They were highly motivated and they chose to work. It wasn't that they were money motivated.

Newnham: What was your reason behind giving away shares to your staff and what was the result?

Shirley: Co-ownership with the staff is part of my giving back. I was given so much as a child refugee that what else can I do but give back? And in the company, it started off in something like year three, we had a bonus system so every six months, we would do all the sums and we would say that this amount could be given back to the staff and it was given out pro rata to their earnings. And that was fine but then we had several years where there were no profits to share out at all so twice a year, I would be writing letters to all the staff saying, "Well, we have this wonderful bonus system but unfortunately your bonus this time is nil."

So we got through the 1970s recession and then a suggestion came that we move the company to a co-ownership, not just bonuses so we did that but it took years to make it happen because we were sharing equity, not only with the employees where there is legislation to help make that easier, but with all the consultants and associates so that was very much breaking new ground. And I do believe in sharing the profits. I believe it is a big incentive to entrepreneurs to realize that they can have less percentage of a larger cake if they share in the early days. When you start—I wasn't wise enough to do this but—when you start, you're desperately needing specialist skills for this, that, and the other. And you can't afford to buy them but, of course, if you offer a percentage of the shares, I think it's a very positive thing.

You know, to begin with, it didn't make any difference. I gave away four percent, then six percent, then seven percent, then seventeen percent, and it was really only when I gave, at our twenty-fifth anniversary, I gave a whole chunk which took it up to twenty-five percent that the staff suddenly realized, a quarter of this company belongs to us, and began to take some real interest. And we put a lot of effort into the communication of that with the staff so that it wasn't just cold annual general reports but us talking in confidence with the staff about what was happening with the business.

Newnham: Can we talk about the highs and lows of entrepreneurial life? When you start a business, you put so much trust in the people you hire, but you had a senior member of staff betray you. How difficult is it to not take it personally when this happens?

Shirley: I don't think I'm the right person to talk about this because I was desperately hurt. Really seriously hurt by a breakaway group, who also went in for industrial espionage. This was somebody I had worked side by side with. My husband was the godfather of her son. So I had no idea I was vulnerable in that way. I was just running what I thought of as a family business. I knew the children's names, I knew who had got measles, I knew who was having marital problems. And so it was very personal and took quite a period of time to not only professionalize the business, but to separate myself from the business after that. To separate my finance from the business, because I had taken a personal mortgage for the company and eventually, the company has to take its own mortgage and borrow for itself. So it was a long, painful process.

Women didn't have any commercial experience, so the mistakes that we made were quite basic ones. For example, our pricing started off wrong, and stayed wrong year after year, decade after decade. Pricing was wrong, so we had a profitless prosperity because we were getting revenue and we were growing, but when we looked at the profit margin, it was going down and down. And it needed professional managers to come and really make it professional.

Newnham: In some ways though, do you think your naivety—in that you hadn't set up a business previously—served you well?

Shirley: Yes, it did. I mean I had no financial knowledge at all, so I managed the business on a cash basis. Now, in the short term, that was very amateur, but in the long term, it really allowed me to build market share and get a position in the industry.

Newnham: Let's go back to some of the low points of running your own business, including the recession. You didn't give up, because this was a crusade for you. Can you tell me some of the ways you pulled yourself out of the tougher times?

Shirley: I think that crusade is what kept me going. I can remember sitting at home, actually rocking, and saying, "What am I going to do? What am I going to do? What can I do?" You know my stomach was churning. And why? Because this woman's company would go down and be remembered only as a so-called fair-weather company, which was fine when the market was growing but couldn't survive through a recession. So we cut out pretty well everything except the essentials. A lot of staff went. And, of course, since many of them were freelancers, I only had to say, "Look, don't expect much work from us in the next eighteen months because we haven't got any." And bless them, they would attend conferences and things like that, nicely dressed, unpaid, but saying that they came from F International. So they helped me through that recession.

I also learned then, the art of the liquidator. This business of getting rid of all the bits and pieces that you can manage without—and just focus. Previously, I was just rushing around after anything that moved, but focus is very important. And when the professional managers came in, they underlined that, so I learned that if you don't focus, you're probably not going to make it. And, I think there is a sheer stubbornness that some women have that's very necessary for entrepreneurs.

Newnham: What do you think makes a great entrepreneur?

Shirley: I don't think it's the money motivation, which is what's always quoted in what one reads. But it seems to work best for an entrepreneur when we find something we really care about. We focus on it and let the money follow the pleasure we get from doing that. You know, I went into software because that's what I love. Unfortunately, as an entrepreneur, I stopped doing it because after a very short period of time, I was dealing with cash flow, HR problems, and all the hassle of running a business. And I was paying other people to write the software! But that is what happens with most entrepreneurs.

I used to envy companies that started with two or three people—one marketing, one financial, one technical. But even that doesn't work necessarily, when there is a break up between the three, it can get quite nasty. So it's not easy to make a fortune. It is not easy to set up a company, but it is so worthwhile because you are creating wealth, not only in financial terms, but a wealth of experience, a wealth of friendships… I mean some of the people that I am working with today, I have been working with for years.

Newnham: And what advice do you have for the entrepreneurs of tomorrow? What skills do you wish that you had started out with?

Shirley: Financial skills. I was as green as anything. I really didn't understand money at all as per the example I gave earlier of my costings being wrong, and nobody else corrected it for many years. We only realized after about twenty years when someone said, "Look, you've got all this business. Why aren't you wealthy?"

I believe it's important to surround yourself with first-class people and people that you like. Not necessarily people like you but people that you like. Choose your partner very carefully because there is a lot of stress at home from running a business. Just the other day, actually, I was saying to a woman that my husband was an "angel" on the work-life balance question. And she said, "You are lucky. Mine is still alive."

Information technology, particularly, is so disruptive that even with a very low investment, you can get to millions of people. And the web is so valuable there. One of the things I did was set up the Oxford Internet Institute, which is not technical research but looks at the social, economic, legal, and ethical issues of the Internet. I am also a more than angel investor in the Digital

Giving magazine, because suddenly, with a relatively small investment, you can reach millions of philanthropists worldwide for giving. And these are different things—the points of inflection are just so different to where they used to be.

Newnham: What do you wish your legacy to be?

Shirley: I am so thrilled that my memoir may be made into a film and that might be a legacy that will actually inspire, over the years. And I have two or three years of exciting things to do because I have never made a film before.

My philanthropy, which has gone to the two things I know and care about. And that is information technology and autism, which was my late son's disorder. The majority has gone to autism.

I helped set up a livery company in the City of London which was a £5 million project about twenty-five years ago now. And did a series of projects that included both computing and autism. For example, some virtual reality projects at Nottingham University, to teach people with autism how to find their way around a virtual city. Things like how to find a seat on a bus—things which most people just take for granted, but children with autism have to be taught.

Currently, we are just starting to use robots for teaching pupils with autism. It's a charming little robot that is able to teach life skills to pupils who are without speech, are very, very vulnerable but actually focus well to a robotic teacher. Maybe they are not as threatened. So there's all sorts of things going on. Another charity of mine, which looks after one hundred and twenty-seven people with autism, is now using fingerprint technology, instead of keys, so that each resident can get into their own room with their own fingerprint. They can't get into somebody else's room and they can't lose the key.

Newnham: You wrote in your book, a phrase that really struck me. "I need to justify the fact that my life was saved." Do you still feel like that?

Shirley: That feeling that I need to justify my own existence is as strong today as it was seventy-five years ago. I was five when it happened and about six, seven, eight when I really started to realize what had happened, and my part in a little bit of history. But no, I still need to make sure that each day is worth living.

Many, many people helped me. Strangers helped me. The Jewish and Christian activists that set up the Kindertransport. The Quakers' Religious Society of Friends who funded it when it ran out of money. Catholic nuns who helped to educate me. Once you have been given so much, you realize that you have been helped. But it is now up to me to help other people.

Gwynne Shotwell

President and COO, SpaceX

Gwynne Shotwell *is president and chief operating officer at SpaceX (Space Exploration Technologies Corporation), where she is responsible for day-to-day operations and company growth.*

Gwynne joined SpaceX, a commercial space exploration founded by Elon Musk, as its seventh employee in its founding year of 2002, as vice president of business development, and now holds a seat on the SpaceX board of directors. A private company famed for its innovation and disruption of an entire industry, SpaceX became the first private company to successfully launch, orbit, and recover a spacecraft in December 2010. It also has a multibillion-dollar contract with NASA to deliver astronauts to the International Space Station (ISS). SpaceX is also working on a next-generation transportation system to take people to Mars in the near future.

Prior to SpaceX, Gwynne spent over ten years at Aerospace Corporation, where she held positions in space systems engineering and technology as well as project management. Before that, Gwynne was the director of Microcosm's Space Systems Division, where she served on the executive committee and was responsible for business development.

Gwynne holds a bachelor of science and a master of science in mechanical engineering and applied mathematics from Northwestern University. She has authored papers on a range of subjects, including spacecraft design and reentry vehicle operational risks.

© Danielle Newnham 2016
D. Newnham, *Female Innovators at Work*, DOI 10.1007/978-1-4842-2364-2_11

Danielle Newnham: What is your background? When did you first get excited about engineering?

Gwynne Shotwell: Since I was little, I was interested in machines. In third grade, I was riding in the car with my mom and wanted to know how the engine worked. My mom bought me a book to explain, and after that I got obsessed with engines, gears, and differentials. I don't know where that book went....

While in high school, I went to a Society of Women Engineers event at the Illinois Institute of Technology. It was a panel event with a group of women engineers, and after the talk I went and spoke with one of the panelists who firstly, she was wearing the best suit out of all of them and secondly, she said the things that were the most interesting to me. She was a mechanical engineer. I felt a connection to her and thus to what she did. That day I decided to become a mechanical engineer.

Upon graduating from Northwestern, I moved to Detroit to work for Chrysler Motors after I was selected to be a part of a management training program. I didn't stay long, as I felt that I needed more education to be a better engineer. I finished my master's degree [back at Northwestern University] and was introduced to the Aerospace Corporation in El Segundo. I ended up going there and spending ten years working on fun projects in space systems engineering. I left in 1998 to work for a small aerospace company, Microcosm, and then I joined SpaceX in 2002. I wanted to be part of the company that was going to change this entire industry. I saw SpaceX as the best possible shot to do this.

Newnham: You were among the first ten employees at SpaceX, starting with the company in its founding year. How were you recruited and what were the early days there like?

Shotwell: I met Elon after dropping off my friend Dr. Hans Koenigsmann from his congrats and goodbye lunch. He had just left the company I was working for to join SpaceX. Elon was sitting in his cube and I shared my opinion with him that I thought he needed a full time head of business development—sales. Shortly after that chat, I got a call from his assistant asking me to apply for the new VP of Sales position.

SpaceX was tiny when I joined. There were half a dozen of us, and like most startup teams, we all wore several different hats. I was the seventh employee and head of sales, but I pitched in wherever needed—launch range interface, government and policy, finance. I spent a lot of time thinking about how to build our teams and culture.

Our mission at SpaceX has stayed constant over the years. Elon created SpaceX to revolutionize space transportation technology with the ultimate goal of enabling life on other planets, and we have taken a very measured approach to it. We designed and flew a small rocket, which was the Falcon 1. Then a bigger one, which was Falcon 9 with a spaceship—Dragon version

I—to take cargo to low Earth orbit. Now we are building an even bigger rocket—the Falcon Heavy—and designing the spaceship to be able to carry people—Crew Dragon.

We're also now starting to focus on building the transportation system to get people to Mars in sufficient numbers to create a self-sustaining city on the planet, starting in the next decade.

Newnham: How do you get new employees on board with the SpaceX mission?

Shotwell: We let them live it. The traditional way that companies introduce employees to their mission is to have a bunch of long-winded presentations. With SpaceX, our goals are very clear—certainly no one joins SpaceX wondering what we're building. So for us, the best way to be invested in the mission is to start contributing and getting to know the company as quickly as possible. We try to keep orientation efficient and focused on practical things that will help people to do their jobs well, and then we let them run with the ball.

SpaceX has a relentless drive to be better, so one really important skill for all our employees is the ability to accept critical feedback. When you get that feedback, that's how you improve. But you need to build a culture where people feel empowered to provide that feedback, and they expect to receive it in return—and not have their feelings hurt.

At the end of the day, SpaceX was created to do something that's never been done before: achieving fully and rapidly reusable spacecraft. So every day we were working to innovate, reinvent and improve on the way things had been previously done in the industry, which means we need to constantly think outside the box, and that's what continues to make SpaceX such a challenging but exhilarating place to be an engineer.

Newnham: Can you describe a particularly bad day at SpaceX and what you learned from it?

Shotwell: I've never seriously thought about quitting in the fourteen years I have been here. SpaceX attracts a particular sort of person who is energized by creating something important over the long term. You'll have days that don't go to plan and aren't great—this I promise! But if you can focus on the mission and know you're surrounded by great people that are all driving in the same direction, you can always press on through. My bad days are almost always when some development occurs and we are going to disappoint a customer. I really hate that and I take customer commitments personally.

Newnham: Can you tell me about some of the major milestones of SpaceX?

Shotwell: The first successful Falcon I launch in 2008 was amazing! Berthing with the ISS in May of 2012 was also a highlight. And the first landing of a Falcon 9 first stage, in December 2015 was breathtaking. There are a lot of important milestones that we've reached over the years, so it's hard to choose and we celebrate the big ones either with a big party [we busted out a lot of champagne when we got to station] or we give people time off to celebrate in their way with friends, colleagues and their family.

Newnham: What's it like to part of a company that experienced such rapid growth, and how does one keep its unique company culture when going through such a transition?

Shotwell: When you're growing, a big challenge is continuing to operate efficiently and quickly. You want to build vehicles at the scale of a large company, but move at the pace of a startup, and it is critical for people to stay connected to the mission. As you scale, bureaucracy and rules inevitably invade but the key is to make sure they all make sense and are not stupid. We actually prefer tools to rules wherever possible.

Internal communication is also key to keeping everyone engaged and hooked to the mission. I spend a lot of time staying connected to the employees. I hold regular "fireside chats" with small groups of employees to answer questions about whatever is on people's minds. I also have an anonymous suggestion box that goes directly to my email, so employees have another way of raising important issues. I also always encourage people to stop by or send me an email if they need some answers. I truly have an open door policy as I sit in a cube. I don't have a door.

Newnham: Can you tell me about the partnerships with e.g. NASA which you played such a fundamental role in?

Shotwell: The genesis of that project was formulated and led by NASA and they deserve the credit. At that time, we were merely bidders. It took incredible vision and relentless determination to pull that COTS [Commercial Orbital Transportation Services] partnership off, and we were thrilled to have won. I think over twenty bidders participated initially and NASA saw the potential in SpaceX. That also took vision. We had to be the underdog.

Once the partnership was formed, it took everyone's effort to make the required technical progress while fighting the good fight [keeping naysayers and bureaucracy out]. It was a historic program and NASA should be incredibly proud. We were honored to have been given the opportunity and thrilled that we achieved our goals.

Newnham: SpaceX and Elon were always under intense media scrutiny. Even now, some press remains pessimistic about your missions. How do you and your team deal with that? How does it affect morale when things don't go as planned?

Shotwell: I don't pay any real attention to the naysayers. At first they said we would never get to orbit. Well we got Falcon 1 there. Then they said we would never get a "real" rocket to orbit. So we did that with Falcon 9—twenty-six times. Then the pundits said we would never get to the International Space

Station. Check, we got that—nine times. Now they say we can't keep up with our manifest. We'll get that done as well. I am motivated by the challenges and I think our employees are motivated by this kind of garbage talk as well. They love proving everyone wrong.

At the same time, while we focus on our business and ignore the smack, we want to tell our story. People are curious about what we do but don't necessarily know a lot about space technology. I think it is important to let people know what we are doing to inspire them about what it means to be working towards building the capabilities to extend human life to other planets. This is going to be one of the greatest challenges in human history, and ultimately it will depend upon the support of millions of people. This is the future of humanity, and we want people to be engaged in the journey.

Newnham: As one of the most innovative companies in the world, how does SpaceX foster an innovative workforce?

Shotwell: First of all, if you keep people focused on the vision, you tend to get great ideas that align with it. SpaceX is a relatively flat organization. Anyone gets to talk to anyone. And the best idea wins—no matter where it comes from. We care about progress and favor results over anything else.

Newnham: How has your role evolved over the fourteen years and what skills are required to perform such a job? What about SpaceX keeps you there?

Shotwell: I started as head of sales. Obviously, we were tiny and so everyone needed to stretch. I took on all customer support, government interfaces, revenue collection, contracts, and legal. Of course I didn't do the day to day in all these area, I just kept an eye on them.

Intelligence, talent, and drive are the most valued skills at SpaceX. You can teach smart people anything, or equally, they teach themselves. If you're the sort of person who believes in what we're doing, and has the drive to make a real impact on the future of humanity, there's no better place to be. And of course it helps to be surrounded by brilliant people every day. SpaceX is a lot like a family, and I can't imagine not being here.

Newnham: The promotional videos for SpaceX, such as for the Falcon Heavy, are always pretty impressive. What some would have considered improbable missions several years ago often become reality at SpaceX. What does it feel like to work for a company like that? And to be part of a team that make these ambitious plans a reality?

Shotwell: A decade ago, the idea of a private space company being able to resupply the International Space Station was just too much. So we didn't focus on that seemingly impossible statement, we focused on getting our job done: building a reliable launch and Dragon system. That seemed far less daunting.

Now we deliver capabilities to orbit and the ISS regularly. Having lived through our early days, and been part of the industry before SpaceX, I don't take any of this for granted. I feel really lucky to be part of something that has moved the industry forward.

Newnham: Reusability. How did that become such a massive part of SpaceX's mission?

Shotwell: Complete and rapid reusability transforms the space industry and is absolutely necessary to allow humans to be truly space faring. Imagine the airline industry if we tossed the airplane after every flight. The cost would be prohibitive and there would be no chance of two-way travel unless you built another airplane on the other side. If we can figure out how to reuse rockets just like airplanes, building a multi-planetary species will become feasible. Otherwise, it is all one way trips which won't do much.

Newnham: A lot of people have an opinion on what Elon Musk is like. What is he like to work with? And what was it about his vision that you bought into when you first met him?

Shotwell: I love working for Elon. He is a data driven, truly deep thinker. He is also hilarious. He takes nothing for granted and never accepts the status quo.

A bad day for you is when you cannot explain why you want to do something in a particular way—that doesn't make a lot of common sense—and respond with "that is just the way things are done." I've been working with Elon for fourteen years now and I've learned so much from him.

Newnham: You are an inspirational and visible role model but there is still a lack of women, in general, in STEM fields. How do you think we encourage more girls into STEM?

Shotwell: The most important thing we can do is expose girls to STEM careers while they're young. When children are young, they believe they can do anything. Stereotypes can also set in early, with children quickly picking up ideas about what kind of careers are "for men" or "for women." So engineering needs to be a field that girls feel is accessible, acceptable, and welcome.

This is where good role models and mentors have a big influence. A study found that of more than 350,000 high school girls who want to pursue STEM, only four percent said they had a mentor encouraging them. That's just crazy. We've got to do better than that. Shoot, I need to do more.

Newnham: And what advice would you offer young women who are already in the field but want to push further into what are often very male-dominated senior management positions?

Shotwell: Never give up on something you want because the path looks hard. If it isn't difficult to get, it likely isn't worth much. Get support and feedback [from people you admire and can trust] to make sure you are on the right path to achieve your goals.

Newnham: You have achieved a great deal in your career and raised a family. Is there such a thing as work/life balance, especially when you are working at such a game-changing company?

Shotwell: Everyone has to make choices for themselves that best fit their situation. I generally don't like to think of it as "balancing." It certainly isn't fifty/fifty every day. I try to apply my resources where they are needed most at that time. Keep in mind this means that you don't break commitments. If I promised my kids I would be at a soccer or track event, then I would be there, but I didn't go to every event. I went to the ones where it seemed they needed/wanted me most. And I rarely missed dinner with my family, unless I was travelling. But after dinner, the kids went to do their homework and so did I…

My husband works his ass off too so there isn't generally too much struggle here.

Ideally, you want to combine your life and your work so you can just live a complete life, with work an integral part of it. If you find the right career, many days your work is honestly going to be the most important thing going on, and you'll want to focus 100 percent. On the other hand, you can end up with a sick child—then that is the time when work doesn't get your focus and your child does. It doesn't mean you care more or less about either. It's just about prioritizing as you need to.

Newnham: When it comes to your career, what are you most proud of and why?

Shotwell: This is easy: Falcon 1 getting to orbit in August of 2008. Getting grappled with the ISS in May of 2012 and then landing the Falcon 9 first stage on land this past December [2015]. Three incredible moments for us.

Newnham: What's the best career advice you have been given?

Shotwell: Take risks. The safe path isn't the most fun, or satisfying, and rarely yields the highest outcomes.

Newnham: What are the most important lessons you have learned in life which were useful at work?

Shotwell: Care about people.

Newnham: Who/what inspires you and why?

Shotwell: Honestly, the people that work for me inspire me. And Bono.

Newnham: What do you wish your/SpaceX's legacy to be?

Shotwell: Humans living on Mars.

Majora Carter

Cofounder and CEO, StartUp Box

Majora Carter is the cofounder and CEO of StartUp Box, a social enterprise on a mission to enable and empower people from low-status communities in America to join the tech economy. Opportunities and support offered through the enterprise include employment in quality assurance testing, lessons in financial literacy, community events space, gaming tournaments, mentorship, and a Wi-Fi café.

Majora also founded Sustainable South Bronx and Green for All. Both organizations were built to help move communities out of poverty through green-infrastructure projects, policies, and job training. In 2007, while running Sustainable South Bronx, Majora introduced MIT's first-ever mobile fab lab to the South Bronx, where it served as an early iteration of the "makerspaces" that have since evolved.

Majora has also worked on diversity projects for tech companies such as Google, Etsy, and Cisco. She is a graduate of the Bronx High School of Science and an advisory board member of the Bronx Academy of Software Engineering High School.

Danielle Newnham: Can you tell me about your background?

Majora Carter: I grew up in Hunts Point, in the South Bronx in New York City, which in the 1970s and 1980s was a time when the city, like everywhere around the country, was dealing with a tremendous amount of financial disinvestment. Landlords, at least in this part of the world, were literally torching buildings, committing arson, instead of trying to find money to reinvest in them. So the phrase "The Bronx is burning" was completely associated with my youth, because the area at the time was filled with what seemed to be

© Danielle Newnham 2016
D. Newnham, *Female Innovators at Work*, DOI 10.1007/978-1-4842-2364-2_12

spontaneous fires combusting. And The Bronx itself lost about sixty percent of its population because of the combination of the fires, the impact of highway construction, and people vacating as quickly as they could.

It was a really difficult time. It looked like London in 1945. There were definitely issues of crime and people, like my dad, who owned a house, were left behind. The house was pretty worthless and it was not like he could sell it to anyone, so we couldn't move someplace else. We were stuck there. There were six of us kids living in the house at the time.

Newnham: I have read that because of what was happening there at the time, people made it their mission to get out of the area. Was that true for you?

Carter: Certainly, I was planning my escape from the South Bronx since I was seven years old. That summer, the buildings at either end of my block burned down, which meant they were completely uninhabitable, and everyone I knew who had lived in them had left. They were just gone. This happened pretty much overnight. Then at the end of the summer, my brother was killed, which was just horrible. And then a little while later, our dog died. So I was done. I just wanted to leave. I used education as my way out. I was a smart kid and I knew it. I was just following that path of trying to be "somebody" by leaving the neighborhood. This is the type of brain drain that goes on in our low-status communities. And I was a part of it. So I went away to study, but I did come back. However, I didn't come back because I had any altruistic aspirations for the community. I came back because I was starting graduate school and I needed a cheap place to stay. That's the only reason.

I had come back occasionally because my mother cooked really well, so that would have been a reason to come too, but there was no way I wanted to live there. And it was funny because I lived this life for a number of years, where I would leave the house super-early just to get out of the house and I wouldn't get back until late at night. Or I couch surfed or whatever because that was more important to me than coming back to my neighborhood.

But I did eventually come back and stayed. That was because I started meeting people in the community doing arts related programs, and I was like, "There are artists in The Bronx?!" It was really amazing meeting people who were born and raised in The Bronx and who were hanging around to try and build a bit of an arts renaissance right here. I just fell in love with the people and the space and I thought, "Wow, I *could* stay here."

Newnham: It then became a mission for you to regenerate the area. How did your involvement evolve?

Carter: Well, there was a point when our city and state were planning on building a huge waste facility on our waterfront. And I knew two things. One, arts alone wasn't going to save us. And two, we really did need to be involved with a level of community development that proved people who were in this community had value—serious value. And unless we did that around the environment and economic development, no one was going to pay any attention to us. No one was going to care. And I knew that intrinsically. So initially, I think I was focused on the environmental side, which I knew connected to the economic side. I did things like focus on transforming abandoned spaces. Well, they weren't abandoned spaces; they were actively used as illegal dumps. But I focused on transforming them so that they would become public spaces that people would want to see. So that was kind of fun.

And then in 2000, I worked on the first waterfront park that we have had in the neighborhood in sixty years. Then I started focusing on things like how to create job training and placement systems where people can see both a personal and a financial stake in the development of the environment and want to support it. I did a bunch of projects like that—probably from the late 1990s up until 2008 through my own non-profit called Sustainable South Bronx. I loved it but for my own professional reasons, I decided to move on. I really tried to play out the environment and economic solutions approach in other parts of the country, and I did. I realized that real estate development was key to the transformation of low-status communities, and really looking at economic drivers was an enormous part of it. Making sure that communities were prepared for it opened up new and interesting challenges too.

Newnham: What kind of reaction did you have from the community when you carried out these transformational projects? From the perspective of those in power and those living in the area?

Carter: I think at first people on the ground didn't think it was possible. There were definitely some diehard people who just loved the idea but for the most part, people were just like—let's see if it works. Fortunately, no one was actively opposed to this type of work, which was great but they certainly weren't going to help either because I think on some level, people felt very demoralized and it just seemed like too big a project. Like, nobody developed parks - I mean, come on. And so for us to say, that yes, we are going to create some jobs in the environment was just as fanciful and flighty as anything else. But that's why we just had to do it and prove what was possible.

Newnham: Which you did. Can you give me an idea of the results from doing these projects? What did success look like?

Carter: It looks like a beautiful, world-class, award-winning park on the river. It looks like people who were in the revolving door of the justice system haven't been back because they have been working in the environmental field, and in the case of technology, it means that there is a storefront right in the middle of this economically challenged community in which there are people working in technology. And thousands of people walk by that door front, look in the huge glass window, and see people working. They may not know exactly what quality assurance [QA] or software testing services are, but they know that there are black and brown people in that space and that they are a part of the tech ecosystem, earning money. And that little part of the tech ecosystem is in a part of the community they had given up on a long time ago.

Newnham: So how did you come up with the idea for StartUp Box and how did you get it started?

Carter: I think it was back in 2012 that we became convinced to develop something in technology. I had just started the non-profit at this point, after having worked in the private sector, and because I was thinking more along the lines of this being a traditional workforce development project, it really did seem like it should be part of the public sector because there we were trying to figure out how to get more people in low-status communities involved in the tech economy. We had spent a lot of time and money trying to figure out projects that really should have been considered more of a philanthropic pursuit. So that's why I started the non-profit—hoping someone else would support doing some of this work, because it was killing me.

What was interesting was that we knew tech was a huge economic driver and we needed to figure out ways to get from low-status communities to the Bay Area. I think the original path we took, though, was very similar to what a lot of folks think, which is just, "Oh. Let's just teach kids to code." But we realized there were already way too many people doing this. The field was getting crowded and we would have not been able to do better than what was already out there.

We started thinking about people other than "kids", and trying to get tech companies to locate up here. We found a company that was really progressive. We thought it would be so great if they came to the South Bronx. But they expressed concern over competing for talent - which is already tight, and would be made more so by moving to a location with dubious lifestyle amenities. For example, there wasn't a place for coffee or anything like that, so we realized it wasn't happening, and that we would have to do something on our own instead. So we did.

We were really excited to learn about quality assurance because one of our advisors was the head of game development at Nickelodeon. He was lamenting about his problems and their off-shore quality assurance team. They would hire game developers to create content for them, but the production schedule would always falter during testing. And so they were wondering, why is it at that point—the cheapest part of the software development pipeline—that it gets stuck?

Then you realize that a lot of these developers were using offshore options. And between the different time zones and the different cultural competencies available to Western software testers, projects would literally just get stopped.

So that added a lot of time to the development, but if we were able to develop a service that competed with these offshore options, and added some value, we knew we could do quality assurance and other software services in the same time zone and with the cultural fluency. This could possibly be used as a way to perform a soft onboarding process for people in our community. Even though we would take 100 percent control of the hiring process and provide our clients a service, there would still be valuable interactions between our team members and our clients.

Elements of QA are entry-level, but we were hoping to give our clients reasons to look at, and empower talent as people that they could hire away from us. For us, that was the social part of our mission—not just to keep a whole bunch of people in entry-level tech jobs, because that's not what we want. We are providing a meaningful way for people who live in low-status communities to connect with people who are already in the tech field.

Tech talent diversity in the US is abysmally low. It really is one of the most undiversed sectors within the country. We really thought that the people who would come to us looking for work would be straight out of jail or underemployed, but we were not expecting people to walk through our door with computer science or other bachelor degrees and top notch training. We would look at them and say, "You are overqualified for this job."

That's when we realized that a major reason why there is a lack of diversity in the tech sector is because people hire who they know, and we are a still a segregated country in many ways. So let's just say a CEO of a tech company has this commitment to diversity. Their HR people are thinking, "Well, my job is on the line if I don't get qualified people hired." And most of them are white, so they hire who they feel most comfortable with, which is generally other white people. Period. And that is just the way it works. These people are not overtly racist, just products of our society.

So that's why it was important for us to develop a company in which our team members could have access to the people who were doing the hiring, but not just in an interview. It's relationship building at no risk spread out over time.

Newnham: And you are doing it in other ways aren't you, including mentorship? How are people benefitting from this?

Carter: Yes, mentors are often the first step to getting people hired. In terms of the benefits, the first is that the individual gets paid per hour and that's awesome. Since they are all local, they get the additional benefit of being able to walk to work or a very short commute which is also wonderful. And it also gives them access into the tech world so then they are exposed to a tremendous amount whether it is a product success or failure and different aspects of the tech world because our clients are so varied. They get to meet these awesome people who can help them build their careers which is in many cases more valuable than training or direct education.

That's effective on an individual level but also, what's great for other people in the area is that they get a huge amount of pride from knowing that a company like this is in the community. Again, we strategically located the company in a corner storefront, and we really did that for a communications purpose, so that people could see people inside working in technology.

What we didn't know was that particular corner was a pretty hot corner in terms of crime. It was vacant for so long and you realize that, especially in low-status communities, places that are inactive become magnets for not nice things. And this particular space had been vacant for around three years. And I remember being shown bullet holes in our roll down gates. I had no idea, and we had been in the space for more than a year at that point. Obviously they were old bullet holes, because that's what used to happen there, but it acts as one of those reminders that this used to happen when you don't build a positive type of community infrastructure.

Newnham: You're not a woman who starts small. You have a mission and then go above and beyond. Can you tell me more about StartUp Box's extended reach—i.e., the game tournaments and Birch Coffee?

Carter: Actually, we always start small by launching beta versions - before the press is invited in. Your ideas might seem great to you, your team, and your advisors. Hitting the real world with anything always teaches you a lesson or two....The tournaments were a way to recruit talent. Our CTO, Lancelot Chase, was hired specifically because he was a professional gamer who had done QA work on games for several years, so he had good intel on the industry. He knew we needed gamers who are really comfortable with playing video games, comfortable in front of computers for long hours, and people who thrive in the face of defeat. Those who will try, fail, repeat, and not go home, but will keep going through every level until the end. He knew that the best way to find these people was to hold gaming tournaments.

At the time, I had no idea that gaming was so big. In the States, it's bigger than the movies. And I had literally no idea, nor did I know that "competitive gaming" was a thing. When I heard about it, I thought, "What? People sit around together in a tournament and play games?" and they did and it is a huge industry and we realized that if we had the game tournaments, people would just come out and play together.

So that was Lancelot's idea for recruiting people and it was great way to see personalities because you can learn a lot about people when they are playing a video game, especially competitively. Are they good? Are they willing to offer advice? Are they able to communicate what they need to when working with someone on QA? And it is also a very happy experience.

Another thing about hosting gaming tournaments in a marginalized, low-status community is that it creates space they can feel happy and confident and really secure in. That's when they think "Oh, maybe this is something I could do." We watch them play and inform them about the tech stuff we are doing and suddenly, you're talking to a different person because they are feeling more confident and less demoralized than if you just approached them on the street. That's why we use the gaming tournaments as a talent recruitment tool.

The other part of it was again, not knowing about this world but trusting my team, that there was an enormous amount of intergenerationality. People who would come to gaming tournaments, like parents would come with little kids and grandparents, and there was a tremendous cross-section of people that would come to them, including police officers, which was another really interesting way to build community, especially in these really difficult times when awareness of police brutality is becoming so acute.

My company has built up a relationship with the local police and I have spent all of my life and all of my career working in the field of community development so you have got to know everybody. It was the police who were more concerned about us hosting tournaments, and it was really funny because the first one we had was overflowing with a couple of hundred people who were going in and out of our little seven-hundred-square-foot space.

What was really fascinating was that the top police brass turned up and, the chief inspector at the time pulled me outside. He was pointing out people and saying things like, "That guy is a total knucklehead. That kid probably needs a little support but is a good kid. That guy, honestly we watch him all the time because he is a bad, bad dude." And, "Oh, you know who that is? That's so-and-so who runs the daycare center and she's here with some of the kids that she's in charge of." And so he was amazed at the cross-section of people who were in the room. He was also favorably impressed because he knew that a community that hangs out together is a safer and healthier community. And I said, "Dude, a game tournament did that." It was really awesome.

We were giving reasons for the community to be in fellowship with each other. And I don't mean to sound all churchy about it, but that essentially is it.

Then there was the development of a social "third space" which is -- not where you live or work but where you can have meaningful interactions with other people, beyond your home and your work. We don't have many of those, and we haven't had one on our main commercial strip for decades. We also haven't coffee shops since I was at high school in the 1980s, so these third places are important because, on some level, it's what keeps people staying in our community and having positive interactions with each other and we didn't have that. So we built a coffee shop.

We eventually partnered with Birch Coffee and ended up seeing how fabulous it was to work with these guys who have an unbelievable commitment to coffee but also the way in which coffee shops can be used to build community.

Newnham: Can you tell me about your future plans for StartUp Box? What is your mission?

Carter: Our mission is to expand StartUp Box, and the concept, to other cities around the country because we know that wherever there is a thriving tech sector in a city, we also know that not too far away from there is a not so thriving, low-status community, and we really believe that developing a StartUp Box in those areas is exactly what connects people to those communities. And we know there is business to be made and so we are pitching, actually we are more than pitching, we have been approached by a few cities around the country who have identified StartUp Box as a way to economically diversify tech communities.

Places like Philly, and Austin, and the Twin Cities—we are looking to develop public-private partnerships there to help facilitate the development of a StartUp Box in each of those areas. If we can launch this in five cities, our research shows us that we could create, in just those five cities, about five hundred direct and indirect jobs, and about $7 million in revenue, which would be fantastic, especially for those in low-status communities, so we are really excited about that.

I also think that there is so much more that we can do. And I really do think that the path we are on in creating these successful models for economic well-being will have a ripple effect. These are opportunities for us to self-gentrify communities for us, and use that as a model for other parts of the country.

Newnham: Do you ever get frustrated that you have had to take it upon yourselves to do this?

Carter: Yes, always. Always. That is the most frustrating part of this because what we do is not fiction. It is really based on market research and a real understanding about how we need to be investing in low-status communities. Sadly, I feel, and not just in New York but all over the country and also outside the country, there is a real reticence to invest in wealth creation for residents of low-status communities. And because of that, what we experience is brain drain, so we lose the most talented, hard-working ones because they are constantly being extracted from communities.

I think it's great that folks are given the opportunity to thrive, but we also need these aspirational role models in place. We also need their ability to reinvest in their own community. So this is the problem. The time is a little past due to build models for why people would want to stay and invest back into their own community. That isn't there now.

I think if there were real public-private partnerships to facilitate that, it would be amazing.

Newnham: What are you most proud of and why?

Carter: I have done a lot to be proud of, but I think the main thing is that we are developing this approach to economically diversify low-status communities to reduce brain drain. These interventions that we do, whether it is looking into and creating models that build economic drivers, such as our tech company, or create the type of spaces that people want to be in like nice cafés, those types of things are exciting for us because they prove out the model that *you don't have to move out of your neighborhood to live in a better one.*

Elizabeth Feinler

Director of the Network Information Systems Center, SRI International

Elizabeth Feinler *is a pioneering information scientist and the former direc-*
tor of the Network Information Systems Center at the Stanford Research Institute
(now SRI International), which she joined in 1960 to work in the Information
Research Department to assist in developing projects such as the Handbook of
Psychopharmacology and the Chemical Process Economics Handbook.

In 1972, Elizabeth joined Dr. Douglas Engelbart's Augmentation Research Center
(ARC) to work on the ARPANET Resource Handbook. Elizabeth was principal investi-
gator for the Network Information Center (NIC) project from 1974 to 1989. During
that time, Elizabeth's NIC group worked on the Advanced Research Projects Agency
Network (ARPANET), which evolved into the Defense Data Network (DDN), fore-
runners to the Internet.

The NIC provided ARPANET users with various support services, a directory, a
resource handbook (list of services), and the DoD protocol handbook. It was also
Elizabeth's group who managed the first host-naming registry for the Internet and
developed the top-level domain naming system of .com, .gov, .org, .edu, and .mil,
which is still in use today.

© Danielle Newnham 2016
D. Newnham, *Female Innovators at Work*, DOI 10.1007/978-1-4842-2364-2_13

*Elizabeth became the director of the Network Information Systems Center at SRI in
1986. She left there in 1989 to work for Sterling Software Corp.*

*At Sterling Software Corp., Elizabeth worked as a contract network requirements
manager at NASA Ames Research Center, where she helped develop guidelines for
managing the NASA Science Internet (NSI) NIC and the NASA websites.*

*Elizabeth was inducted into the Internet Hall of Fame in 2012. Since retiring, she has
been a consultant at The Computer History Museum, where she donated, organized,
and detailed over 350 boxes of archives from the Engelbart and NIC projects.*

*Elizabeth was the first in her family to graduate from college, which she did in 1954
with a Bachelor of Science degree in chemistry from West Liberty University.*

Danielle Newnham: Can you tell me about your background? What were
you like growing up?

Elizabeth Feinler: I grew up in Wheeling, West Virginia, on the island during the time of The Great Depression. Money was very tight and no one in
my family was wealthy. Both of my grandfathers and my step-father's father
lost their businesses in the depression. My father became an alcoholic, so my
parents separated when I was about two years old. We then went to live with
my mother's parents who ran a boarding house, and my mother then worked
as a clerk in a shoe store. When I was seven, my mother remarried. My sister,
half-brother, and I lived with my mother and stepfather, a steel worker, until I
went off to college at eighteen.

My life was a little schizophrenic as, early on, I spent weekends with my father
and paternal grandparents and week days with my mother and her parents.
Life at home was organized. I had chores, was expected to help out, be responsible, be courteous to the elderly boarders, and do well in school. No heli-
copter mom here. If I got a bad teacher or thought I got a bad deal at school,
the message from home was, "Deal with it. No one's life is without problems."

On the other hand when I was at my father's house, all stops were out. Movies,
ice cream and candy, circuses, favorite foods, presents—you name it. My sister
and I were spoiled rotten there. My grandfather had owned several theaters
in town, and even though he had lost them in the depression, and had to go
back to work in one as a ticket taker to make ends meet, as a courtesy to him
we were allowed to go to all the movies in town for free.

I was interested in art and my uncle, who was a commercial artist, gave me
paints, brushes, and paper he no longer needed. Dad made us a doll house,
desks with swivel chairs, and games for us to play, and my two aunts gave us
old clothes and costume jewelry to play dress up or "movie star."

Needless to say I had a rich Walter Mitty–like fantasy life. The movies had
some strong women in them then—Betty Davis, Ingrid Bergman, Mae West,
Joan Crawford. Barbara Stanwyck, Carole Lombard, Vivien Leigh—and they
served as role models because I saw so many movies—sometimes eight or
ten in a weekend.

I went to public schools, liked school, and did well. I was shy, but had many friends. I met one really good, lifelong friend in second grade and am still good friends with her today, although she now lives half way across the country. We went to grade school and high school together, were college roommates, I was in her wedding, and we worked our way through college together as assistant librarians in the college library.

As kids, we studied together and played together. We liked nature study and went on nature hikes and roamed the river bank or went to the library. Kids weren't allowed to read adult library books, and we had read most of the kid's books so my mother wrote to the librarian saying I had her permission to read any book in the library and the judgement to evaluate what I read, so I was issued an adult library card. I liked murder mysteries and historical novels. The science section was minimal, but we thought it was great. We liked "ologies," and being kid-like, adopted a new "ology" every month—ornithology, geology, ichthyology, herpetology, microbiology, etc. Actually, I think we liked the importance of the long scientific words as much as the science itself.

In high school, I did the usual high school activities—dated, danced, hung out with friends, followed the big bands, worried about my appearance and being popular, and tried not to be labeled a "brain"—another schizophrenic activity. I always wanted to go to college, but didn't think it was possible, as no one in the family had that kind of money. However, in my junior year, I decided I was going to go somehow or other and started looking for scholarships.

There were almost no jobs for women in those days and what there were paid very little, so I worked at all the jobs I could get—baby sitter, car hop, clerk in the local department store, copywriter for radio ads, china decorator in a local glass factory, seamstress making slipcovers and drapes, and so on.

I was lucky enough to be awarded a full scholarship in advertising design at the University of Cincinnati, a co-op school where one could work a semester and study a semester, and thus work one's way through. I was so excited and took a train to Cincinnati to accept the scholarship only to find out that you could not co-op your freshman year. I didn't have the money for room and board, so I had to give up the scholarship. This was a very low point, but I was still determined to be the first person in my family to go to college, so I enrolled in West Liberty State College, which was close enough for me to commute and live at home. I was working two jobs and trying to go to college, which obviously was not going to work for very long. In my second semester, the college librarian offered me a staff position as assistant librarian, which allowed me to work full time at a reasonable salary. We worked nights in the library, so I had time off during the day to take classes. The art department was minimal, but the chemistry department was reasonably good, so I majored in chemistry.

I did graduate work at Purdue in biochemistry and completed course work for a PhD. However, I was worn down from living on $130 a month and not happy with opportunities for women in biochemistry at the time. So I decided to work a year and make some money to proceed, I was amazed to be wined, dined, and Sweet Adelined at the American Chemical Society job fair in Miami, where I had more than twenty job offers. *Sputnik* had just gone up and the US was frantic for scientists of any stripe—even women—to play catch-up with the Russians. I accepted a job at Chemical Abstracts, which in those days was on the Ohio State campus.

Newnham: What did you do there and what prompted the job change to SRI? What was SRI like back then?

Feinler: The job at Chemical Abstracts [CA] was an information job. I was assistant editor for microbiology, botany, sugars, gums, and polysaccharides for the *Fifth Decennial Index*. This was a huge information undertaking and piqued my interest in handling large data projects. We did the indexing by reading the reprint or its abstract and dictating appropriate index entries, which were then transcribed by secretaries onto 3x5 index cards, re-reviewed by us, and stored in order in vaults before being sent to printers for printing. None of the process was computerized. CA was just thinking about automating at the time, but neither the right software nor computers were available yet.

As a single person, Columbus, Ohio, wasn't somewhere I wanted to spend the rest of my life. We jokingly said Columbus was "centrally located in the middle of nowhere." I read in *Chemical and Engineering News* about a group being created at SRI that paired information specialists, in my case chemistry, with research teams. The specialists searched the technical literature, then gathered, and organized the information pertinent to the research team's needs.

This appealed to me and California seemed like a happening place, so I wrote and asked them to hire me. They wrote back to say they were interested, but did not have a job at the time. It was a long shot, so I forgot about it and decided to go off on a grand tour of Europe with my roommate. Right before we left for Europe though, I received an offer from SRI, which I accepted starting a week after we returned from our trip. When I first got to California, I couldn't remember where I was, because I had been in so many strange cities in such a short time.

SRI is a non-profit research establishment frequently referred to as a think tank. When I arrived in 1960 it was, and still is, involved in all kinds of research projects and was a very exciting place to work. It did contract research for the US government and private companies, and even for other countries. Projects were typically a couple of years long—some shorter and some much longer—so workers often needed specific information in a hurry.

Our group was a service group i.e., we were farmed out to projects because we knew the literature sources and could quickly collect and organize whatever was needed. None of this was done with computers yet, it was all done by brute force by collecting reprints and written material and condensing the information onto myriad numbers of 3x5 index cards, or yellow-lining the reprints, or whatever format suited the researcher's needs. My first project was a physics project producing a compilation of charge transfer reactions, about which I knew nothing. However, the research group gave me a quick tutorial and we published the compilation—and I got my sea legs at SRI.

Newnham: What led to you working with Doug Engelbart's team?

Feinler: I moved up to be manager of my service group and as such worked on bigger and bigger information projects, such as the *Handbook of Psychopharmacology* for the National Institutes of Health, and preservation of biological specimens for NASA Skylab. On one project on fire retardant chemicals, I decided we needed computer help, so worked with two programmers to develop a bibliographic searching system on a General Electric timeshared computer.

Doug was anticipating bidding on the Defense Advanced Research Projects Agency [DARPA] Network Information Center [NIC] project for the ARPANET [forerunner to the Internet], so he dropped by to see what I was doing. He had developed NLS [oN-Line System], which was an amazing system at the time of the late 1960s because it had almost everything we do today on computers—programming, text editing, mixed text and graphics, remote teleconferencing, debugging, hypertext, font selection, document production, the mouse pointer, and on and on. He wanted to use this system as the basis for the ARPANET NIC project.

I saw his system as a great breakthrough for using computers to handle information across networks, so asked him to hire me. He said he didn't have a job for me at the time, so I dismissed the idea. A few months later he appeared in my office and said he had a job for me now, and asked me if I wanted to transfer to his group. I asked him what the job was, and he said he wanted me to produce the *ARPANET Resource Handbook*. I asked him what a resource handbook was, and he said he didn't exactly know, but he needed one in six weeks for DARPA's demo of the ARPANET in Washington, DC. So that is how I joined Doug's group.

Newnham: What did you think of NLS the first time you sat in front of it?

Feinler: That I would crash the system. After I learned to use it, I thought it was a very useful and creative tool, with everything right at my fingertips. It had text editing, programming, debugging, a journal system, a database system, email, a consistent user interface, searching, hypertext links, teleconferencing, mixed text and graphics, the mouse pointer, and on and on. Some features were experimental at the time, while others we used on a daily basis. It did most of the things we do today. However, the software was unfortunately way ahead of the existing hardware at the time.

Newnham: Going back to NIC. What was its purpose?

Feinler: The NIC was primarily an information hub for the ARPANET/ Internet. At first, in the early 1970s, it dealt mostly with paper distribution, as there were no protocols for file transfer or email. Once email, the first "killer app," was developed then most interactions were done by email or information servers.

The NIC published the *ARPANET/DDN Directory* [essentially a phone number and email address book of network users and personnel], the *ARPANET Resource Handbook* [a directory of computers and resources available for use across the ARPANET], and the *DoD Protocol Handbook* [a compendium of the protocols or technology upon which the Internet was built].

Over time, we provided a twelve-hour-a-day telephone hotline, maintained the official host table, developed the top-level domain naming system, ran an audit trail and billing system for the DDN, administered the telephone access to the DDN [TACACS], maintained an online and hardcopy library—both at SRI and at the Defense Communications Agency [DCA] in Washington, provided the first netwide WHOIS name server, were the official distributers of the *Requests for Comments* [RFCs, a network technical note series], ran a large computer facility, and coordinated various official working groups, such as the Network Technical Liaison and Host Administrators. It was through these groups [Liaison and Host Administrators, as well as the Network Technical Working Group] that we all kept in touch. The NIC relayed info and problems out to these groups. And they kept us informed of happenings and problems at their sites or in general. The NIC also made announcements on behalf of our sponsors to the user community.

Newnham: Can you tell me more about your role within NIC and how it evolved over time?

Feinler: I joined Doug's group in 1972 as an information scientist to produce the *ARPANET Resource Handbook*, a compilation of computer and program resources available at various government and university centers that were accessible over the ARPANET.

There was a funding hiatus in 1972 and funds were cut drastically. Many of the NIC staff were laid off or left SRI. Shortly after that in 1974, I became the Principal Investigator for the NIC project, and the NIC became a separate project from Doug's NLS development work. At that time the NIC had a budget of $100,000 and a staff of two or three people including me. Trying to keep the project alive for $100,000 was really hard. Everyone worked many more hours than they were paid, and trying to run the NIC from California on a ten percent pie-slice on a BBN computer in Boston almost caused me to resign. The successful cutover to the TCP/IP protocols was probably the most significant milestone.

Doug's group was sold off to Tymshare Corp. in 1977, but I remained at SRI to run the NIC and to evolve its networked methods of information handling. DCA took over the day-to-day operation of the ARPANET, and after 1984, the ARPANET became one arm of the much larger Defense Data Network [DDN]. The scope of the NIC project expanded considerably, and I moved up to be director of the Network Information Systems Center at SRI.

When I left SRI in 1989 the NIC had a staff of more than forty, we ran a computer center with a DEC-20, Foonly [DEC-10 lookalike], and Sun servers, and had a budget of about 11 million dollars. This was a very big project at the time, especially for a woman.

Newnham: Speaking of that. What was the ratio of men to women back then?

Feinler: Almost all programmers were male. Although I wasn't a programmer, so I was usually accepted. Maybe it was my nickname "Jake." People didn't always know whether I was male or female.

There were several women working on the NIC project as we grew. Many worked their way up, so it was hard to get them proper recognition. I made them task managers and gave them substantial budgets to manage, as well as responsibility for the task. It was hard to ignore a manager with responsibility for a million dollar task—male or female. Sometimes I had to find out on the sly what men were making for a given job, then insist a woman doing the same job get equal billing and pay.

Newnham: Going back to the NIC. What were some of the major challenges you faced and how did you overcome them?

Feinler: I would say the greatest challenge was too many users and too little computer capacity. Another challenge was that the ARPANET/Internet was still being developed, as it was fast becoming a valued user utility, and the two purposes were not always compatible. At first, computers were huge in physical size, expensive to maintain, but small in actual computer capacity, and in most cases their use was spread very thin in many directions.

Many host computers on the early ARPANET/Internet were being used for other purposes than just network research, so it was difficult for their staff to pay allegiance to all the administrative demands. For example, the NIC maintained the official host name table for the ARPANET/Internet. We could ask a site to implement something important to the ARPANET/Internet, but it might not respond. Some sites did not install a complete host table on their computers, because it took up too much space or was too much work. Consequently, some email could not be delivered, and the NIC got complaints. This is one example of many similar problems.

The NIC resolved these problems by working together with local site staff, and technical gurus, when needed. In this case we developed an automatic server to update site host tables more easily, and pointed out the advantages of having a complete host table installed. Later we worked with network gurus to switch over to the domain naming system in place today.

By the time I left SRI in 1989, computers were small in size and much greater in compute power, but capacity was still a problem because the network had grown exponentially. Today capacity is obviously no longer a problem.

Newnham: How did the inevitable spurts of growth and change affect you and what you were doing?

Feinler: The NIC grew as the network grew. At first, there was myself and one other person, and no programming support. We had to ask Doug's programmers for help, largely as a favor, to get anything fixed or changed. In 1974, I was able to hire a programmer and the NIC began divorcing itself from using Doug's NLS system, other than for text editing and some of its database programming.

At that time we began offering many more services via network information servers, as these were more efficient and did not require a login or prior training. We did not have a dedicated computer and had to work in a sometimes minuscule pie-slice on a rented computer.

In 1984, DoD officially adopted the TCP/IP protocol suite and the NIC project expanded greatly. At that time, we obtained the DEC-20 and Sun servers, began transition of our software to the C programming language, began implementing the domain naming system, added many new features to the WHOIS server, and began collecting the audit trail and billing data for the DDN.

Also, by this time almost all network services except the telephone hotline were provided online. In addition we provided written documentation on request or by subscription to users all over the world, who were not on the Internet, but were interested in the packet-switched technology.

An ideal size for an informal research group at SRI is, in my observation, about twenty people. After that more structure is needed, and this was true of the NIC group. Our contract was laid out into specific tasks, so I appointed task leaders for each task, added a contract administrator to help track expenditures and deliverables, and hired a manager for our expanding computer facility. When I left in 1989, we were a group of more than forty people.

Newnham: What was it like working with Doug? Have you any anecdotes or fond memories that you care to share from your time working together?

Feinler: Doug was my mentor and a friend for many years, until he passed away a year or so ago. He was a quiet, thoughtful person with a mission and a passion to augment human intellect through a symbiosis with computers. He was all ears if you wanted to talk ideas, but could become a turtle in its shell if you just wanted to complain, and there was lots to complain about early on. I remember going to his office once with a veritable litany of woes. The system was down, computer was slow, I couldn't get time on a workstation, no programmer was available to fix things, and on and on. I was on a roll. He listened until I finished my rant, and then quietly said, "What are you going to do about these problems?" I got that he didn't hire me to bitch. He hired me to think my way to a solution.

Newnham: Can you tell me anymore about the systems that you were using during this time?

Feinler: As I mentioned, we started out with Doug's NLS system, which had many great features, but was way ahead of the computer capacity needed to deliver it to a whole network of users. At first, the NIC project had a pie-slice on a crowded DEC-10 and then a DEC-20—both at SRI. Then we were switched to Tymshare machines, then to a machine at Bolt Beranek and Newman [BBN] in Boston—which was virtually impossible—then to a purchased in-house Tymshare Foonly, and finally, to a purchased DEC-20 running TOPS 20. When I left, we were converting some activities to SUN servers, but still had the other two machines. We used a variety of programming languages—mostly L-10 and C or C++. We wrote our own DBMS and programs for many of the NIC servers. The domain naming system was adapted from Paul Mockapetris' Jeeves program.

Newnham: You were working at SRI at the dawn of the Internet. What was it used for in the early days and how did those working to create it think it would evolve?

Feinler: Computers were very expensive when the ARPANET/Internet began. *Sputnik* had gone up and the Cold War was in full swing. At first it was anticipated the ARPANET/Internet would be used for resource sharing. Scientists would be able to access large computers in real time across the network, and not have to travel to a distant site to use its computer. When email was developed—along with text editing, file transfer, and computer printing - everyone started using it for communication, document production, and text manipulation.

Meanwhile, packet-switching as a networking technology was proving to be superior, so funding moved from resource sharing to advanced protocol development. The ARPANET/Internet was unusual in that it had a rather robust user community at the same time protocol development was going on. The users and the developers often clashed in their priorities.

At first the network was strictly funded by the military. Then other government agencies began to use it. Other networks like BITNET and UUCP [Unix-to-Unix Copy] net found ways to exchange email with the ARPANET/Internet, then finally NSFnet was created and countless students were using the network. Meanwhile, personal computers were flourishing, LAN protocols were developed, the web was developing, the world was wanting and/or getting on, and the government was still footing the bill. Thus, the decision to allow commercial traffic and let the Internet pay its own way.

Newnham: I understand security/privacy wasn't such an issue back then, but what were issues? What were the things people worried about early on when it came to the Internet?

Feinler: Speed and congestion were major concerns. Protocol changes, especially the switch to TCP/IP—a major technological event—meant sites had to change a great deal of software. Some didn't make it and left the net. Users were often caught in the middle and couldn't get their day-to-day work done. At the beginning, developers were the main users, and they wanted transparency so they could build and test things out across the whole net and work freely back and forth. Then, many students crept onto the net one way or another, some legitimate, others because it was the best game in town, so security was kind of added on rather than built in. "Hackers" in those days were apt to hack into a system, find a flaw, and tell the developer as a favor so the developer could fix the problem. Few were trouble makers, they just wanted on.

When personal computers began being used for office work and before LAN protocols, users still had to send and receive email on host computers, so these were hopelessly bogged down. Flaming was a problem, but flamers were often jumped on by others and told to "knock it off." If the flamer was part of an online working group and didn't stop flaming after a warning, they could be removed from the group. Many email systems used different conventions and user terminology, so getting email from one network to another was a challenge.

Newnham: How did your work evolve as the tech evolved?

Feinler: Mostly we went from paper and hardcopy documentation to doing most everything online. Also, the transition away from NLS and the transition to TCP/IP were a challenge. We built our own software based on the premise that NIC users were episodic users—i.e., they did not have the time or inclination to spend learning how to use what we offered, so it had better be obvious to start with. Needless to say keeping up with the email and ever expanding user community was never ending and exhausting.

Newnham: I have heard from others that the real activity online happened at night. What was it like in those days?

Feinler: It was great fun. The computers were so wedged during the day that night was the only time any real work could get done. Night users were usually students working on their theses or programmers trying to run programs along with whatever kid hackers that could worm their way on. We "chatted" back and forth by typing, and took breaks to talk and exchange network gossip and ideas.

I once traveled to MIT where I had a Chinese banquet with about fifteen people who were network friends, but whom I had never met in person. It was mind boggling! I sometimes did a rollover where I worked all night then stayed to work the next day to cover phones and daytime happenings. The hours of four to five a.m. were the worst. I drank a lot of Cokes and Mountain Dew.

So it was exhilarating and frustrating at the same time. Everyone wanted the network to succeed, so there was great esprit de corps, but things often broke, or were painfully slow, or mismatched so that meeting a deadline was a gamble. We all worked very hard though and took pride in what was evolving.

Newnham: What turned out to be the most surprising discovery during this time?

Feinler: I thought the sociology of the network was even more interesting than the technology. The Internet completely changed the way people communicate and perform knowledge work, and the web has put the world's knowledge at everyone's fingertips. Who would have imagined terabytes of capacity on an iPhone? Or for that matter, who would have imagined iPhones themselves? On the other hand, I am still waiting for an electronic storage system that can outlast paper.

Newnham: Can you tell me about the TCP/IP vendors guide and its importance?

Feinler: Commercial companies were not allowed on the ARPANET/DDN [at that time, a privately owned government network] unless they were directly involved contractors. As the network grew from a research network [is packet switching a good idea?] to an operational network [users using it to do their daily work] the government wanted to be able to buy commercial off-the-shelf [COTS] products, that were compatible with TCP/IP protocols. And vendors wanted to sell the government such products. However, vendors weren't allowed to advertise on the DDN or other government networks, because it would have given them an unfair advantage over vendors that did not have access to these networks.

The NIC tried to bridge this gap with the vendors guide, a NIC publication that listed companies with TCP/IP compatible products. However, we were not allowed to recommend any one product over another because of the unfair advantage rulings, so it was just a list. I mentioned to Dan Lynch that someone needed to bring buyers and sellers together, which eventually led to the Interop trade shows where vendors had to demo their products over TCP/IP, and buyers could evaluate them.

Newnham: Besides the technical challenges you have mentioned, what were some of the other challenges that you faced and how did you overcome them?

Feinler: A problem with contracting was the constant turnover at DCA. Another was introducing new DCA, and other new government entities, to the Internet culture and way of doing things. The methodology was not top down or military spit-and-polish, albeit very effective. DARPA and DCA did not always see eye to eye because the objective of one was research, while the objective of the other was operating functioning networks. My personal challenge was email. It was never-ending and more than anyone could keep up with. I had nightmares about missing something really important, as I quickly eyeballed what I could hopefully ignore.

Newnham: You left SRI in 1989 and contracted for NASA. Can you tell me about why you left and the projects that you worked on for NASA?

Feinler: I was burned out. I had just renegotiated the contract, so the group was funded. I wanted to do something else, or actually do nothing at all for a while. I had been invited to be a visiting scholar in Brazil and I was going to do that and travel around South America for a while. Unfortunately, the day I was in Washington introducing our clients to my successor, Dr. Frank Kuo, my stepfather had a heart attack and died. My mother was partially blind and could not live alone in Florida, so instead I spent the next year or so, primarily focused on family and personal matters.

I then attended an IETF meeting at NASA Ames and ran into Bill Jones, a former technical liaison. He asked me what I was doing, and I said nothing, so he invited me to come to work for the NASA Science Internet [NSI], which I did. I did a variety of things there. I served as a requirements manager for NASA scientists based at the large ground-based telescopes, such as Aricebo and Ceretola. I helped transfer the NASA NIC from DECnet at Goddard to the Internet at NASA Ames. I helped establish ground rules for managing a website at NASA. I wrote proposals and so on.

Newnham: Looking back, what part of your career are you most proud of and why?

Feinler: I am proud to have had a small role in the development of the Internet, a technical phenomenon that has changed the way the world learns and communicates. I also think the conversion of the whole network to the TCP/IP protocol suite remains impressive. This was a monumental technical undertaking in which we participated.

I am glad to have had the opportunity to foster careers for several people in my group, who started from the ground up. I always expected people to do their best, and they almost always did. Several went on to do very well. I was proud that I gave them their start on the NIC project.

Newnham: What do you think about the way the Internet went? Did you see the tipping point coming?

Feinler: Well I knew that the government was not going to continue paying for all of it, and that the web was another "killer app" that changed everything. It was too useful to do away with, so commercialization was an obvious solution. I did not anticipate that naming and addressing would become a multimillion dollar business though.

I hope the Internet will maintain net neutrality. My fears are that porn, cyber espionage and crime will bring it down. We need a body of international law worthy of the task of controlling these. I worry about the gap between those who have access versus those who do not. And I also worry about people's ability to separate facts from opinions, and recognize that the two are not the same thing.

Newnham: What advice do you have for women entering the tech field and hoping to play a part in its future?

Feinler: Speak up and ask for what you want. Keep your focus on the job at hand and the best way to get it done. Forget the male/female debate unless you are being treated really unfairly. And if you are, hone your skills and move on to a place that respects you and your contribution.

Newnham: You've been heavily involved with the Computer History Museum. How do you hope its collection will inspire future generations?

Feinler: It is great fun to take people there, especially kids or old timers, and see them light up when they recognize familiar artifacts or eras. I donated more than three hundred and fifty boxes of archives about the early Internet and Engelbart's work to the museum. So I hope future students will be inspired to learn about all we built way back when—and continue innovating.

Newnham: What do you wish your legacy to be?

Feinler: I never thought of myself as important enough to leave a legacy. I hope people consider me a person of integrity. I am proud of the work we did and the career paths that I was able to create for young people, particularly women.

Yasmine Mustafa

Cofounder and CEO, ROAR for Good

Yasmine Mustafa *is the cofounder and CEO of ROAR for Good, a wearables company, currently creating Athena safety device. In discreet situations, it messages friends and family with your GPS location. Or, in emergencies, it also initiates an alarm. The company's mission is to reduce attacks against women and address the underlying causes of such crimes.*

Prior to ROAR for Good, Yasmine founded 123LinkIt in 2009, an affiliate marketing company that she later sold to marketing company NetLine Corporation. Yasmine also sits on the board of Coded by Kids, which helps inner-city kids learn how to code. She founded the Philadelphia chapter of Girl Develop It, an organization that offers low-cost web development classes predominantly to women.

A refugee of the Persian Gulf War, eight year-old Yasmine Mustafa and her family were rescued from a Kuwaiti bomb shelter in 1990 when the American embassy burst in, searching for her little brother, who had been born in the United States and therefore an American citizen. Twenty-two years later, she was awarded US citizenship. Yasmine has a degree in entrepreneurship from Temple University in Philadelphia.

Danielle Newnham: Can you tell me about your background?

© Danielle Newnham 2016

D. Newnham, *Female Innovators at Work*, DOI 10.1007/978-1-4842-2364-2_14

Yasmine Mustafa: My parents are Palestinian, but they didn't want to raise a family in such a dangerous location, so we moved to Kuwait. My four siblings and I were born in Kuwait, and my little brother was born in the US. He is the reason the American Embassy came looking for and rescued us amidst the ravages of the Persian Gulf war.

To be honest, I don't remember much about Kuwait. I remember the war the most, obviously, because that was a huge event in my life and that was when everything changed for me and my family.

What I can also remember from that time is being around family. My family was always close by. I remember that because coming here, that was the one thing I missed most—not having uncles, or aunts, or grandparents, or cousins. It was something that I took for granted in Kuwait—that they would just always be there.

But I mainly remember the war—the tanks, the bombs, the planes, the panic that followed, running down into the shelter every time the siren blasted, and being whisked away and brought here.

Newnham: And what was life like for you once you came to the United States?

Mustafa: I came over when I was eight and it was a culture shock—everything was very different. When I got on the plane to come here, I was more excited than afraid because I had never been on an airplane before. I don't think it really hit me that we were never going back.

The first thing I noticed when I came to Philadelphia was how incredibly busy it was—how the buildings were so close together and the skyscrapers, which we didn't have in Kuwait. I had never seen an Asian person or a black person—everyone in Kuwait looked like me. And even people walking dogs around as pets—I don't ever remember seeing a dog in Kuwait. So I was like "Whoa, this is so different." I wondered how two places in the world could be so different.

When we came here, we didn't speak any English so we didn't really communicate with anyone outside of the family, and it wasn't until we were put into English-as-a-second-language classes that we started learning the language. When I originally came here, I was put in fourth grade in the first school because that was my age group but because I didn't speak any English, they just gave me coloring books and crayons and put me in the corner. So every day, that's all I did. I just colored.

I also remember my parents being very stressed about what we were going to do because when we came to the US, we couldn't get our money out of the bank. My father was an engineer and unsuccessfully tried to find a job. He didn't realize that educational degrees don't always transfer over. So that is something he struggled with because his identity was that of a successful engineer. Coming over here and learning that he would have to start at the bottom again was really tough for him.

Newnham: When you arrived, was the intention to go back to Kuwait at some point?

Mustafa: I am not sure. As a little kid not knowing, I thought we would go back one day. I thought once things got better and Saddam left, we would go back to our home and our family, and then when we didn't, I never questioned it.

Newnham: How did your father find work in the end?

Mustafa: My dad ended up buying a 7-Eleven store outside of Philadelphia because he couldn't get a job as an engineer. And the store was across the road from the middle school and high school that I attended, so I became known as the "7-Eleven girl." I used to take candy from the store and then sell it for twice the price at school.

And when I was like fifteen or sixteen, I was a hostess at a diner. I ended up redesigning their menu and then I started asking other diners nearby if I could redesign their menus.

Newnham: When did you get into tech?

Mustafa: Not until I was around twenty-four. I had gone through four major changes in college because I couldn't decide what I wanted to do. I went from mechanical engineering to graphic design to psychology, and then, finally, entrepreneurship. And as part of the entrepreneurship program, you have to do two internships. I was doing one that I didn't really like and my friend was doing one that he loved, so I asked if he could get me an interview which he did, and I got it. The school wouldn't let me swap my internship so I decided to do it anyway, on top of the two jobs I had at the time. It was at an early-stage tech consultancy firm.

It was a very small company run by a man named Skip Shuda. His passion was helping entrepreneurs, and he helped them with everything from writing their business plan to putting together the pitch deck, to fundraising, and market strategies. Everything you can think of entailed in starting a company. I remember being enamored by these entrepreneurs that would sit across the table from me and share their dreams and aspirations, and what they wanted to do to make the world a better place. I just wanted to be one of them.

At the very beginning, I didn't understand a lot of what was going on, so I used to write notes in my notepad. Then Skip and I would meet afterward and I would have him explain it all to me. From there I worked my way up. When I graduated from college, he offered me a job, and two years later, we became partners in the business.

I mainly focused on marketing while I was there—ideas, strategy, and implementation. And while doing that, I got the idea for my first company— 123LinkIt. As we were running a tech company, we wanted to establish ourselves as thought leaders, so we started a blog. I would write about things I was learning or things I had experienced while meeting with clients. Then I took it over completely and it ended up becoming one of the top 100,000 blogs according to Technorati, which was a blog directory at the time.

So things started taking off with the blog and we started getting a lot of traffic. One day, someone suggested that I could make money while blogging, which I didn't know about, and the idea of making money from something I was already doing was really appealing to me. It was especially appealing, because at the time, back in 2007, I was barely scraping by. I was making very little money. So he showed me what to do and I put some ads up and some affiliate links. A couple of months later, I wrote a blog post called "The Top 20 Entrepreneurial Quotes." It was the most trivial blog post I had written—all the other blog posts had taken me two or three hours, but this one took me twenty minutes and I wrote it on a whim. But, of course, it was the number-one most trafficked post I have ever had. I don't remember how many views it had, but it was on the front pages of Digg and StumbleUpon. It was everywhere.

It really took off. A couple of months later, I got two checks in the mail and they were from ads that we had put up and forgotten about. So this gave me the idea for 123LinkIt. At the time, it was a very convoluted process to add ads to your blog, especially affiliate ads, because you had to go and find an affiliate network. You had to apply to be accepted. You had to go look for advertisers, and then apply for them, and also wait for them to accept you. Then once they did accept you, you had to find the links to the products, and then go to your blog and add the links to the source code. It was an eight-step process and extremely time-consuming. I couldn't find anything that did it better.

So as I started making more and more money from blogging, I realized there was something there. I said, "This is what I am going to do. I am going to start my own company, helping people make money through their blogs."

Newnham: And how did 123LinkIt make the whole process easier?

Mustafa: We were a WordPress plugin that you would install onto your blog. If you wrote about any products, our software would automatically find the product keyword and link it to the product's store page so people could then buy directly. Then if someone bought something, we would get a commission and we would split that with the blogger.

Newnham: What were your expectations when you started the business? Did you have any idea how you wanted to grow it?

Mustafa: Initially, I wanted it to help people supplement their income and then as blogs really took off, I wanted to help people earn enough so that they could transition from part-time blogging to a full-time job. That was on the consumer side. On the business side, I wanted to grow it to be the number one affiliate software plugin, so that when publishers thought about making money, they would choose 123LinkIt. And eventually I saw us getting acquired by a major ad network.

But one of my biggest struggles and an important lesson I learned is that if you are going to start a company as a solo founder, in an area that you are not familiar with, you are going to run into a lot of trouble. Even if you hire the right people, in technology it is not that easy because the biggest obstacle I had was being a non-technical person running a software company and conversing with developers about what I wanted them to build.

I had so much trouble talking to my developers about what I wanted and what's coming next because I didn't appreciate or realize that there are multiple ways to develop something. So they would come back to me and say something like, "Well, we can do it this way but it will impact this." I wasn't informed enough to know which way to go so I would ask them what they thought was best— which meant I was putting a big part of the business into the hands of these developers who didn't know much about the business, and we ran into a lot of trouble because of that.

It made me realize that I need to at least understand how the development process works. So the first thing I did was start a Ruby 101 group for beginners here in Philly. Anyone who wanted to learn would come together. We would meet on weekends. It went really well for the first couple of weeks, but then everybody started coming to it, even people who knew how to code. I tried listening to them, but it was like they were speaking a different language, I just did not understand what they were saying. And I tried to teach myself but it didn't really work out.

That's when I learned about Girl Develop It [GDI] in New York. I discovered them through Twitter and I signed up for one of their classes. I would take the two-hour Bolt Bus to New York for a two-hour class before I got the two-hour Bolt Bus back.

But it was all worth it because when I finished the course, I knew how to build a website. I thought, "Wow, this is amazing. I feel so empowered. I get it." And so I approached the GDI founder, who was teaching the class, and asked if she had thought about expanding. Six months later, we brought GDI to Philly.

The motivation was that I wanted to learn how to code and couldn't find the resources. Also, when I was trying to learn how to code, I learned why so few women get into coding, and why so many opt out because they don't see other women coders. I also learned about how in middle school, girls get turned away from technology and science and math, and seeing this as a problem, I saw how Girl Develop It could really make a difference.

Newnham: So you were working on both for a time. Then you sold 123Linkit. What is the story behind the sale? And what led to ROAR for Good?

Mustafa: Yes, so I was running 123Linkit and Girl Develop It at the same time and then two years into 123Linkit, at the end of 2011, one of my advisors wanted us to white-label what we were doing for his business which was part of NetLine, a B2B lead generation company in Silicon Valley. And it was taking a while for our team to do it so then jokingly we said, "Why don't you buy us?" The next day, he called me to talk about an acquisition.

Part of the acquisition required me to work with NetLine, so I ended up working there for a year and a half. But in April 2012, I became a US citizen and from that moment, I started thinking about traveling. I thought, "I have been working since I was nine years old. I need to take a break and not work so hard for once in my life." It was the first time I wasn't bound by my circumstances. I wasn't shackled by being an illegal immigrant or working two jobs to get through school.

There was a period of my life between being eighteen years old to when I was twenty-five, which was really, really tough. My dad left when I was eighteen. He booked a one-way ticket to Jordan and left, and he took everything with him—including all the family savings. He left us with nothing. It was also then that we learned we were illegal immigrants because we didn't have the proper paperwork to get jobs. In actuality, even though we had been brought here as refugees, we didn't have any rights. Something had slipped through the immigration system, which meant we were not Americans and really not welcome. So that period was really tough because all of us had to work under the table. I made five dollars an hour for eight years of my life. I worked two jobs, sometimes three jobs, just to get by.

But then I became a legal resident and that is when I started planning the trip that I took almost five years later. I was almost thirty and decided I wanted to travel the world and have time to myself. At first, I planned to go away for a month, then it was two months, then it was three months, and then I thought, "What the heck, let's make it six months" to make up for all the times I could not do this. Because when I didn't have paperwork, I was really worried about flying and traveling—in case they didn't let me back in.

And so, at the beginning of the trip, everyone was really excited for me. They were like, "Yeah, Yasmine, you deserve it. You should do it." But when I booked it, they said, "Are you frigging crazy? What were you thinking? You can't travel alone as a woman!" But I did it.

I left to go to Ecuador, where I did full Spanish immersion for the first month. I went to Spanish school four to six hours a day and I stayed with a Spanish family who spoke no English at all. The first month it was a deep-dive, so hard, but really great. And then from there, I started travelling and went to different places in Ecuador, Colombia, Argentina, Chile, Bolivia, and Peru. It was life-changing. Everything I had wanted and more. And as simple as it sounds, it was then that I realized, deep down, we are all the same. It doesn't matter your race, religion, or gender—we are all the same.

And one of the recurring themes I experienced during this trip was that everywhere I went—and I know it was because I was a solo female traveler—I would hear these horror stories. Someone would tell me a story of a friend they had or a fellow hostel guest that had been sexually assaulted or harassed. It just became this conversation that would recur again and again everywhere I went. So I became far more aware of how big an issue it was and how prevalent the issue of violence is against women.

Then a week after I got back from the trip, I picked up a newspaper and learned that my neighbor had been raped. She had gone out to feed her parking meter when she was grabbed from behind, dragged into an alley, severely beaten and brutally raped.

So thinking back to my trip, it was just like a lightbulb. There had to be something we could do about this. So I started thinking about what women do now to protect themselves and how they use pepper spray, tasers, and knives, but the problem with those tools is that you have to take them out of your pocket or your purse in order for them to work. So I started to think about how we could take those tools and make them wearable. Why not embed something into a bracelet or a necklace so that if you ever need them, they would be right there?

But actually, it turned out to be a terrible idea because we did some surveys and spoke with a lot of women and we learned that women actually don't like pepper spray or tasers because they feel like they might use them against themselves accidentally during an attack, so they would harm themselves instead of the attacker. But also, they were worried that they might be overpowered and their own self-defense tool used as a weapon against them.

And then digging into it more, we realized that self-defense tools are made by men for women, not taking into account the specific needs of women. So that's when we said we need to go back to the drawing board and make something that cannot be used against the person wearing it, but could assist them in getting help in some way. And so that's how Athena came about. We realized that if we made something that looked nice, women would be more likely to wear it. If we made something that could deter an attack and if it can notify family and friends when you press it, it could be a better alternative to self-defense tools.

We got together and found some police officers and self-defense instructors to help us figure out the main components of what should be in the device. Then we prototyped it and held self-defense classes and focus groups and iterated from there. And Athena is what came out of sixteen months of research and testing. Essentially, it is a pendant that you clip on to your waist, purse, or as a necklace and when you're in trouble, it has two modes. One is SilentROAR, which is when you feel anxious and nervous, and you think someone may be following you and you want someone you know to watch over you. So you tap the button three times and it sends your contacts a text message with your location so that they can watch over you. Then if you feel safe again, you can notify them that you are fine. So it's sort of like a virtual bodyguard.

The second mode is for emergencies and you need help right away. You hold the button for three seconds, which activates an audible alert messages your friends and family with your location. Right now, we are engineering Athena to call an emergency number as well, whether that be campus police, or 911, or whoever you want it to call.

Newnham: Why ROAR? What is the significance behind the name?

Mustafa: Well, a big thing for us is not to be fearmongering, so we focused on empowerment. We wanted to create a female empowerment company. And so when we were trying to come up with a name, a Katy Perry song came on, called Roar, which is all about female empowerment. And when we started brainstorming, we also thought about the Helen Reddy song, I Am Woman—"hear me roar." So it just came together and we said, "We have got to call it ROAR."

The device even has an alarm mode that you could say roars, so it just made so much sense. We added the "for Good" because of our social mission impact message, so we became ROAR for Good.

Newnham: What's the technology used in Athena?

Mustafa: It uses Bluetooth low-energy. We have two buzzers in there and six LEDs. It syncs up to your phone and once you have added your designated contacts, it will send text messages to them using Twilio. All everyday technology, but used innovatively to help protect women.

Newnham: Can you tell me more about why you decided to crowdfund Athena and the lessons that you learned from doing so?

Mustafa: We had a lot of focus groups and self-defense classes where we learned a lot. And we had a lot of women say "This is great. I can't wait to buy one." But there is a world of difference between someone saying they would buy one and them actually purchasing it, so we wanted to do the crowdfunding campaign to really test out the demand and get validation.

We launched it in October 2015 and our goal externally was $40,000, which, if we achieved, we knew we were onto something. Internally, we had a goal of $100,000, which would mean over a thousand devices sold. But we hit our goal of $40,000 within two days. The $100,000 goal within ten days. And then we finished the campaign with almost $270,000 in preorders. So by the middle of the campaign, we knew that, yes, people do want this. There is demand for this and we knew then that this was a company that we were going to continue building.

Newnham: That must have been a great feeling. What were the first steps you took once you reached the final sum?

Mustafa: We had a manufacturer but the one we had picked couldn't handle the volume, so we had to find a new one. And then we had to go through the design-to-manufacture process, which was taking our prototype and making it something that could be manufactured. This meant tweaking the design so that it is easier to build and less expensive.

We ended up finding Flex—they used to be called Flextronics—and they make ninety percent of today's wearables. We didn't think they would work with us because they are a really big company. They had revenue last year of $26 billion, but they work with select startups. They loved our story and believed in our potential. We went over our financials with them and they said OK.

Newnham: How have you found the process? And what lessons have you learned along the way?

Mustafa: The top lessons are to focus on the brand and the storytelling aspect of it, because we would not have been as successful if we did not have a good story to share with people, not just Athena the product but the whole idea of wanting to run a company that will one day go out of business. Our whole goal is that we make a better version of self-defense tools with Athena but then we invest the proceeds we make from it into empathy education to right the balance and prevent the assault so that one day, there will be no need for pepper spray or tasers or even Athena.

I think we would have preferred to be further along with our prototype or at least aware of how long we needed for DFM- design for manufacturing before the campaign ended, because by the time we got validation from the campaign's success, we were behind on delivery. So that was also a tough lesson to learn.

Another lesson was in international orders, because we accepted them without doing much research on them. They have been a really big challenge because we didn't know anything about duty, or customs, or VAT [value added tax]. There are just so many nuances that we didn't anticipate. For example we recently learned that shipping products with magnets is not allowed in some countries. So there are all these nuances for international shipping that we didn't anticipate and that I wish we had looked into.

Newnham: Would you recommend that other startups use crowdfunding as a way to validate their idea?

Mustafa: Yes, depending on what your product is. If you are looking to build a lifestyle business, I think crowdfunding could be great for the initial pop of interest. It is really great for marketing. And if you are looking to build a sustainable company, you want to be a for-profit. And it's going to be a full-time job. Spend a lot more time getting everything right beforehand and thinking through what is going to happen after the campaign so that you plan for the best- and worst-case scenarios.

Newnham: How much of your founding team was in place when you started the campaign?

Mustafa: When I came back from South America, and that rape happened, I called my cofounder, Anthony Gold, and told him what happened. He said, "How do I help you with this? I want to be a part of this." So we joined forces and we hired some engineers and an industrial designer. When we launched the campaign, we were four full-time people.

Newnham: And how was the company funded pre-campaign?

Mustafa: Last year we were accepted into Dreamit Ventures, which gave us money, interns, design help, legal help, accounting help—so that's how we lined up the team. And then we raised a small friends-and-family round of $200,000, which included $100,000 from one local investor who really loved what we were doing, and $50,000 from Ben Franklin Technology Partners which is focused on starting and keeping companies in Pennsylvania.

Newnham: What have some of the highlights/low points been so far?

Mustafa: Every time I have a prototype in my hands, I cannot believe that we are building something that started with an idea. It's pretty astonishing. But other than that, it is very complicated. There are many, many stages of building hardware where for each step forward you take, you can take four steps back. Because you can make one change that you don't think will impact anything else, but then you prototype it and you have to test it, and then you find out it has impacted something totally unrelated. And then you have to figure out what happened, and then prototype it again. It's an incredibly time-consuming process. Especially as we are building a potentially life-saving device, so we don't want to take any shortcuts. We are solely committed to quality over cost. We are spending the time, money, and resources to ensure that we are building something that will absolutely work.

Newnham: Is Athena a solo product or are you planning a suite?

Mustafa: Yes, we are planning a suite. One of things that surprised us about the crowdfunding campaign is how many people who came forward and said, "Hey, I would love something like this for my kids," or "…for my parents." And those products require different feature sets. For example, young kids don't normally have cell phones, so we have ideas of working on a 3G chipset so that kids can use it without a phone.

We have even heard from adults who said they want a version where they don't have to use a phone with it. And then for senior citizens, we have heard from them saying they love our product as an alternative to all the existing "I've fallen and can't get up" kind of tools. And "I would want it waterproof so I can wear it in the shower." We have even heard from people who want it for medical conditions such as diabetes or dementia, so definitely, we want to come out with different products for different people.

Newnham: What would you say are some of the highs and lows of being a founder?

Mustafa: The highs are creating something. I don't know any other feeling of knowing you have contributed to building something. That sense of satisfaction and purpose you get knowing that what you are doing is making a difference and helping people. When I think of the highs, that's it. And the lows for me are because it is a rollercoaster. In the same day that we announce something huge, something will go very, very wrong.

So it is very up and down and it is also very hard to separate work life with personal life but that is partially the entrepreneur too. To me, it's all consuming. It's hard not to think of my work and what I do every day. The only time I don't think about it is when I am doing yoga.

Newnham: Have you ever felt like giving up?

Mustafa: Yes, sure. With 123LinkIt, I wanted to close it a couple of times. That's when having an advisory board and mentors is a huge help because just like any highs and lows, they last for brief periods of time and quitting is a consequence of a low, but it can be a fleeting feeling and it doesn't mean it will persist. My mentors and advisors are great at helping me figure what the deep cause is, what's really going on, and how we overcome it so that the feeling of helplessness passes and I am re-motivated and re-energized.

Newnham: Speaking of mentorship, how important do you think mentors are to young women looking to get into tech?

Mustafa: Studies have shown it is really important. When women don't see other women in leadership positions, they don't see themselves in those leadership positions. So having women in science and technology is really important for helping women not self-select out of those fields. And that's why, for example, with Girl Develop It, the fact that it is women-run and women-focused, means that as these students are coming to our classes, they see that they are not alone. Even though the media tells them that it's mostly white men coding in a basement, and that in films the women don't like science, it's completely untrue. And so that is why it was really important to us with Girl Develop It—to surround the organization with women role models, women teachers, women volunteers. It's why representation matters.

Newnham: And how important is it to get kids coding?

Mustafa: It's interesting today because babies learn how to swipe on iPads before they learn how to talk. And kids are huge consumers of technology but they don't know how it works. That is troubling because as technology becomes more advanced, we are going to have more jobs in those fields. And if there isn't an increase of people getting into those fields, we are going to have more demand than there is supply—which is already happening. So I think it is important and for schools to have it as a requirement, especially. It should be a necessity rather than an elective.

Newnham: What are you excited about when it comes to the future of wearables?

Mustafa: I am excited about the fact that as technology advances, things get smaller and smarter. When we were first starting out building Athena, we wanted to add a microphone and a camera and we couldn't. We had to sacrifice those features because they would have made the device too big. We had to make compromises over the design because when we did testing and focus groups, we found that women didn't want to carry something that was too heavy or too bulky. And if we had made Athena with all the features that we wanted, then it would have looked like Flavor Flav with his clock.

So I am just really excited about how quickly technology is advancing and how seamlessly wearables are being integrated, such as the Google and Levis connected jacket. So I am excited about incorporating wearables into clothing and having them seamlessly be part of your everyday life.

Newnham: What are you most proud of?

Mustafa: You know when you do stuff and to you, it's just that you are doing what you have to do, what you enjoy doing. But then other people are inspired by it. When people reach out and say they found my TED talk inspiring or "I found your perseverance inspiring," I am not very good at taking compliments but that makes me proud. And when I get emails saying something I did encouraged someone to do something, I actually save them in a folder. When I am feeling down, I go and read them because now those words motivate me.

Newnham: Finally, if you could go back in time, what would you say to a younger Yasmine?

Mustafa: You know in TV shows and movies, it always seems like it is going to end perfectly. Well, I remember being young and thinking, "Why aren't things ending perfectly?" So I would tell her that life is not like that. No matter how much you plan things, life has its own plans and the key is to know that and adapt. You can still have plans, but really, life, work, relationships—it's all about adapting.

Judy Estrin

Founder, JLabs LLC

Judy Estrin *is a networking technology pioneer, prolific entrepreneur, and author. She has cofounded eight technology companies, including Bridge Communications, a network router, bridges, and communications servers company; Precept Software, Inc., which developed video streaming software; Packet Design LLC, an incubator that spun out networking technology companies; and JLabs LLC, which stands for Judy's Labs.*

Judy became chief technology officer at Cisco Systems following its acquisition of Precept Software, Inc., in 1998.

Prior to founding her own businesses, Judy worked at Zilog, where she contributed to the design of the Z8 and Z8000 microprocessors. She went on to lead the team that developed one of the first commercial LAN (local area network) systems.

Judy is currently on the board of directors of KQED and The Medium Corporation. She has also served on the board of directors for The Walt Disney Company (1998–2014), FedEx Corporation (1989–2010), Sun Microsystems (1995–2003), and Rockwell Corporation (1994–1998).

Judy is the author of Closing the Innovation Gap: Reigniting the Spark of Creativity in a Global Economy (McGraw-Hill Education, 2008), which explores key concepts of innovation and how leaders can foster innovation to ensure future economic growth.

© Danielle Newnham 2016
D. Newnham, *Female Innovators at Work*, DOI 10.1007/978-1-4842-2364-2_15

Judy holds a Bachelor of Science degree in mathematics and computer science from UCLA and a Master of Science degree in electrical engineering from Stanford University. While at Stanford, Judy worked with Vint Cerf's team that developed the TCP/IP protocols, which form the underlying technology of the Internet.

Danielle Newnham: What is your background? And what were your influences growing up?

Judy Estrin: I grew up in a strong scientific, technological, engineering environment. Both my folks were PhDs in electrical engineering. My mother got her PhD in electrical engineering in a year that I think there was maybe one other woman in the country that got a PhD, so it was an academic environment and very intellectually supportive.

I had two strong role models in that my mother, as I said, was a PhD and engineer, as was my father who was also very supportive of my mother. I am the middle of three girls. My older sister is an MD [doctor] and my younger sister is a professor of electrical engineering and computer science. I was fortunate to grow up in an environment that fostered my interest in engineering and technology. We were encouraged to believe that we could do anything we wanted to, therefore I didn't have these obstacles in my mind that made me think I couldn't or shouldn't pursue things. I grew up believing I could, essentially, enter a man's world, which at that time it was very much so.

On the other hand, because it was a very, very academic environment, the fact that I ended up becoming an entrepreneur and expanding into the business side was a surprise actually, even to me. Some people have stories about how they were entrepreneurs from the beginning and that they had a lemonade stand or something similar, but I didn't. As a kid, I really didn't focus on business or even my future career. I focused on learning, my studies, and schoolwork. In high school, my passion was folk dancing. I performed and taught folk dancing. I had no idea that I might want to be an entrepreneur. I did love computer science, which I was exposed to very early.

As I was growing up, I had a very hard time writing, so another one of the surprises in my career is that I ended up writing a book. I was always more focused on the math and computer science side. I never thought that I would come to enjoy writing. As I said, I came from a very intellectually supportive environment and one that created a lot of drive. The messages we received growing up were to always keep learning, always do the best you can and learn from your mistakes. If you get an A-, focus on why it wasn't an A? So always try to do better.

Newnham: When did you first sit in front of a computer?

Estrin: I am of a generation where most people didn't have a computer growing up because there were no personal computers, but I was fortunate enough to be exposed to computing in middle school and high school because my father was involved in the field from its inception. He worked with John von Neumann at The Institute for Advanced Study at Princeton and then started the computer science department at UCLA. He was one of the very early computer scientists before computer science was even a recognized discipline.

So we were exposed to computers early. I can remember when I was in high school my father bringing home some tapes with video of FORTRAN courses on them. FORTRAN was an early computer programming language. And, of the three girls, I was the only one interested in watching them.

Newnham: You then went on to study at Stanford. Can you tell me more about your work there?

Estrin: I did my masters at Stanford and my adviser, Vint Cerf, was one of the "fathers" of the Internet. At that time, they had just finished the specification of TCP [Transmission Control Protocol], which became the underlying protocols of the Internet. The specs had been written and they were at the point of developing and testing the prototypes when I got there. My specific role with Vint's small research team was to help with the initial TCP testing.

At times I had to get up at three a.m. to test, because some of the main people we were working with were researchers at the University College London. We were trying to match the time zones so some of the time we did it early in the morning. We would test sending packets and then talk via a Teletype machine as to whether that packet had got there or not. This would have been 1975.

The TCP protocols allowed different types of computers to reliably exchange information across multiple networks. We each would run an implementation of the code, have our test computers exchange information and then we would need to validate whether or not it got there. In today's world, when you send information from your phone what's happening is all of the data is going into these packets or envelopes of information that go zipping around the Internet. Well, the Internet didn't exist then, we were creating the initial infrastructure of what was the Internet, and it started with a small number of computers exchanging information in these new ways.

Newnham: And how did it feel to be present at the dawn of the Internet?

Estrin: It was a wonderful experience working with an incredible group of people. We realized that what we were doing was interesting and exciting but I think that few actually knew that it was going to be this life-changing. It is hard to know—you might hope—but it is hard to know what the eventual impact of technological breakthroughs will be because success is about more than the technology itself. And at that point, the Internet work was focused on connecting computers in an academic and a government setting to share information. So I think that the hope was that it would be important but it has ended up being just so much more significant than I ever anticipated.

When I was at Stanford, I was involved in the Internet work. But at that same time another important technology was being developed, Ethernet, which is the technology that connects computers in a local arena. When people talk about Wi-Fi, when you connect your computers together in your home—that is an evolution of Ethernet, as opposed to the Internet. I can remember well a Stanford seminar that I attended where Bob Metcalfe presented his early Ethernet work at Xerox. My career in the network industry involved commercialization of not only Internet products but of local area networks and Ethernet, which also ended up becoming ubiquitous and critical to how we live our lives.

If you think about the invention of electricity, at one point it was just, "Oh, I can transmit these electrical signals." And now it is something we take for granted. So, it is amazing to look back at the early networking years and see how quickly things have evolved and much our lives depend on this technology.

Newnham: After Stanford, you start at your first startup. Can you tell me more about it?

Estrin: Yes, Zilog was a semiconductor company. They built microprocessors, which are the chips that are at the heart of all of our computers. Zilog had spun out of Intel and was competing with Intel in that space. They had started a new group to build computer systems which I was part of. When I first went there, I was working on the design of the central processing unit of the microprocessor. I then led a team that developed one of the first commercial local area networks.

When I graduated with my master's degree I interviewed at HP, Intel, and Xerox, and then talked to this little company called Zilog, which one of my professors was involved with. I went to Zilog—not because I had any thoughts about being an entrepreneur, but a friend of my father's told me some of the smartest people he knew were at Zilog. So I decided to go where the smart people were.

Today, many people say, "I am going to go to a big company, or I am going to go to a small company because I want to become an entrepreneur" but this was more about I wanted to work with really smart people. And when I was at Zilog, I got a sense of what it was like to be part of a small, focused, fast-moving team. I moved into management more quickly than I might have at a larger company. That gave me a sense of what a small dynamic team could achieve and started me on my entrepreneurial path.

When I was there, I also met my ex-husband, Bill. After a few years, he wanted to start a company and I decided to start it with him. This illustrates a consistent aspect of how my career developed—I really did not plan it out. In general I am a planner, but when I think about how my career evolved, a lot of it was about being open to take advantage of opportunities. And making decisions based on people and doing interesting stuff that I hoped would be substantial and make a difference.

Now, many young people want to become entrepreneurs but it wasn't that common in those days. I was twenty-six and Bill was thirty-one. He was tired of working for other people, some of whom he did not respect. He wanted to go start something and be the boss. He was more business focused and I was more technology focused at that time. We both believed that the new networking industry would be important and co-founded Bridge Communications.

Newnham: Can you tell me more about Bridge and what work you did, as well as if there were any lessons you took from Zilog to your first startup?

Estrin: Yes, so Bridge was one of the very early companies focused on the networking space and we sold products that interconnected computers and people through local area networks and also, sold products that connected networks together. The name Bridge came from the idea of bridging two networks.

One of the main lessons I had learned at Zilog was that it is not enough to have a great idea or product. The project I was involved with was almost exclusively technology-driven. At the time we didn't have a clear sense of what problems we could solve and did not have resources focused on figuring it out. Early on in my career, I had an appreciation for technology and not much of an appreciation for marketing or sales. There are times when you have to focus more on technology and push through objections because early on often people do not know what technology can provide them. So you don't want to be completely driven by what people think they want now. But you don't want to be completely driven by technology without thinking about how to package that to solve real problems either. You need the balance between the outward-facing and the inward-facing aspects of a technology company. Or you can have the best technology in the world but nobody wants it or the people who might don't know you exist.

When we first started Bridge, Bill had much more business experience than I did and I ran the engineering side. When we started shipping the product, because it was a very new market based on a new technology I ended up spending a lot of my time talking to large customers evangelizing the new local area network technology and explaining what our products could do. This was the beginning of me expanding my scope into the marketing and sales part of the organization. And a couple of years into Bridge, I took over marketing and sales in addition to engineering.

Newnham: How comfortable were you moving away from the engineering side?

Estrin: I wouldn't say I so much moved away but expanded. At first, I was a bit uncomfortable with the idea because I had grown up thinking that technology was all that mattered. But by then I realized how important the marketing and business aspects are— not instead of the technology, but coupled well with the technology.

But, in terms of actually doing the job, I was very comfortable because most of my career had been about communicating and problem solving—I like to communicate and I like people. As you look at how to solve a customer problem, or an organizational problem, or a technical problem, there are some skills that are transferrable between them. So it ended up not being as hard as I thought. It was more a psychological barrier that I had to get over.

Newnham: What were some of the bigger obstacles that you faced in the early days?

Estrin: The company ones are the natural ones—it took us a long time to get funding because this was a completely new technology. Closing early customers was hard, we were really creating a new market as we were introducing the technology. So there were funding obstacles, there were market obstacles, and there were competitive obstacles. And this was the first time that both Bill and I were doing this. We were learning how to build a company, which was both a wonderful and scary experience.

From a personal perspective, there were two key things that I learned over that period of time having to do with decision making that I continued to develop as I moved forward. One of them was that sometimes you have to make decisions without all of the data. As an engineer, I wanted the perfect amount of data before I made a decision. I needed to get comfortable with a more balanced approach of not going to the extreme of just making decisions without facts or data, but knowing when you've done the best you can, and have to make the best decision you can, when it is time to move on. So learning how to do that and not overanalyze. I also needed to learn that not everyone was going to be happy with every decision I made or like me all the time. This doesn't mean you need to be obnoxious. I know some leaders believe in leadership through intimidation, but that's not my style. I did have to learn, however, that I couldn't take everything so personally and sometimes, I had to make a decision that was for the best for the organization and for most people. And there would be some people who might not like it. I could offset this some by treating them with respect, and explain the decision as well as I could. There is often no way to make everybody happy all of the time.

Newnham: You took Bridge public. Was this something you had wanted to do all along?

Estrin: It was pretty clear when we started the company that it was going to require significant funding. When we decided to raise venture capital, it meant that the path would either be that we were successful enough to go public or get acquired, or we would fail. Meaning it was the type of company that needed sufficient funding that it probably wasn't going to be able to be bootstrapped.

And it was hard to fundraise, especially that first round because nobody knew us. It took us six months and lots of rejection. After the first round, when we had successfully shipped product it was a little easier and then for our second company, it was a lot easier because once you're successful, then people are much more willing to fund you.

Newnham: Bridge was then acquired by 3Com whom you then merged with. Why did you leave? And why join Network Computing Devices [NCD]?

Estrin: Combining with 3Com made a lot of strategic sense but it was one of those mergers where people issues ended up complicating things, the details of which could be a book in its own right. So one of my pieces of advice is that with mergers or any type of partnership, be sensitive and realistic about potential people issues and not ignore signs because you want a deal to go through. It was considered "a merger of equals," meaning we were supposed to co-manage the resulting company but we did not agree with the 3Com management team on the direction the combined company should take. The resulting conflict ended up being very difficult for everyone involved and after about nine months, we decided it was the best thing for the company and us to leave.

When we left, we had planned to take some time off, to have a break after a very intensive five years building Bridge and a difficult time during the merger. We were about to leave for a trip to London when someone—a friend of a friend—asked if we would meet with a team with a cool new product. It was five people who had put together a prototype for what became Network Computing Devices' first product. They were having trouble raising money and they needed an experienced executive team. We were very excited about what they were doing and pretty quickly agreed to join them as CEO and executive vice president and our trip became more work than vacation. Then, with the five of them, we went on to raise the company's first round of funding.

NCD was an early player in the network computing market. Our X terminals were graphics devices that communicated with computers over the network. Again, as with Bridge, we were ahead of the market. Entrepreneurs innovate in different ways. Sometimes you come up with a product by looking at what someone else is doing and you do it cheaper or better or sometimes you look at a market that someone's created and you come into it and can scale in a different way or have a different distribution strategy. Our companies, Bridge, NCD and Precept, tended to be companies that were more forward looking focused on creating new markets.

NCD sales took off more quickly than Bridge. We took the company public in 1992 and a year later Bill moved to the role of chairman and I took over as CEO. In 1994, the company was doing well but we made a very hard decision to leave and I recruited somebody to replace me as CEO. The decision was driven by our personal needs, we had been pushing hard for a very long time. My son was four and we felt like we needed to do something different.

At the time, I think I said I would never start another company because we really needed a break. We took a couple of months off, and then it became clear that we wanted to re-engage in some way. At first, we looked for something that we could do part-time, we weren't going to start another company. We were going to advise other companies, and then we came up with the idea for Precept and started it about six months after we left NCD.

At the time, my younger sister was doing research in networking at University of Southern California. Some of her work involved a new technology called multicast. I was reading some of her research and anticipated that it would enable new applications for networking.

Precept was one of the first companies to stream video over the Internet. The term IPTV [Internet Protocol television] was actually the name of our product. We were among the first people to coin that term, which has now become generic. The technology was very successful. It was based on multicast capability that Cisco was pushing—an infrastructure change that allowed us to transmit video in a more efficient way. But when we started to go out and sell the product we found that Cisco was marketing this feature in their datasheets and white papers, but most customers were not deploying the multicast feature for a variety of reasons. Because the infrastructure wasn't there, our growth was a little slower than we had hoped. We were too early in terms of the product. We were in the process of trying to figure out how to adjust when the consumer Internet market started to really take off.

And frankly, the overall tech industry shifted from being heavily technology-driven to strongly market, and even hype driven in 1995. We realized that critical mass would be very helpful. For a small company to get out into the marketplace in an area that Microsoft and others were about to enter—we needed to do something. We already had a sales relationship with Cisco and this led to discussions around whether I would become Cisco's CTO if they bought the company.

Cisco was interested in the technology that Precept had to offer, but also Cisco's CTO at the time wanted to go on leave and they were looking for a replacement for him. So it became a dual thing: if I were willing to become Cisco's CTO, then they would buy the company. It was the right thing for me to do for the shareholders of Precept. To be honest, I wasn't looking to become the chief technology officer at Cisco or give up my role as CEO, but I figured it would be an interesting experience. And, as I mentioned earlier, my most important career moves came from being open to something. It wasn't my plan but it was the right thing for the shareholders. And I thought it would be a fascinating experience—and it was both fascinating and challenging.

I was there from 1998 to 2000. During that time, Cisco grew from eighteen thousand to thirty-six thousand people. I was responsible for legal, mergers and acquisitions, in addition to being the CTO. And one year in, I also took over the responsibility for their centralized software group. So it was very exciting, a completely different experience for me to work in that size company. Cisco was in such a high-growth and dominant position in the industry, whereas I was used to being the entrepreneur, the underdog.

It was challenging to work at a high level in such a different culture from what I was used to. A company's culture is a reflection of the leadership. And I am not judging— it's not good or bad—but a lot of the decisions, and the management style, and the way things were done there were different from the way I would have done them. And sometimes it can be good, because diversity of thinking and approach can be very powerful, and sometimes it made things very hard. Also, large organizations have a certain amount of political jockeying, which is inevitable, and although I initially found it interesting, because I like people and like to figure out how to work with different people, it got frustrating when it impeded my ability to get things done.

I had agreed to stay for at least two years at the end of which I started to examine whether or not I wanted to go back to being an entrepreneur. I exited in a smooth way working with the CEO to put together a transition plan. And that worked well for Cisco and it worked well for me.

Newnham: What was it like being a woman in tech at that time? Did you come across other women in similar senior positions? Or were you like a lone wolf?

Estrin: I was often the only woman in the room, or at the table. There were very few women at the top, and for sure, even fewer with technical backgrounds. A lot of the women were in communications roles, or employee relations, or maybe marketing. But very few had come up the technical path, which both helped and hurt me.

But I had grown up in an environment where I watched my mother being one of the few women, so I didn't think about it a lot. I just did it. The fact that I had a deep technical background gave me credibility. There were lots of instances where when I entered a room people may have discounted my capabilities, but I would establish respect through my technical credentials or business credentials. By the time I went to Cisco, I had several successful companies under my belt, so it wasn't like I was climbing the corporate ladder.

But there is no question that it was a different time. And there wasn't as much conversation about diversity then. There were the beginnings, but people are more vocal about it now, which is good. It is also sad that today we are still having to talk about the scarcity of women in tech.

Newnham: What was next for you?

Estrin: After Cisco, we founded Packet Design, which had a very different business model. Packet Design was a technology incubator where we could work on several projects in parallel with the plan to create companies around ones that were ready for market. We developed some really interesting technology and we did spin out a few companies. But our work was focused on advanced networking technology and a year in, the networking industry collapsed with the bursting of the Internet bubble and this negatively impacted our progress.

The business model was experimental, and it semi-worked, but it turned out to be more challenging to spin out technology and companies than we anticipated. So it was lot of lessons learned. Also, a couple of years into Packet Design was when my ex-husband and I split. That time was marked by a fair amount of turmoil, both personally and professionally, but we worked through it.

I then created JLabs—Judy's Lab, which is basically a vehicle for the multiple things I do primarily focusing on innovation and leadership. From 2012 to 2014, I was also involved in a startup co-founded by my son, David, called EvntLive, which was sold to Yahoo!.

Newnham: You have cofounded more successful tech startups than most. What would you say are the key ingredients?

Estrin: I think it's about solving a problem that is of value to the marketplace and understanding and matching your funding and distribution strategy as well as your patience level with that idea. So if you have something that is forward looking, you need to have enough funding and enough knowledge, distribution, and patience to know it is going to take time. If you've come up with an idea for something whose time is right now, you have to move more quickly and make sure you get a product out that you can then rapidly improve and adapt.

There is a movement towards lean startups, getting products out immediately, and scale fast/fail fast - all of these things that have come from, in some ways, the consumer Internet market. These concepts aren't wrong, but they are not universal. It is about matching your patience, funding, and strategy with the idea that you have, and matching that idea with value. If you are in the medical, pharma, or biotech business, things take longer than if you are building an app. If you are doing an app in which if you fail, no one is going to die, you can move quickly. But if you are building a self-driving car or developing a new drug, then you need to have a different approach.

I think it is important to understand the value that you are bringing and in what time frame. Luck and market timing have a lot to do with how successful you are, too. Also, people should remember that entrepreneurship is risky and not easy. We often only hear about the companies that succeed or those that fail spectacularly, but there are so many that just don't quite succeed or fail softly. It is good to know that going into it.

Lastly, it's all about leadership and culture and people. Entrepreneurship is how you get a team to effectively work together on something. So, all of those things are important.

Newnham: And what qualities do you look for on a founding team?

Estrin: It depends on the company. If it is something that takes a lot of development and a lot of technology, then you want a team that has deep technical backgrounds, as well as the ability to lead and bring a product to market. If it is something that is going to be in development for a couple of years, then often the founding team doesn't need to understand sales, because it's first about getting the product to the point where you can sell it. But if it is something that is going to quickly come to market and it's really a distribution or scale play, then you want a founding team to have business and sales expertise early-on. If it is a manufacturing play, then you need to understand about those strategies.

There is no magic. People talk about entrepreneurship like it's one thing. Entrepreneurship is a state of mind. It's about being entrepreneurial, taking risks, dealing with ambiguity, being agile, and being able to adjust to things that happen. I try to figure out whether or not there is a match between what they need to succeed and what the team has.

I also look at cohesiveness in the team, because startups are tricky and take a lot of time so you need really good communication. One of the classic things that happens with a lot of startups is that you end up with the team not getting along and sometimes people succeed in spite of the friction but often it can slow things down.

Newnham: In your book, you talk about different levels of success. How do you define success? And is there anything you would add to the book now?

Estrin: The meaning of success for me has changed over time. I think the important thing for all entrepreneurs and non entrepreneurs is to figure out what matters to you, about what drives you, as opposed to letting the world around you define what success means. To some people, success means money. To some, it means the 'most money'. And to others people, it means 'enough money'. Some measure their success by their impact on others, perhaps those less fortunate. To some people, success means recognition, which for a scientist might be peer recognition but for a celebrity, or celebrity CEO, it might be mass recognition. Success might come from feeling like you are doing interesting work and solving problems. Success might be having a work-life balance that allows you more time to do the life part and not just work. And what success means to you may change over time.

Personally, I have never really been driven by the money. I've always understood that companies need to return money to their investors but was always more driven by solving hard problems, doing interesting work and being around interesting people. Making money was nice, no one is ever going to complain about making money, but it wasn't the way I measured success. The various motivations people have is what makes working with different types so interesting.

Newnham: What are you most proud of and why?

Estrin: My most fulfilling role has been that of being a mother. But in my career, I would say Bridge, our first company. And while I have loved lots of things that we have done, that stands out to me as just an unbelievable experience—building a team, building a culture, bringing a new product to market in an environment that was very different from today's. I loved it.

And, even though it is different from the rest of my entrepreneurial career, writing my book was a really big accomplishment because all of my life I really thought that I couldn't write. I was literally blocked, but I broke through and learned to write and how to have a voice.

Also, I really enjoyed my board work. Both Disney and FedEx are unbelievably innovative companies. It's an honor to have served on those boards. I learned so much and felt like I was able to contribute. And to be affiliated with two such large important companies with international scope—that was fascinating.

So if I had to pick an entrepreneurial highlight, it was probably Bridge. Although, like you love all of your kids, I loved all of my companies. And, in terms of challenges, writing the book was almost or more challenging than any of the companies I started.

Newnham: What advice would you offer women getting into tech and/or founding their first startup?

Estrin: My advice is to believe in yourself and jump in, take the risk. You can do it and can be successful. But also be realistic about the environment so that you can navigate around the obstacles. There is still a lot of gender bias. You don't want to stop because of it, but you also want to figure out the best way to navigate any given situation.

The fact of the matter is that there is a lot of failure that goes into the success—small failures and big failures—but both success and failure will help you move forward if you learn from them.

Martha Lane Fox

Founder, Doteveryone

Martha Lane Fox *is the founder and executive chair of Doteveryone, an organization that champions digital innovation and inclusion.*

Martha was appointed non-executive director of Twitter in April 2016. She is a non-executive director of the Bailey's Prize for Fiction, the Creative Industries Federation, the Scale-Up Institute and the Open Data Institute.

In March 2014, Martha was appointed Chancellor of the Open University and became a crossbench peer in the UK House of Lords in March 2013.

In 2007, Martha founded her own charitable foundation Antigone, which supports the technology needs and ideas of charities in the education, health and criminal justice sectors. Martha also serves as Patron of AbilityNet, Reprieve, Camfed and Just for Kids Law.

Martha cofounded lastminute.com with Brent Hoberman in 1998 and served as its group managing director from 1998 until 2004. The company joined the London Stock Exchange in 2000 and remained successful despite the burst of the tech bubble. Sabre Holdings acquired lastminute.com for £577 million in 2005.

Also in 2005, Martha cofounded and became chair of Lucky Voice, a private chain of karaoke bars in the United Kingdom. Martha was appointed Commander of The

© Danielle Newnham 2016

D. Newnham, *Female Innovators at Work*, DOI 10.1007/978-1-4842-2364-2_16

Most Excellent Order of the British Empire (CBE) in the 2013 New Year Honours for services to the digital economy and charity.

Martha received a BA in ancient and modern history at the University of Oxford.

Danielle Newnham: Where did you get your entrepreneurial spirit from?

Martha Lane Fox: I think there were probably two things. Both my parents did entrepreneurial things. My dad was an academic but he was always starting businesses on the side, so he published both history and gardening books. I remember being quite small and stuffing envelopes, helping him with work.

And my mum. When she went back to work, she started in a small business run by my godparents and then she went off and started something with my godmother, so I think it was always around us. I can honestly say I think my parents would have been more shocked if I said I wanted to be a banker or a lawyer than I wanted to start my own business.

Newnham: How did you meet Brent and what led to the idea for lastminute.com?

Lane Fox: It was Brent's idea. We met at a strategy consultancy called Spectrum. It was my first job. Brent's second or third job and he had talked about the idea a lot. He talked about it as a user. As the customer, which is the most important thing, and then very generously, when he left, we talked a lot about whether or not we could do it together and he said that we both needed to get more experience which we then did and then we started lastminute.com in 1997.

Like every business, there were struggles as you're advancing on all fronts. You're trying to raise money which is a huge struggle, especially against the backdrop of there having been no Internet businesses really. We were trying to build the technology. So again, especially difficult when there had been no Internet businesses prior. We were trying to hire people and all of this stuff, not just the complicated backdrop of the cycle in which the Internet was at that moment, but also just the whole usual business struggles. So it was kind of this hell-for-leather tactic of the two of us trying to get just that bit further on any one of those fronts.

The challenge was also not only selling lastminite.com as a concept, but also selling the concept of e-commerce—and that the Internet was likely to stay and be successful.

In my first job, I had worked in a strategy consulting company that was pretty much nearly exclusively focused on the impact the Internet was having on media and the telecom business.

Newnham: Did you raise funds straight away?

Lane Fox: Yes, we did. Yes, we were lucky in that we both had flats that we could rent out rooms in so we could have some income. But we went out to raise £600,000 pretty quickly, which was to get us to the first generation of the site and to the concept Brent came up with, which didn't actually shift the whole time we were doing it.

It was all about the nice things to have at the last minute to have a great time so that was hotels, flights, theater tickets, and restaurant bookings, and everything to be able to help the supplier clear the inventory at the last minute and the customer to have an easier experience. And the brilliance of his idea was that it just could not exist in another form such as paper or telephone or any other form. This was an idea facilitated by the Internet and that was immensely powerful.

There were of course challenges though. The industry was new, so a lot of the challenge was the industry itself. There were not a lot of people that would even invest in Internet businesses, so we quite often ended up in traditional or old-fashioned investment companies, which did feel very male-dominated. I was used to working in media and telecoms in the startup Spectrum, which actually had a very balanced number of men and women as cofounders. So I was quite surprised to come into a sector, particularly the banking and investment side, where we saw so few women.

Newnham: Did you experience sexism?

Lane Fox: It's a tricky one I think in as much because as latent as sexism I got, it would also be slightly insane to suggest that we hadn't benefitted in many ways from me being a young woman. You know, it attracted attention—not the sort of attention I wanted. It was incredibly sexist on one level but it meant that if I went to an opening of an envelope, it was in the papers. And sometimes, they would even cut Brent out of the photo. Unbelievable! So of course I wish it wasn't so. But did it help the business? It would be completely disingenuous to say it didn't help. It was hard though.

Newnham: When did you decide to IPO?

Lane Fox: 2000. It just kind of seemed inevitable—the bankers were all over us. The Internet boom in America was just going crazy. Businesses were going public all the time. There were not many e-commerce businesses in Europe and we were well known so we just raced towards it.

Then there was a stock market crash, so everyone was valued as though they were going to survive. And clearly that was not going to happen, although clearly we did.

Newnham: What lessons did you take from the business?

Lane Fox: Well, Lucky Voice was the next business, but what I have started since then is charitable stuff. I always find it interesting when people don't think people who start social enterprises or charities are considered proper entrepreneurs. Actually, I would argue that it is much, much harder because you don't get paying customers, which means you have to scrabble around to get the money in a completely different type of way.

What I think I specifically learnt from lastminute.com was the power of the Internet, which I realize sounds quite a stupid thing to say, but we were really there on the cusp of seeing how this technology could just fly. And I think from that, I learnt that even as an ancient modern historian and someone who didn't really understand coding, understanding technology and embedding it at the heart of everything that I was to do is, and was, phenomenal.

The second thing I learnt I hope was a generosity of spirit. You know, Brent had a generosity of spirit in that he shared his idea with me. I hope that the way we constructed the business was around generosity of spirit also. I personally think that if you have to fire someone, make it as nice as you can. If you have to make people redundant, don't be too mean on terms. Life is too short. The world is a big and scary place very often, so if you can do one small bit to make it a bit lighter, then I think that's important. Especially as a founder/entrepreneur/owner. I feel quite strongly about that kind of stuff.

I also think hire people better than you was pretty much a thread going through everything we did. We didn't always manage to find the right people but not being scared of hiring people that could probably do your job better is quite a good lesson generally because you'll get just that much further.

Newnham: At the height of lastminute.com, how many people did you employ?

Lane Fox: A couple of thousand people but they were based all over Europe. At one point, we had people in about fourteen countries.

Newnham: And how hard was it to walk away from a business that you had put so much into?

Lane Fox: It wasn't actually which I know sounds awful but I think I had always had it in mind to move on. I didn't have quite the same emotional connection to it as I did going into it. I think that when I left I was thirty-one, although I felt like I was a hundred and one, and the world seemed big and exciting. I think it would have been extraordinary if a twenty-five-year-old girl had wanted to stay in that business forever and ever and ever. I respect people that do. I look at the outlying examples, like Mark Zuckerberg, who is clearly an entrepreneur extraordinaire. I respect people that stay in their businesses, and can grow with it, and grow the team around it. But I don't think that's my special skill.

Newnham: After you left lastminute.com, you were involved in a horrific car accident. How did the accident change your path?

Lane Fox: Do you know what? I really don't think it changed me. Obviously, physically it did dramatically. It curtails what I am capable of doing, but I really don't think it changed my brain. I think there is a narrative that people kind of look for when you have "a major event and then things change," but I don't feel like that. What it made me do is work differently, which made me have to think about a different set of things I was going to do.

But when we started lastminute.com, we were looking to support charities from our very first board meeting in our broom cupboard. It was always important for me to have the for-profit and not-for-profit stuff closely side by side. But I guess what the accident did was that it meant I couldn't work from nine until nine in a consistent way, so I found a new way of working that was a bit more easily achievable. I started off with starting a charity and that kind of work.

Newnham: You have had more than one successful company. What skillset do you think is most useful to an entrepreneur?

Lane Fox: I think self-awareness is a pretty big one. I think being able to challenge yourself and not feeling frightened when other people challenge you because being demonic or thinking you're completely right all the time or thinking your idea is absolutely foolproof because you think it is brilliant is foolhardy. And I think the capacity to be part of a team, which I don't think I always got right at all but I think I am getting it more right as I go on, and building a team is really, really important. So, I think that is the first thing—a high EQ.

Then I think an absolutely religious focus on the product itself because you will always be the person that has that more than anyone else. Brent had it in lastminute.com. I learnt a lot from him. I hope I had it as well. I had it certainly in terms of the brand and the culture and stuff. And again, with Lucky Voice, to have a religious view on what the business is like. And even though Doteveryone is different, as it is more charitable, a relentless focus on what it is is absolutely vital. And that comes from the top and filters down and that sets the tone. In the end, you are only as good as the product you are creating.

Finally, boldness and fearlessness, because I think it is scary and difficult. And ostensibly, I much prefer starting things in pairs or groups because it is lonely and difficult. And you have to be quite bold and think: I've just got to pick up the phone to call that person again and again until they answer, or I'm going to go to this conference where I know no one, or I'm going to ask this person for money, or go on this TV interview—or whatever the thing is. So I think boldness and fearlessness are also important.

Working in a startup is very often such a hardcore working environment. I don't mean working all hours—I think that is a misplaced thing about successful startups. But because you haven't got the luxury of big support networks of bigger organizations, so you have to have somebody you're following—as in the leader, the entrepreneur, who feels fearless enough that they will give you air cover, look after you, take the shit, and all that stuff.

Newnham: Is it harder for women to do this, do you think?

Lane Fox: The numbers point to it, don't they? I think there is still just a bias against women. And in the predominantly male venture capital community, they are more disparaging of you, because you hear examples again and again and again. I mean, why are so many bloody gadgets funded by VCs? Because they want to fly them around their garden. And why are there so few actual real innovations around some of the things women would like? It's beginning but it has taken a long time.

Well, I think it is because if you go along and say you've got this brilliant idea for a menstruation something-or-other, they're going to run a mile. I think it is just the way of the world. So yes, of course I think women have it harder. Also, if all the actual technologists are all men—I think eighty percent of the world's software engineers are men—and because if you want to do anything in technology, you need them, then that's a hard dynamic sometimes. Because you play in to all the worst preconceptions about women and their ability to do shit, make shit, get shit done which is just crap really but it is just a cultural thing.

Newnham: So tell me more about Doteveryone.

Lane Fox: Yes, we a new kind of digital organization. We are a charity seeing what is broken about the Internet in the UK right now and showing what's possible. I believe that if we focus on the "everyone" part of the Internet and really go much further and much faster, the UK could be something quite extraordinary. But there are no organizations championing us, the user's voice, in the way Doteveryone will. So you'll get lots of Google lobbying and lots of Facebook lobbying—not because they are bad companies but because they are companies. But where's the universality piece and where's the bit that embeds what the Internet might do for all of us beyond the next commercial startup? So that's what I am interested in and that's what we're doing. I think the UK has a remarkable opportunity because we do a lot of stuff brilliantly and if we can capitalize on that, knock down some of the barriers, of which gender in technology is one, I think we could be an even more successful digital nation.

Newnham: And how are you proposing to do that?

Lane Fox: We are working on four areas. The first is building our awesome partnership network to encourage people to talk to each other and get further by joining up the dots. We are very lucky to have convening power—we've got cross sector, public private and social, charity, individuals and organizations, so that's something quite powerful in just building that network.

Then we are doing interventions around three areas, which are digital skills for everyone, at every level, fixing the gender gap in technology and building products and services for social good.

Newnham: If Doteveryone is successful, what does the future of tech look like?

Lane Fox: I like to imagine a world where the Internet has enabled a radical redesign of how we use our public services, not the government-type digital services which I was heavily involved with, as you know, which did a brilliant job of making not very good digital services better, but actually organizing ourselves around the Internet will be the organizing principle of our era. I think the country that manages to do this will have huge gains.

So I believe that if everyone is successful, we will have more people who are able to get more work by being online, get higher paid jobs, and have more tools at their disposal to be able to battle some of the complex situations that we all face.

Secondly, I think that we will have a more successful and creative set of public services and connections between us all in society because an example is we're building this project in end of life care because palliative care is a massive challenge for the country and takes up a huge percentage of the NHS [National Health Service] budget but it is still very unimaginatively offline. Again, not because anyone is doing a bad job but because of experience and time. And so you can use the tools of technology—not to make everything digital but often quite the opposite. To give people more time for face to face.

It is just about modernizing and improving services. I think we have done a good job of thinking how that happens to industries, but not yet how that happens to society.

Newnham: How do you work with companies on diversity?

Lane Fox: Well, I just joined the board of Twitter. And we at Doteveryone are doing lots of things with our partners, such as Sage and Google on the 5050tech program. We work a lot with the corporate sector as well. I always try to go to as many things as I can to talk about this. I am increasingly refusing invites that are only women, because although those networks are great and really important for women—and I don't want to be disparaging about them at all—but personally, I think I am most helpful in making sure that men are a part of this conversation and changing stuff because that is really important.

Newnham: And how important do you think mentors are?

Lane Fox: I absolutely believe in mentors. I think it is really valuable. I don't think it has to be just women for women. I have personally had a couple of more senior men than me as mentors myself. My first boss from Spectrum is a really great guy and we'd regularly have lunch where he always challenged me.

You can find mentors in unlikely places. I think it is quite good to have mentors who don't look like you, because they can challenge you and help you. So yes, mentors are great and whether it is formal or informal, I think it is always a good idea to ask someone to be a mentor. I mean, lots of people find me and I try to do something. If I can't meet, I suggest we have half an hour on the phone. People often say yes because most want to help. So think of your questions carefully, ahead of calling, and work out what you might want to get out of it.

Newnham: You mentioned earlier that you have joined the board at Twitter. Can you tell more about that?

Lane Fox: Well, I am a non-executive, so we don't meddle. We support the CEO, challenge the strategy, hopefully offer challenge in the right places, show a different point of view, bring a bit of a European perspective. I am only the second woman on the board, so hopefully a noisy voice.

I feel it's a massive privilege to be on the board of such an iconic company. I really think the platform is so endlessly fascinating and I hope I can be of some use and make some contribution.

Newnham: What advice do you have for young women who are looking to get into tech?

Lane Fox: I think the thing that strikes me again and again about the difference between 1997/1998 and now, nearly twenty years on, is the ability to get going much more quickly than we could. I mean, tech was still hard then and you didn't have such easy tools. Yes, there was no Google and you can't really start a business without a relationship with Google. But, on the other hand, there are so many quick ways to build something now. Even I, without my technology skills, can knock up something in WordPress or put up something quite quickly. And that's a remarkable shift in quite a short space of time.

So I would urge you that if you have an idea, get out there with something very cheap and test it on people. Don't build a huge expensive thing and go "Ta-da!" Just get going and test it, and you'll learn more by doing than by doing a big reveal and not actually getting out there and seeing that users want it. So that's what I would urge people to do.

I would also say be fearless because I get intimidated still when I do things now. I can't imagine what it is like for people at the beginning of their careers who haven't had all the opportunities and luck that I have. Please know that we all suffer from low self-esteem and you just have to try, and smile through it, and be confident because I absolutely guarantee there are some awesome women out there who are poised to do some brilliant things.

Manuela Veloso

Herbert A. Simon University Professor

Manuela Veloso *is the Herbert A. Simon University professor in the Computer Science Department at Carnegie Mellon University. She is the incoming head of the Machine Learning Department, and she has courtesy appointments in the Robotics Institute and Electrical and Computer Engineering Department. She researches in Artificial Intelligence and Robotics and founded and leads the CORAL research laboratory, which studies autonomous agents that "Collaborate, Observe, Reason, Act, and Learn." Manuela is an IEEE Fellow, an AAAS Fellow, and an AAAI Fellow. She is the past president of the Association for the Advancement of Artificial Intelligence (AAAI) and RoboCup. Manuela and her students research with a variety of autonomous robots.*

Manuela's long-term interest and research into multi-agent and multi-robot research has also seen her and her team exploring robot soccer. She cofounded the RoboCup Federation, which launched its first games in 1997.

Manuela received her Licenciatura in electrical engineering and an MSc in electrical and computer engineering from Instituto Superior Técnico in Lisbon, Portugal. She also has an MA in computer science from Boston University and a PhD in computer science from Carnegie Mellon University.

Manuela has co-authored numerous papers, predominantly around the subject of intelligent, autonomous, mobile agents.

Danielle Newnham: Can you tell me more about your background?

© Danielle Newnham 2016
D. Newnham, *Female Innovators at Work*, DOI 10.1007/978-1-4842-2364-2_17

Manuela Veloso: I grew up in Lisbon in Portugal and I was interested in math since I was four years old. I always loved my arithmetic, very much more than anything else. So when it came to college, I first thought of just doing a degree in math. But my father is a mechanical engineer and he advised me to do engineering, so I took a degree in electrical engineering in Lisbon in the 1980s. And then after I finished my degree, I became very interested in computers.

I did my master's thesis on database theory, still in Portugal. And then in 1984, I came to the United States. I did a master's in computer science and a PhD in computer science, which included artificial intelligence [AI] and automation. I went from math to becoming very interested in computers to then being very interested in the problem of automation—automation of decisions and all sorts of AI technology. So that's what led me to the research I am doing now on artificial intelligence and robotics.

Newnham: Was there a specific incident or experience that sparked your interest in automation?

Veloso: Yes, it's a good question. I remember for my master's thesis, I was involved in entering all the information for a factory. It was a factory that built and sold refrigerators and freezers in Portugal. It was all done manually from the orders to the suppliers and handling the customers, and then they gave a grant to the university to have a computer automatically generate these lists of parts and the orders. When I was doing that, I became very interested in how much could be done automatically.

I also became interested in the fact that the orders were very repetitive. And so, from everything, it seemed you could learn some statistics such as eight out of ten orders were of this type. We are talking about 1982, so this is the beginning of digitalization for a lot of companies. It was clear that all of those actual computations we were doing could be more and more automated. It was the very beginning of data science. I became fascinated with what computers could do to process data, to optimize decisions, and to support humans with a lot of data.

So that's why I became so interested with the problem of decision-making. In fact, my interest in AI has a lot to do with the decision-making and learning which came from doing the digitization of the factory's processing. My PhD thesis was actually on planning by analogy ["Learning by Analogical Reasoning in General Purpose Problem Solving"], which meant that the computer would generate plans or solve problems by using similar past problems and extracting the solution to those, and also trying to generate new solutions to new problems by basically analogy and adaptation of previous past solutions.

It was really a very problem-solving PhD thesis because I was so influenced by the fact that the problems were not just to be solved once, but it was a learning curve. You have to learn to solve one problem. And then next time, you have to solve another problem, so you apply the learnings from the previous problems and try to always do better, based on this system. That's basically how I got interested in artificial intelligence and automation, and planning and learning. It was based on the realization in that company that things were repetitive. Always slightly different—they were never always exactly the same. But their slight differences meant that the technology, instead of doing it from scratch, could make it easier to learn from and make it better and easier and quicker.

That's what motivated me—not a science fiction book or anything like that, because I was never interested in science fiction growing up. No Star Wars or Star Trek, or imagination of future worlds. I was very driven by the way people solve problems and how much I realised computers could help complete tasks in people's lives.

Newnham: What came next for you? And were there many women in the field when you started?

Veloso: Well, I have been a professor since 1992 at Carnegie Mellon University [CMU] so I joined the faculty immediately. Carnegie Mellon is number one in computer science and robotics in the world and a lot of work we do is research with excellent students and we teach of course. But it is basically about not being "afraid" of thinking about new problems and thinking about really avant-garde ideas. I have always been on the research side since 1992.

It has always been that the number of women is a considerable minority compared to the number of men but at Carnegie Mellon, it has been addressed for a long time. What happens is we have undergraduate students who are students doing their bachelor's degree and then we have the PhD and the master's students, as graduate students, and then we have the faculty so these are very different tiers of education. For our undergrads at CMU, the percentage of women has dramatically increased. We were thirteen to fifteen percent in the 1990s, but the incoming computer science class in the Fall 2016 is forty-seven percent women. That is remarkable.

I think what is interesting is that when the students come, they feel that they will be more welcome because there are more women here, and so the number increases each year. Now, unfortunately, this is not necessarily the case for graduate students. The graduate students are still thirteen to fifteen percent—maybe eighteen percent at most. And if you go up to the faculty, I think we are ten percent women, so it just gets lower. And if you get to the department heads, and the deans, and leadership of the university, maybe it's like two or three percent.

In fact, I just became head of the Machine Learning Department, but there are currently no other women heading any of the other departments in the School of Computer Science. In electrical engineering, the department head is a woman too. We would like to keep women in the pipeline all the way to the leadership level.

Newnham: Why do you think the numbers aren't increasing?

Veloso: I don't know. The only thing I can tell you is that I try my best to be a role model. I try my best to encourage women wherever I go but, as women, we can only do so much so this needs to change from the top. I will tell you something. At a very famous robotics conference, ICRA in 2015, the complete organizing committee was women—just women. It was sixty women and it was wonderful to work with those many women in leadership. It makes a huge difference.

Newnham: You are behind the CORAL [Cooperate, Observe, Reason, Act, and Learn] research group and CoBots [collaborative robots]. Can you tell me a bit about both?

Veloso: When I became interested in artificial intelligence, there were many areas of research within it, like natural language processing, vision, machine learning, planning, machine translation, information retrieval so there are many, many areas. I became interested in intelligent robots, in the sense that they would be able to sense. That is, they would be able to perceive the world through cameras and sensors and then make decisions by themselves and move.

So I have always worked on autonomous mobile robots. That has always been my research and continues to be. That's not just looking at a vision problem but vision combined with decisions. A robot would see an open area and knows it has to get to that room and that it has to go forward and take a right if we are researching on autonomous robots inside of buildings. So we are talking about in a human environment, not in space, not on the roads, not underwater. I have been working on these autonomous robots for a long time. And on top of that, I have always worked on more than one robot so that is why my research group is called Cooperate, Observe, Reason, Act, and Learn because we research on intelligent agents that can collaborate with each other.

Really, it is because we are looking at the problem of more than one robot coordinating, so collaborate and observing, because they have to see, and reason because they have to plan their optimized path to reach their goals and optimize actions, and then act because they move and then learn to improve their performance. They keep doing so they need to learn from each experience.

I started that research in 1992 and I have been working on different problems within this spectrum ever since, including robot soccer and CoBots. These CoBots actually move in our building. We have four of them and they are autonomous in terms of not hitting obstacles and finding their way in the building and being able to arrive at their destinations on time, which requires all sorts of scheduling and all sorts of route planning, and also localization and navigation in the building.

One of the most unique things about CoBots is that they ask for help when they need help. That became an important contribution as what we call "symbiotic autonomy." And we understood the need to ask for help, after I realized that robots will inevitably have limitations in the sense that they are not able to open any door, or they are not able to press elevator buttons, or pick up all objects. And therefore they are able to do many things by themselves but when they are not capable of a particular action, they proactively ask for help from humans. They can also access the web for information they need for a task, or they can send an email to a human and say, "I am in front of an obstacle and I can't go around it and the obstacle does not move," or "Where are the keys?" "Can someone come and help me?" So the main thing here is that they are embedded or in a symbiosis with the environment where they are, which includes humans, and the web and other robots, and other remote humans.

This is major in terms of researching AI, because we see now an AI system that is capable of resourcing to the outside, to other sources of knowledge and other sources of actuation to get a complete complex task done. And then when someone helps them press the elevator button, they can then get the elevator themselves, and get out and continue with their task. It's just a little bit in the middle that they cannot do, and then they go on.

Newnham: What software and hardware are you using?

Veloso: The CoBot robots are essentially a computer on wheels so a computer on a stand and at the bottom of the stand is an omnidirectional base with four wheels, which means that the robots can move in any direction and can go around obstacles easily. All the hardware for the CoBots was done by Mike Licitra, and maintained especially by Joydeep Biswas. The research on the autonomous has already led to the PhD theses of several of my students, namely Stephanie Rosenthal, Brian Coltin, Joydeep Biswas, and Richard Wang.

Newnham: Obviously, within the university, I am sure people have gotten used to them. But when you have visitors greeted by the CoBots, how do people generally react to them?

Veloso: You are right. The people at the university got used to them. Although they really don't use them as much as they could, because they still see the CoBots as one of my research projects, whereas they could use them and ask them to help with tasks.

And the visitors, they accept the robots very well. I have to say most or maybe all the visitors who come to my office are escorted by a CoBot. They come in the elevator and the CoBot is waiting at the elevator hall, with a message on it saying, "I'm here to take to you to Manuela Veloso's office" and then the visitor just follows the robot all the way down the corridors to my office. And the visitors appreciate it, because I think it is the only place in the world where you are escorted to a location by a fully autonomous mobile robot.

We are also doing research into having the robots interact through speech with the people. But first of all we needed to focus on the safe and reliable navigation so that the CoBot could autonomously traverse our buildings. Such robust localization and navigation was the core contribution of the PhD thesis of my student Joydeep Biswas, which led the robots to have navigated for more than 1,000 km fully autonomously. We are now working on enabling the robot to interact with humans and answer their requests, plan for their requests, and describe which decisions it has made.

Newnham: These robots are clearly collecting data the whole time. How is that being used and fed back in?

Veloso: In terms of mobile robots, they move around accurately knowing their position in the map of the building. If the robots carry a sensor on them to capture, for example, humidity, or Wi-Fi strength, or anything, they can actually collect data. The thesis of my student Richard Wang addressed this data collection by the autonomous robots.

The robot produces very accurate maps of sensed data in the building with the precise location because they accurately know where they are. Then they annotate those precise locations on the map with all sorts of information that they capture in the sensors, at different times of the day so they accumulate very finely accurate data. For example, the data on the Wi-Fi can be used to select locations for the access points.

So for the future, one can imagine these robots helping humans, such as architects and building designers, to decide where the temperature is low or the noise level is high and how to address this.

Our CoBots can do very accurate indoor data collection, and this is really interesting in terms of the contribution of mobile robots in a physical space.

Newnham: You have been working on this for twenty years. What surprised you? And what were some of the obstacles?

Veloso: A surprise was the acknowledgment that this robot technology—computer on wheels with sensors—inevitably have limitations. Even with many advances in the coming years, I think that it's going to be very hard to have an intelligent mechanical robot handle all the complexities of the world, be it opening any door or picking up any object. Or it's going to be very hard to have a computer that will understand everything we say.

So I think that it was a big breakthrough for me to realize that all these intelligent creatures or intelligence will include asking for help. So, what I am trying to tell you is that if we include, within the intelligence, the ability to know what you don't know, and go to the web to find out or call someone or call another robot. Instead of thinking we are going to be able to have machines that do it all, which understand the words of Shakespeare and understand all of the images, was to actually say the opposite. What if they don't understand but now we can help and eventually they will learn from the help we give them? And so eventually they become better through experience. Through these years, with CoBots, that was a major novelty and "surprise" for me.

Newnham: You said earlier that people in the university are not using the CoBots as much as they could. How do you think we better prepare humans to interact with robots?

Veloso: I think it requires a good company to take this over. It's not going to be through Manuela at Carnegie Mellon, it's going to be like a genius of some company that magically make these robots of common use. I think it really needs a great company to make these mobile creatures be accepted and be useful and be available to humans.

Robots will need to be functional and interact well with humans. If we would swipe the screen on the cell phone and nothing would happen, we would not be willing to swipe it. It's because it gives us so much function that we adapt and appreciate new technology. We need robots that are functional and useful.

Radia Perlman

Inventor, Spanning Tree Protocol

Radia Perlman *is a distinguished inventor, network engineer, software designer, IEEE Fellow, and respected author. Radia has made countless contributions to the Internet, including creating the algorithm behind STP (Spanning Tree Protocol). Her innovations enable today's link-state routing protocols to be robust, scalable, and easy to manage. Radia improved the spanning tree–based Ethernet by designing TRILL (TRansparent Interconnection of Lots of Links), which allows the Ethernet to make optimal use of bandwidth.*

As an undergraduate at MIT, Radia undertook what was known as an Undergraduate Research Opportunity within the LOGO Lab at the MIT Artificial Intelligence Laboratory. While there, working under the supervision of Seymour Papert, Radia created TORTIS (Toddler's Own Recursive Turtle Interpreter System), a children's version of the educational LOGO robotics language.

Radia's seminal books, which were hugely successful, include Interconnections: Bridges, Routers, Switches, and Internetworking Protocols (Addison-Wesley Professional, 1999) and Network Security: Private Communication in a Public World (Prentice Hall, 2002). Radia also holds more than a hundred issued patents.

Radia has taught at the University of Washington, Harvard University, and MIT. She has a BS and an MS degree in mathematics from MIT, and a PhD in computer science, also from MIT. She was inducted into the Internet Hall of Fame in 2014 and the National Inventors Hall of Fame in 2016.

© Danielle Newnham 2016

D. Newnham, *Female Innovators at Work*, DOI 10.1007/978-1-4842-2364-2_18

Danielle Newnham: Can you tell me about your background?

Radia Perlman: I don't think there's anything remarkable about my background. I grew up in New Jersey with an older sister. Family values were critical thinking, hard work, non-discrimination, living frugally, and not displaying wealth, being very against classism. My father especially had a good sense of humor. I was pretty shy and quiet, but very ambitious academically.

Once "penmanship" stopped being part of my grade, after grade three or so, I was able to get A's in everything, and really cared about my "perfect record." To get A's in history, which required memorizing meaningless names and dates, I wasted so much of my childhood cramming for history tests, scoring 100, and then promptly forgetting it all right after the test. I liked to read, play piano, definitely not into sports, either playing or watching. In addition to science and math, I enjoyed foreign languages and creative writing.

I really didn't have close friends until college. I didn't have much in common with the girls, who seemed to be into clothes and gossip and boys. And the boys didn't seem to want to interact with girls except as girlfriends. There were some mean people in our class who mercilessly picked on some of the kids and even some of the teachers. I managed to mostly stay out of their way and not be a target, but I was quite traumatized by seeing their cruelty. I felt a little ashamed of myself for not confronting the bullies, but I wasn't sure what I could do that wouldn't make things worse for the kids being picked on. I did try to be nice to the kids being picked on when the bullies weren't around.

I enjoyed science, math, and languages. I liked reading and writing, but was stressed about the subjective grading [as opposed to science and math, where if you got the right answer, you'd definitely get a good grade]. I really hated history. I hated phys ed [physical education], which seemed like endless choosing teams, with me being the last to be chosen, standing there all embarrassed while the captains choosing the sides spent longer and longer agonizing over which of the remaining people they should choose.

As an adult, I feel like a missed out on a lot. Phys ed ought to be about physical fitness, and it wasn't until I was much older that I realized how important and enjoyable that can be. And history is fascinating if one thinks about things rather than regurgitating quick facts. I really wish that school, and families, would teach how complex the world really is, and that there is seldom a complete right/wrong.

I always liked logic puzzles, and every science or math class as mentioned before. My high school chemistry and physics teachers both had an interesting style of teaching. They'd introduce a new topic by giving us a quiz and seeing how much we could figure out ourselves. I was always excited when they did this. The rest of the class hated it, and felt it was unfair to be quizzed on something they hadn't been taught but I think it is a fantastic way of teaching—making you think about how to do stuff before being fed the recipe for getting the answer. But I've never been excited about technology in the way that people attribute to "engineers." I never built anything or took anything apart. I still do not like fancy gadgets. I get mystified by new user interfaces in rental cars and hotel showers.

Newnham: I understand both your parents were engineers, with your mother a programmer. What kind of influence did that have on you? And how unusual was it for women to code in those days?

Perlman: I'm sure it was extremely unusual for women to be programmers. My mother was first a "Girl Friday," a term for "secretary" or "admin" back in the day. She got her job with a "mathematician" title by answering an ad that was "Help wanted: male." In those days the help-wanted ads were always separated into "Help wanted: male" and "Help wanted: female."

My mother helped me with my homework and cared about academic achievement. However, she didn't teach me how to program, and I didn't have a computer.

Newnham: You ended up at MIT. Can you tell me about your time there?

Perlman: I started as an undergraduate in math, stayed for graduate school in math, dropped out having done all the requirements for PhD but not having even started on a thesis, or even having an advisor, and then ten years later, I went back, this time in computer science, and I did complete a PhD. I expected to be average at MIT. I'm always amazed at how kids who were the best at high school are devastated when they aren't the best in college, particularly a very competitive college. But expecting to be average, I was quite happy that I was always comfortably above class average.

Some interesting anecdotes: There were extremely few women when I was there. Then I majored in math. I'm not sure what the other women majored in but very few majored in math. Then after my freshman year they no longer required women to live in the one female dorm, because that was greatly restricting how many females could be accepted, and most of the dorms, except the female dorm, became co-ed. I moved to a dorm that was supposedly co-ed, but with so few female students at MIT, the co-ed dorms were pretty much all male. So basically, after freshman year, I didn't see any women anymore.

I noticed a weird phenomenon though, and someone else mentioned the same thing so I know I wasn't imagining it… I was quiet and shy, and just wanted to learn. I was in a large lecture class, probably freshman physics. The professor would keep staring at me after he'd made some point, expecting me to nod that I understood, and then he'd move on. This made me self-conscious, so I'd sit in a different place the next lecture. But he always seemed to find me and stare at me for that nod. I really didn't like it, it made it harder for me to concentrate on learning the material, and I finally thought I'd go on strike and refuse to nod. So, the next lecture, he stared at me, and I just looked down, or stared back, but didn't nod. This got him really flustered and he then said "Is there a problem, Miss Perlman?" I was mortified, and decided, fine..., I'll function as the class nodder.

Another anecdote that very elegantly illustrates a famous computer problem known as "the dining philosopher's problem." Basically, that problem is a cute way of explaining that there might be a bunch of processes that each need certain resources in order to make progress, but some of the resources might be reserved by other processes. Until a process has all the resources at once, it can't make progress. There can be a deadlock where all the processes are waiting for resources, and not releasing any that they'd reserved.

Anyway, at MIT, there was a class in digital hardware. The hardest thing about it was that there was not enough equipment. You'd have to build something, and have the teacher look at it and check it off, before you could be done. You'd have to try to assemble all the things you needed by walking around to other students and saying, "Can I borrow the scope?" or "Do you have any extra AND gates?" I was the only female in the class, with a bunch of really shy nerds who had never spoken to a female before. I discovered that there was nothing I could ask that they wouldn't agree to in their shock at being spoken to by a female. "Sure, you can take the scope. Do you need a kidney?" So I got my project signed-off very quickly, feeling kind of guilty. But then I decided I owed it to the world to help the other kids, so I'd pick a kid and say, "I'll help you finish." I'd find all the things he needed, and then he'd get his project checked off. After doing this for maybe one-third of the class, there were enough resources that the rest of the kids could finish on their own.

So MIT was fine when I was an undergraduate and when I was taking classes in grad school. It was kind of miserable though when I needed an advisor to start on a thesis. The math department did not assign you an advisor. I'd have to knock on doors and say, "I need an advisor." And all the professors would say, "Well, I'm incredibly busy, and I'm such an important person." So I never wound up with an advisor.

Newnham: Being one of few women in your college courses and in your field, how did that affect you?

Perlman: Mostly, I don't notice. It feels very natural to me to be among mostly men. I don't tend to think about gender, really. I'm just me. And my friends, who are mostly male, are just them. When I think of the word "woman," I think of someone in heels, and makeup, and fancy clothes, which is definitely not me. When I think of the word "man," I think of the lumberjack on the Brawny towels package, which is definitely not any of my male friends either.

However, one problem, especially in college, was being around all these very vulnerable, shy boys. I'm very approachable and I never wanted to hurt anyone's feelings, especially these super-shy boys. I couldn't marry them all, so I always needed to have a boyfriend so I could say I was attached, rather than telling anyone I wasn't interested in spending more time with them personally.

Another problem was sometimes feeling like I was representing my gender. I abandoned the work I'd done with programming languages for young kids because I wanted to be taken seriously as a real scientist—and something involving cute little kids seemed not like "real science."

But another problem is that, as a kid, I never paid attention to how I dressed. I'm totally mystified when I go to a hotel room as to what all the little bottles of lotions are for. So it might have been nice to have had more female friends to help me learn that sort of stuff, for the occasional times it's important to dress the part.

Newnham: Can you tell me about your earlier jobs?

Perlman: Well my very first job was a summer job when I was a teenager, as a waitress at a deli. It was a very complicated job. Not only did I have to take the orders and make the sandwiches, but there was a deli in front with all these long round things, and someone would ask for a quarter pound of provolone….And I didn't even know if that was a meat or a cheese. All these unfamiliar foods—all with names that sounded the same to me. And to me, pretty much, all people look alike. So I'd be rushing around, and someone would say "Can you get me an extra fork?" I would, but then when I got the fork and looked at the customers, I'd see a sea of identical looking people and I couldn't figure out which one wanted the fork.

People would say, "Are you new?" and I'd say yes, and they'd give me enormous tips to encourage me. At the end of the first week, the owner took me aside and said, "I'm sorry, honey. I can tell you're trying really hard, but you just don't have the brains. I'm going to have to let you go."

I was incredibly upset at the concept that I… had… been… fired… from… a… job. I had no aspirations of a career as a waitress, but I thought this would haunt me for the rest of my life. That every job application would ask, "Have you ever been fired from a job?" And I'd have to say yes. Luckily, nobody's asked me that though.

Maybe even earlier than that I would get gigs as a piano accompanist. But my real first job, I suppose, was in the LOGO lab as a system programmer, writing utilities such as debuggers. LOGO is a language for teaching kids to program. I got inspired to try to teach all the concepts to much younger kids. The first thing that I designed and built was called the "button box," which had big buttons with pictures in contrast to LOGO, which used the regular keyboard where you'd have to type "forward 100". There were several boxes that plugged into each other, starting with one with the direct commands—forward, back, right, left, toot your horn, turn your light on, turn your light off, pull your pen up off the paper, put your pen down onto the paper—and ultimately one that allowed you to program, with four buttons: start remembering, stop remembering, do it, and forget it. If things were confusing, you could unplug the more complicated boxes and get back to the familiar. For older kids and for adults, the button box system was a wonderful introduction to programming. And after spending a few minutes on it, people found the regular LOGO language much easier to learn.

But the younger kids didn't understand the programming. They'd either hit start remembering, and then be in awe of the beautiful display that stored the commands, with pictures such as a light bulb for "turn your light on," ignoring the turtle. Or teachers would try to get them to focus on the turtle and ignore the screen, and ask them to "teach the turtle to draw a square," at which point the kids would think the picture the turtle drew was the program. They'd be confused as to why the turtle might turn the wrong way first, or stop to toot its horn, when it was following the set of commands they'd used, but they didn't remember which commands they'd used.

So the next thing I did I called "the slot machine," which consisted of several long Plexiglas boxes with slots on the top for storing commands. Each box was a program. Commands were about the size of credit cards, with a picture on the top and something machine-readable on the bottom. You programmed a box by filling it with commands. There was a big button on the left of the box and hitting that caused a light to go on in the first slot position. The turtle would execute the command there, and then the next light would go on. The boxes were different colors. So, for instance, a command that was red would mean "leave this light on and execute everything in the red row." So the programs could call each other or do recursion.

Going from there to network protocols was totally unplanned. I was in grad school, and had done everything but a thesis, but never had an advisor, and I had no idea how to start on a thesis. At this point I confided to an old friend that I was kind of stuck in grad school, and he said, "How about joining our group at BBN" [Bolt, Berenek, Newman, a government contractor that developed software for network equipment]? And that turned out to be designing routing protocols for the ARPA packet radio network. And so it was then that I discovered that I loved protocols. But the real opportunity for changing the world was when Digital Equipment Corporation [DEC] offered me the job of being the person to design routing for DECnet. It was exactly the right place at the right time.

And by the way, and as I mentioned earlier, I wound up returning to grad school ten years after dropping out. I got a PhD in computer science. It was so much easier the second time, when I had more self-confidence. I'd become an expert in network protocols and it was easy to do a thesis.

Newnham: Can you tell me more about your time at DEC? And what led to you coming up with the algorithm behind the Spanning Tree Protocol?

Perlman: Like I said, Digital was the perfect job at the perfect time in history. The head of the group, Tony Lauck, was incredibly smart and I learned a lot. He also posed wonderful questions. One of my first suggestions as routing architect was to change over to a protocol similar to what was in the ARPANET [*Advanced Research Projects Agency* Network]. Tony said, "Hmm. I'm not convinced it's stable. Can you prove it's stable?" And indeed when trying to prove it was stable, I realized it was not. That was one of my first papers—showing that it wasn't stable and how to redesign it to make it stable. He also proposed that I figure out how to make "transparent bridges," that moved Ethernet packets around, find a loop-free subset of the topology.

He also challenged me to make it "scale as a constant" [meaning, the amount of memory and computation necessary to run the algorithm should not grow with the size of the network]. That was ridiculous. Nothing's a constant. Maybe linear in the size of the network. But that was when I figured out the spanning tree algorithm, which also, amazingly, scales as a constant.

But the whole spanning tree Ethernet stuff was really a kludge, invented out of necessity because people left out the real routing stuff—the stuff I had been working on, despite my trying to argue with them that they still needed the routing layer. I assumed the spanning tree stuff would last a year or two until there was time to redesign the networked computers to do it the "right way" but as it turns out, because the world settled on IP as the routing header, people still need Ethernet to create a flat cloud in which computers can move around and keep their address.

Newnham: What was the dawn of the new age?

Perlman: It was just some computers hooked together, and you could do email, and file transfer and remote login. I certainly could not have imagined things like Internet search, and things like eBay, where you buy random stuff from little merchants all over the world.

There was also a great resentment by some of the programmers at MIT when the administrators added passwords to login. What if someone had a bug in his program and he wasn't around? How could you look through his directory for his code and fix the bug?

Newnham: Going back to the lack of women in your field – was this ever an issue for you? Do you think female inventors get appropriate recognition for their work?

Perlman: Not really, though if I remember, it was really hard to find a women's bathroom in the math department of MIT. I'm sure there are times when subconscious bias causes a hiring manager to just not be impressed by someone who doesn't fit their image of an "engineer." And I do sometimes wind up interacting with people who are pompous bullies, and that's really annoying. They do well for themselves in terms of impressing management, but they are toxic to people around them, and I have yet to meet anyone like that that is actually good, technically. But I've worked with both male and female bullies, and I've worked with a lot of wonderful, brilliant, collaborative people of both genders too.

In college, there was also an opportunity to spend a year in Antarctica programming a Nova computer. It sounded kind of intriguing… a real adventure. But when I asked, they said it was only for men. So it was not really discrimination, but with a small number of people cooped up for a whole year, they'd decided it would be easier to just have men.

In terms of female inventors, it's not so much "female" that prevents some innovators from getting the recognition they deserve. I think some people— of both genders—are relentlessly self-promoting, and they get lots of recognition, usually way more than they deserve. Others, who just quietly do good work, are often underappreciated. The only reason anyone has heard of me is that I happened to write my first book, Interconnections. It is because the book is what everyone learned the field from. Anyone in networking would have had that book on their shelf.

Newnham: You often talk about approaching design differently, perhaps because you're not "in love with technology." What do you mean by that? What is your approach?

Perlman: I think about problems before diving in and trying to implement something. I also boil the problem down to the basic concept, removing all unnecessary details. And then wind up with a really simple solution. The other nice thing about hating technology is that I design things that are super easy to use, since I sympathize with people like myself that don't want to have to learn a million things in order to use something.

Newnham: You wear many hats as software designer and network engineer. What skills does it take to do those jobs?

Perlman: People bring their own skills, and the ideal team is one where people's skills complement each other. My particular skills are being able to focus on the heart of a problem, ignoring irrelevant details, to think outside the box, and to be able to explain things very clearly.

Sometimes a job involves a very specific thing you have to build in a very short amount of time, with all sorts of annoyances like lack of documentation, bugs in other components, etc. Then one needs to focus on the one thing you are doing. But if you aren't in a crunch mode like that, my advice is to be intellectually curious and try to learn things, even if they're not "what you need to know now." Also, constantly question why things are the way they are. And try to think of alternative designs, and compare them. Don't believe things that you hear or read, because a lot of it is wrong. So rather than accepting "this is the way things are" and memorizing that, exploring alternatives often leads to innovation.

Newnham: Can you tell me about your current role at EMC? And what's your view on data security and its future?

Perlman: At EMC I'm consulting with various groups doing networking and security things.

There are a lot of interesting aspects of security. To some extent the world has ignored the concept of malicious participants. So, there is the wonderful Internet search, and you can find lots of information. But how do you know whether it's correct? And there are so many ways of mining information for bad purposes. Like people that post pictures of their vacation, while they're on vacation, which lets burglars know their home will be vacant.

One thing that people assume should be kept very carefully secret is medical records. Sure. But if you're travelling in some obscure country, and fall unconscious, I think you'd like anyone claiming to be a doctor to be able to access your medical records in order to help you.

Newnham: Finally, what are you most proud of?

Perlman: Well, there's the routing stuff. I made a form of routing called "link state routing" robust, self-configuring, and scalable. And of course the spanning tree algorithm. And my thesis on how to make networks work, even if some of the components are misbehaving. I've also done stuff in other areas, for instance, designing how to allow data to have expiration dates, so that after the expiration date the data is completely unrecoverable, even if backups exist.

I'm also really proud of my books. I don't just regurgitate details of the deployed stuff, and I don't drown the reader in acronyms and irrelevant details, or a lot of formalism. Instead, I look at individual problems conceptually, like, "How would a computer plugging into a network obtain an address?" And I discuss several different options, with trade-offs, and only then, do I mention how it's done in various protocols—not just the ones that are currently deployed, but ones that have had interesting approaches, even if those protocols are no longer used. But anyway, I'm quite proud of being able to make sense out of very muddy fields full of misconceptions and ill-defined buzzwords, make it understandable and thought-provoking, and entertaining as well.

Sampriti Bhattacharyya

Founder, Hydroswarm

Sampriti Bhattacharyya is the founder of Hydroswarm, an early stage startup that designs artificial intelligence–enabled underwater drones to perform a myriad of tasks, including port security, marine exploration, and ocean mapping.

Sampriti is also the cofounder and director of the Lab-X Foundation, a non-profit she started in 2012 in her native India to offer hands-on engineering training to those in developing countries.

Sampriti has an MS in aerospace engineering from Ohio State University and a BS in electrical engineering. She is about to complete her PhD in mechanical engineering at the Massachusetts Institute of Technology (MIT), with a minor in business. Her previous experience include working with NASA on intelligent aircrafts and designing innovative nuclear reactors using particle accelerators.

She was named one of the Forbes 30 Under 30 Class of 2016 in Manufacturing, Connected World's 2016 Women of M2M, and Robohub's Top 25 Women in Robotics 2014.

Danielle Newnham: Can you tell me about your background?

© Danielle Newnham 2016

D. Newnham, *Female Innovators at Work*, DOI 10.1007/978-1-4842-2364-2_19

Sampriti Bhattacharyya: I was an absolute rebel when I was young. I was born and raised in Kolkata, India, and I didn't take the traditional route of child prodigy going to MIT. Instead I went to a very small engineering college in India for my bachelor's in Electrical Engineering. And through various adventures—and misadventures—I made it out to the United States to do an internship and then grad school and now to finish my PhD at MIT.

My mom worked as a senior lecturer in a college and that was really very uncommon in India at the time. She even had a PhD in political science, which is even more rare! She was probably one of the very few women I knew who worked, because women didn't used to work in India at all—it was a very patriarchal society. Anyway, my parents didn't get along that well so they separated when I was pretty young, which was a little dysfunctional, because in our society, that was really not acceptable at the time either. So my older sister and I grew up with my mom. And one thing I really remember learning from my mom was that I didn't want to be a housewife. I wanted to have a career.

I was a bit of a loner off doing my own thing all the time. I was always fascinated by aerospace and I was also a creative kid, always writing poems and very artsy and imaginative. Rebellious too, and got into trouble all the time. And by the time I was in eleventh and twelfth grade, I messed up and my scores were pretty bad. But, unlike other kids who focused on grades, I really enjoyed learning new things. I didn't travel abroad when I was younger, so my knowledge of the world came from our tiny TV. Movies and the shows on the Discovery Channel about space exploration and science caught my interest, and by middle school, all I wanted was to be an astronaut. In high school I did this science exhibit called Mission Mars, which got a lot of attention, so I always had this ability to come up with ideas and get people together to do something cool.

I graduated high school and I went to a small engineering school in Kolkata. I knew at that time that I would not be able to be an astronaut anymore because schools like the one I went to just made IT engineers—those whose jobs are from America and outsourced to India. But I was still passionate about space, so I started studying astrophysics on the side, as a hobby. It was something I just enjoyed and never assumed it would find any relevance in my resume.

I was really interested in the Spirit and Opportunity mission to Mars. The Spirit got stuck on Mars because its solar panel was covered with dust, so it had issues with power. I started thinking, "Why can't the solar panel just rotate towards the sun to track the sun so it always gets it? And can you have a mini filter to blow off any dust." Whenever I see problems, I like to think about the solutions.

Then my boyfriend at that time went to the Indian Institutes of Technology and went to UC Berkeley for his internship. That was the first time I had had heard of an internship. I had never even been on a plane, but I knew I wanted to do an internship. So I ended up writing five hundred emails to every lab. I also used to sneak into the physics conferences whenever people from America came to talk, so I emailed all the contacts I had made at those, too. Out of the five hundred, I only received four replies, and finally, one worked out. My first internship was at Fermilab, a particle physics and accelerator laboratory, in the suburbs of Chicago.

After my first internship, I really loved engineering. It also changed my perspective, because when you live in India, you see this Western world as a whole new world. But I soon realized we're all the same—we were just a bunch of people wanting to do cool stuff. I then returned home and the next summer, I graduated and was called back by Fermilab to work with them again. So that was good, except I still had a bit of Indian mentality, which made me think I should get married. It is almost implanted in you that a woman's fulfillment in life comes from marriage and kids. Even though I was a bit of rebel, I still thought a little like that. So in between internships in the States, I would return home to pursue my then-boyfriend to marry me, but his mom would only allow an arranged marriage, so it didn't work out.

I then felt like a total failure because I had failed in what I thought was one of the biggest missions in my life, which was to get married, so I decided to do something that would terrify me and that was backpack around India on my own. I was twenty-two and went from Bombay to the Himalayas, and then I got stuck in landslides. My goal had been to go to the highest lake in the world, but there was a cloudburst that killed one thousand people, and I was on a bus on my way there when it happened. It was one of the most life-changing points in my life and it made me a stronger person. It also made me realize that there are so many things in the world that need attention and that could use more help.

So after that, I applied to grad schools and got accepted to do a master's in aeronautical engineering at Ohio State University, thinking that maybe there was still a chance that I could be an aerospace engineer. I was entirely funded by Fermilab. Initially, I was working on particle accelerator stuff, but my big project thesis was on a new kind of nuclear reactor that can produce energy out of radioactive waste. It was a very inspiring project and a very inspiring idea because we were using particle accelerators beyond just for science. And that is when I started looking at big problems like radioactive waste, which no one knows what to do with.

But a part of me, as an aerospace student, still really wanted to work with NASA, so I write to NASA and ask about doing an internship there. I told them about my background and what I have done, but their response was, "Sorry. NASA only takes American citizens." So I get on LinkedIn and search for anyone I can find who definitely isn't an American citizen but works at NASA. I then send another two hundred emails, because if I want something, I have a hard time hearing no. I just always think there is a way.

I found out that NASA does take a small amount of people who are not citizens. I asked my advisor if he could set up an interview for me because I knew that if I could have an interview, I had a good chance of getting in due to my background. So, after two hundred emails and an insane amount of pestering, my dream was accomplished and it was one of the happiest days of my life. I got a three-month internship at NASA Ames in Silicon Valley. I worked on flight control—so how to land planes when they have had their wings and tail broken. But the tricks I learned there I also applied to the research of the particle accelerator for my master's thesis on mining nuclear reactor waste for energy, which ended up getting a fair amount of attention. And so I wanted to come to MIT to build it.

Newnham: How did it get attention?

Bhattacharyya: I guess there are two things I have learned. You can do research and you can keep it so technical that most people don't relate to the big impact and the influence of it, or you can actually talk about what you do so that it explains the importance to anybody and everybody. When I talked about my research or put posters up at conferences, I always included all the technical stuff but I also always included an intro about the magnitude of impact it would have if we were to do it. And I am very passionate when I find a solution. I really connect to what I do.

And I did some very impressive work as a master's student. I worked very hard on the technical part and even when I went to conferences where I put my posters up, I think I was really enthusiastic because I saw a clear problem in the world and I wasn't shy to work on it.

We are so bent on solving little, little problems like developing apps and then developing another one, but there are big problems that need to be addressed and we are not solving them. So even though I was young, I did not see why I should take a proactive step in voicing my ideas. So that helped and I got good recommendations. I think that's what got me into MIT.

Newnham: So tell me about MIT and what you are doing there.

Bhattacharyya: So I come to MIT and think, OK, let's build this nuclear reactor. Wait, I can't build this nuclear reactor because I am a foreign national. And the thing is, at the end of the day, deciding to build a nuclear reactor requires so much more political involvement. So instead of being in the nuclear engineering department, I ended up in the mechanical engineering department where there was a professor named Harry Asada, who was building robots for nuclear reactors but not the same type of reactors. Do you remember the Fukushima disaster in Japan when there was a tsunami that led to a nuclear meltdown?

Newnham: Yes, I do.

Bhattacharyya: Professor Asada was building small, egg-shaped robots to go inside the nuclear reactors and monitor cracks. I thought, "OK, let me stay attached to the nuclear reactor by working with him." So that's what I did. He hired me for underwater communication because this is a boiling water tank in which the egg-shaped robot goes in. I had an undergraduate background in electrical engineering and expertise that was relevant for this research. But when I actually started at MIT, he decided to change his mind and said we weren't doing communication anymore, we're just going to build a different type of robot. I have never done any core subjects on mechanical engineering before—I just picked the department based on the research. So I'm staring at him when he says this, thinking, "But I have never built a robot!" I go to the lab and there are fourteen guys and me. Fourteen guys and me—that is the lab.

So I essentially become the most hated person in the lab because I didn't know how to build shit. I barely knew how to turn the drilling machine on. My professor was so disappointed in me. We are on good terms now, but I still remember my first few months at MIT and thinking I don't belong here. And it's true. I probably came from the smallest college. Everyone else there is probably from other Ivy League and top schools and are prodigies. And I went to a teeny-weeny college somewhere in India. So it was really hard.

During the very first semester, my professor said, "You are the slowest student I've ever had." So I thought about leaving because I couldn't take it. I thought about doing economics instead because, at the time, I had a non-profit and I wanted to find a mathematically-orientated method for a sustainable non-profit.

Anyway, all in all, I decided to stay, but then the bigger problem was the qualifying exams—and qualifying exams for mechanical engineering at MIT are notoriously hard. I mean, getting into MIT doesn't guarantee that you can study at MIT. After a year and half, you have to take a qualifying exam and you have to pass in three areas, which are oral, written, and research. And with your research, you have to show really good research acumen. So I was freaking out, and at one point, thinking I have nowhere to go and this was everything I wanted. There was a time when I was fifteen that I used to see Harvard and MIT on the TV. I used to dream of being under some other sky. So now I am here and I have to put one hundred and twenty percent in and give it all I have got to make it happen.

I studied for three months and I passed. I passed the hardest exam, which I never thought I would ever do, because you look back and you have been told so many times that you are not good enough.

But I can remember the day I went to Facebook and saw Mark Zuckerberg. He was standing by the desk as I was sneaking in with a friend to get free food while I was at NASA. And I see this guy who is just a few years older than me and I think about how he has the same amount of hours in a day as I do, right?

So if he can do something like this, then why can't I? I guess that is the one question I always stumble upon: Why can't I? That "why" drives me crazy. Why can't I do it? What's stopping me?

So I passed my qualifying exams and got to stay at MIT, but the thing that bothered me about my PhD was that I always wanted to be an entrepreneur. I wanted to start something by myself. I was in California and I was reading about the Navy's military marine mammal program in 2014. With seaports, there are many big ships and small ships, so how do you guarantee that they don't contain any threats? It's impossible. They can carry nuclear weapons. They can carry contraband. But there are so many boats, so how will you scan them? It's not people carrying them in their pockets. It's attached to the propellers and the cavities. So what the Navy in San Diego does is it trains dolphins and seals, which have biological ultrasounds. They can send ultrasound echoes and see if there is a reflection pattern from the ships.

Newnham: So you started thinking about this. How did you take it forward?

Bhattacharyya: Well I was spending four years of my prime twenties on a study but I didn't want my thesis to just be another book in the library. I wanted to do something that would actually be useful for the world. When I was reading about the marine mammal program, I could see that it was impossible. It is not scalable but you can have robots and/or you can have autonomous underwater vehicles [AUVs], like torpedo ships, which cost millions of dollars. Or you can have remotely operated vehicles [ROVs] but they can get snagged in propellers.

But if you use little egg-shaped robots like mine, you can move them on ship hulls and spread them below the ship. They can detect contraband or even narco-submarines. You can know what's coming and even detect against other threats, such as mine countermeasure and so on and so forth, because these drones act like a moving intelligent distributed sensor network. My particular PhD is about a robot that can even go on surfaces, underwater, and skim on it. So it can go on surfaces and beam a sensor to see if something is hollow or if there is something hidden. This is not millions of dollars. It is much, much cheaper.

So I wrote this in the introduction in my research paper, which was just for a research conference, not any startup stuff, but it got a lot of media attention and then became very viral. This was in September 2014. And then VCs reached out to me but I explained that I was still in school and doing my PhD. It was also when the Malaysian Airlines Flight 370 went missing. I was thinking, "It's 2015 and people talk about robots taking over, and yet we do not have the technology to find a massive 737 airplane that drowns in the water?"

So as I mentioned before, when I see a problem, it's not like I want to start a company—I just want to know what can be done to solve that problem. I guess it's because I am an engineer. I think about how to break it down to the physics of the problem and I return to the question, why can't I? Don't tell me there is no answer. Why is there no solution? So you breakdown the physics of a drowned airplane and it is pretty simple. It is only giving out sound echoes, so all we need to do is find the sound echo. OK, what's the search area? It is 120,000 square kilometers. And what are you using to search the area? You are using a bunch of ships and one autonomous underwater vehicle, which is a Bluefin-21. But one Bluefin-21 that goes at five nautical miles to travel such a big area is a non-optimal solution, because you realize that when it comes to the ocean, you have no right tool to do the right job.

But if you think about the problem of finding a sound ping, all you need is a bunch of cheap hydrophones, sensors—like ears. So if you could throw a bunch of distributed hydrophones, which are not a million dollars but about a hundred dollars; that's all you need. Hundreds of them distributed all over the search area. The problem is that the platform where you would put the hydrophones is three million dollars and you can't do it. So that's when the big problem hit me. Seventy percent of the world is ocean and we know less than five percent of it in much detail. That's less than what we know of the moon's surface! And this is because we do not have a cheap, scalable, and adaptable method of mapping and monitoring large ocean areas. There is no scalable method that can map large areas and get data from in the ocean. We don't know how to do it. And ninety percent of the world's energy resources' life form is in the ocean. We think to get energy, we need to go and mine asteroids. But the solution is in our backyard.

Newnham: Why do you think no one has looked into this before?

Bhattacharyya: I think there are several reasons. The thing is that there are a lot of things we don't look into before we actually look into it. The first thing is what technology is available? Previously, it was hard to make things smaller, cheaper, and scalable, especially for the extreme environment of the ocean. And look, I used to be an aerospace engineer and I heard people saying, "This is rocket science," or "This is not rocket science." And now I say this is not rocket science but it is ocean science, which is a bit harder than rocket science.

Doing anything in the ocean is really hard because the pressure is insane and there is no light or visibility. There is no radio, so you can't communicate underwater. There is no live Internet stream underwater, so you can't send real-time data. On the positive side, I think for most of us, it is such a mystery that we do not even know the huge potential of it. So it requires one heck of a technology to disrupt. It is not easy. People are looking into it and everyone has their own solution. And one or the other has to find the right one.

Newnham: With Evie, your egg-shaped robot, how did you go from idea to possible solution to startup?

Bhattacharyya: The prototype was created as part of my PhD research to demonstrate the idea of an underwater robot that can go on surfaces and so on. That's when I was approached by a couple of accelerators. One was Qualcomm's Robotics Accelerator, where I was accepted, but couldn't go because I had to stay in Boston. I won an MIT $100,000 business competition. I was one of the top seven winners, despite the fact I still didn't have a team. But over the summer, I also got accepted by the MassChallenge Accelerator, where I ended up being a gold prize winner. And when this happens, you start interacting with the users, because my market isn't finding a lost airplane. So, the most important question is who will use it and how?

You start looking at the users and their mission profiles and that gives you an idea about what is needed. I mean, making something at MIT is totally different in specification to what will actually go into the ocean. So you really deep dive into the issues in the ocean such as corrosion and then you look into how you would deploy them. How would you ensure that they can go to three thousand meter depth without running out of battery? There are no maps of the ocean so how do you navigate there?

Once you have picked your field and a couple of mission profiles, then you deep dive to see what technology is needed to bring on board. And the nice thing about prototyping is that you can catch something out, have a new design, and work with your tentative user to see if it is something they want. You have to constantly ask your potential users what they are looking for. This is also the first of its kind, so of course, most people do not really know what they are looking for because it hasn't existed before. But you ask them about the problems that they face. You want to make it all very seamless for your users.

So that is how we got going. We have done several iterations and it is still in the prototyping stage.

Newnham: Can you say who your users/potential users are?

Bhattacharyya: I can't say as it is not public but I can tell you that the application uses range from port security to marine research, aquaculture, pollution, conservation and energy sectors such as oil. But the ultimate goal is to actually have a map of the ocean, just like you have a Google Maps. Imagine if you had 3D underwater maps? You could have "underwater Uber" in the future…

Evie has two parts. A single drone is called a "hydrone" and it can work in groups, like swarms. You can think of it as an intelligent sensor network—essentially, a flexible grid structure that can collect signals over large areas. So they are not meant for fast travelling in the ocean. They are just hanging out there, collecting data. But, at the same time, they can also be used singly—so Evie could follow a diver around. Therefore, the idea behind Hydroswarm is to have a swarm of underwater robots that can map large areas of ocean.

This is important because, for instance, we know that the coral reefs are dying in some places and are absolutely fine in other places, but we don't know why. And we don't know why because we are unable to easily collect large area data from, for instance, two different reefs. Well, we can, but it is very hard and costly. But if you have the mapping, then you can examine the data and the differences. What is wrong in one place that is not in the other? This means that you can then take active steps in ocean conservation.

Another example is fish. We might overfish in one area, but if we knew how the fish population was distributed over the ocean then probably the fishermen aren't going to go and hang out for six months to figure that out. Also if you knew the water had nutrient contents which attracts more fish in certain areas then you can fish in a much more prepared method. You don't have to overfish because you know what nutrients the fish need and how to grow those nutrients so you can replenish in areas which need it.

There are also geothermal vents. Instead of thinking about energy from asteroid mining, there is a geothermal tunnel on the Californian coast that could probably power a large area. In time, we could just extract energy from there. Also medical plants—a lot of medicine comes from marine plants. So, I think considering that life started in the ocean, understanding our ocean would open up the door to so many possibilities, including from an economic perspective.

Therefore the whole point of Evie is to help understand the ocean's contents in a large, scalable way. This is the goal of Evie—to essentially be a drone with a pluggable sensor platform.

Newnham: What has surprised you most during this process?

Bhattacharyya: Oh boy. Every day is a surprise. I think I have become a little more confident than I was, so I guess I learned that I was not entirely stupid. And that I am capable of more than I thought. Another thing is that I got comfortable with trying out new things.

There are two aspects, I guess. One of course is lessons you learn from a technology aspect and the second part is what you learn from running a startup. From the technology aspect, it is really fascinating to see the different things I have learned from different areas of my work, all came together in this technology. A lot of the things I did in my master's or in electrical engineering as an undergrad, it might not have seemed relevant back then but they all found a use in Hydroswarm.

Another important lesson is that the ocean is so hard. It's way harder than space. And it's surprising how little we know about the ocean and what little technology we actually have to deal with anything in the ocean. That was very surprising because after years of space travel, we don't even know how to explore our own ocean. So it was fascinating to see how hard it is but also, it is equally motivating.

Newnham: Can you tell me about your Lab-X Foundation?

Bhattacharyya: That started whilst I was at NASA. It was right after I saw Mark Zuckerberg and Elon Musk's SpaceX. I didn't have any idea about start-ups before that but I was sitting there and thinking about my life back in India, and I thought about how if I didn't do that one internship in Chicago, then by now I would be married with a few kids, and not doing something that I loved. Instead, I was working at NASA, which nobody thought I could do. In a country of over a billion people, many people apply to engineering courses but less than one percent gets into Ivy League schools. I thought, "What if they were given the opportunity to?"

I wanted to create Lab-X to give hands-on opportunities to students back in India and we have brought many students out to do internships in the States and we do workshops with them then they often go back and start startups and be leaders in their community.

Newnham: What advice would you offer a young girl like you, who dreamed of working at NASA or running her own startup?

Bhattacharyya: If you really want something, go out and get it. Don't let anyone tell you what you can or cannot do because it is important to know that your work is something you will spend all your life doing. So pick what you really love. It will be hard and you might fail many times, but the most important lesson I have learned doing my startup is perseverance. Go for what is yours in this universe.

Nothing in my life has been super smooth. And you always feel like you suffer for a reason. But I see my life like a video game, and there is only one quarter to pay because game over is game over. So I think you have one game to play, and in this game, all these terrible things might happen and all these obstacles might distract me and make me think about giving up, but I need to keep my head up high, and look forward, and keep scoring. Because I only have one game to play and I have got to make the best out of it. Right?

Ramona Pierson

Cofounder, Declara

Ramona Pierson is the cofounder and CEO of Declara, a startup that uses artificial intelligence to power its collaborative knowledge platform. Ramona started Declara with Nelson Gonzalez and with $25 million in Seed A funding and a mission to innovate the education sector.

Ramona started her career in the Marine Corps, working on algorithms to help fighter attack squadrons. She was incredibly fit, even nominated as the fittest person on the base by her male peers. But a drunk driver hit her and left her for dead. She was in a drug-induced coma for eighteen months before waking, unable to see, walk, or talk. After more than 50 surgeries and a lengthy rehabilitation process in a senior citizens' home, she slowly started to rebuild her life. She went on to start three companies, all in the tech education space, including SynapticMash, which she sold to Promethean World Plc.

President Obama recently praised Declara for combining "... the power of a search engine with a worldwide network of experts so that we all can learn faster from our fellow citizens and their lifetimes of knowledge."

Danielle Newnham: What were you like growing up?

Ramona Pierson: Growing up, I was very busy all the time. As a little kid, I thought I would be in the Olympics, so I would train every day. All my friends and family would laugh at me while I ran the stadium stairs at the track or football field and did wind sprints. I started doing that after I saw the Olympics when I was five years old.

© Danielle Newnham 2016

D. Newnham, *Female Innovators at Work*, DOI 10.1007/978-1-4842-2364-2_20

When I grew up, the world was a lot different than it is now. It was like Mad Men, with our parents smoking cigarettes, drinking cocktails, and telling us just to show up back in the house by midnight. So we ran around like little animals all the time. These days, parents are so involved with their kids in sports and activities. But when I grew up, my parents would always be surprised when I would bring awards home for playing field hockey or volley ball, or running and track. They just never had an idea that I did anything. Also, I loved to read all the time. And I was always getting into trouble. My brothers and I would always try and build grenades and rockets so we could blow things up. My father had always encouraged that because he worked on propulsion systems.

So we grew up very independent, without much supervision. It was kind of a mix of my parents being super strict with us inside the house, but outside, they didn't have a clue what we were up to. We were raised to be independent and not depend on anybody at that time. My mother was a very competitive person. It's hard to explain but it felt like there was so much chaos in our house as kids. It just felt like I always had to create my own sense of order and discipline, which contributed to my going into the military. So I guess that's why I got into sports, because there was a lot of discipline in that, and order. I always built out a schedule for myself to train, study and focus on, regardless of what was happening in my life.

Newnham: You graduated early and joined the Marines. Can you tell me about the accident?

Pierson: I was twenty-two. I came home from work one night and took my dog out for our usual run. I had no idea then that my life was about to change forever.

I don't remember much but I was running across the street when I got hit by a drunk driver. I flew out in front and then he ran over my legs. Horrible things were happening to my body, but strangers came to me and kept my heart going. Someone used a pen to open up my airway so I could get some air. All of these people helped me and I ended up in the hospital. I was wrapped in ice and put into a drug-induced coma, which I remained in for the next eighteen months. When I woke up, I was blind, I couldn't talk, and I couldn't walk.

Newnham: What was the recovery process like?

Pierson: I was in the hospital for quite a long time and got passed around. But then it appeared that I wasn't going to thrive, so of course the best action for them was thinking about where to put somebody who is probably never going to work or be able to care for herself again. And the obvious answer was to put me into a senior citizens' home. The senior citizens' home had three levels: hospice care for people who are sunsetting their lives, middle care, which has a bit of assistance and social services, and then people who are living independently in those places.

So when I showed up, they were going to put me into the hospice care because they thought I would be sunsetting my life. But there wasn't any space, so fortunately for me, they stuck me in the independent care level. And the senior citizens surrounded me because they didn't think that a young person should be sunsetting her life. They interacted with me as if I were their kid. They literally re-raised me and I think back on that and I thank God that I got the best parenting of my life, as an adult, in that senior citizens' home.

Also, what was interesting was that while I was in the coma, people had put rosaries and crosses on my bed. And even though I didn't know who they were or why they did that, I think back on it now and it's heartening to know that people were thinking about me while I was pretty much out of it. Even though I can't tell you who those people were, I think about those people a lot. Strangers, maybe staff from the home, who had left signs that they were there and had thought about me. That makes me think back and know I wasn't alone through that whole process.

All in all, the recovery process ended up taking close to five or six years.

Newnham: Was there a stage where you just thought, this is it—this is where I'm going to spend the rest of my life? And equally, was there a moment of light when you reached a particular milestone?

Pierson: Periodically, I would feel like I was recovering and doing well, and then something in my health would pop up. I kept having heart problems and I also could not regulate going to the bathroom, so I kept urinating like crazy. Finally, after going in and out of the hospital, the folks who released me were saying, "She's not going to thrive." And they kept telling me that I wasn't going to live six months and that I would suffer from sudden heart failure. But then, accidentally, I ended up with an emergency in a different hospital in Grand Junction and a neurosurgeon there diagnosed me with diabetes insipidus, which is a diabetes around salt not sugar. So once he got me on the right medications, then I started to recover well. So that was definitely a time where I thought I don't know if I'm going to survive, but then, after he diagnosed me, I was able to put weight on and started to thrive physically. And so then I saw the light—that there was actually hope for me.

I never got depressed, because in the beginning, I was really struggling so much every single day just to live to see the next day. And then in the senior citizens' home, when I wasn't struggling with that, they were trying to teach me how to speak and how to do other things. I then realized it was time to get my leg fixed, which seems like such a small thing in comparison to living and dying, but I had two really big problems. One was my left leg, which I had incredible pain in—unbearable pain. So I just had to learn to manage that. And I could not use my left hand very well. If you are going to get a Seeing Eye dog, you have to be able to use your left hand. So I had to struggle with having them release my tendons in my left hand so that I could open and close my hand again in order to have the dog.

I went through a series of surgeries to be able to use my leg. I just recently broke the only part of the bone in that leg that is mine. I went through twenty surgeries on my left leg just to get it to work. Sometimes I wonder if I should have just had them take it off—then I wouldn't have gone through so many surgeries and continue to go through surgeries. But that's OK. It works good enough.

I just kept looking forward. Maybe it was because my childhood was so rough and bizarre. I always ignored what was happening in the house—and my crazy parents—and focused on training and studying. So that might have been a life skill I acquired that helped me to recover.

Even in a startup, I still remain focused on moving things forward and not getting discouraged or distracted. And when you go through things like this, as well as military training, you realize that if you double down and you have the grit and can persevere through things that are terrible, you will be able to tune into things that are important and tune out the things that are noise. So all of that was helpful for running a startup.

Newnham: You go through all of this, and obviously it changes you profoundly, but how does it change you in terms of work and the career path it led you to?

Pierson: I was so young and I did think about work when all of this happened. I thought about what I was going to do for the rest of my life. Sitting in a senior citizens' home wasn't the answer, because in my heart, I believed I needed to find my purpose. What's ironic is I had wanted to become a heart surgeon my whole life, but when I was in the senior citizens' home, I thought now I want to become an educator. I think it was because of the education I was getting from the senior citizens. So I started to think about working toward volunteering in schools. And that was a weird thing because I was blind. When I talked to educators they would always ask me, "Well, how will you teach a classroom if you can't see the classroom and manage kids? Schools would never hire you because you can't manage children."

So I interviewed and talked to a lot of teachers, but I was inspired by the senior citizens, who then said, "Why not become a professor? If college kids walk out of your classroom, you don't need to manage them—just fail them." But, along the way in that process, I also really became energized by trying to understand what motivates people to learn at a very deep level in terms of the neuroscience and biological indicators of learning, because I felt deeply that so many of our organizational structures of the brain and opportunities get shifted based on our own internal beliefs and chemical reactions to our environment. So I went down the path of really trying to understand the neuroscience behind learning.

Newnham: And then you started a business?

Pierson: When I decided to focus on education, I decided to get my teaching certificate so that I could better understand the education process, and educators and all the acronyms they use. And then try to understand the problems that educators deal with. Because why build solutions for something you don't understand? So, when my wife, Debra, moved up at Microsoft, I ended up getting a Gates grant through the Alliance for Education to become a Fellow. I entered into education through that fellowship in Seattle and started to build out something called The Source, collaborative-learning software, for the Seattle Public Schools. The software is still in use today.

So I built a very large data warehouse that brought in two hundred and fifty different data sources or databases to look at the student learning and achievements in a 360-degree view. I then built something called Read Write Technology so that teachers and students could interact with each other. So that's what they used to call social networks—Read Write Technology. And it's kind of ironic, as that's how they used to describe Facebook in the beginning, and then they started calling it a "social network." So I basically built a very early social network for education.

Then I had a not-for-profit, Learning Without Borders, where we were trying to connect educators. This was before people were using the cloud. It connected educators in South Africa with educators in the United States so that we could share best practices and lessons. What we were trying to do was effect change in post-apartheid schools. But the educators there didn't have access to education and professional development.

When I went to South Africa and worked in some of the post-apartheid schools, I realized that because teachers didn't have an education beyond the seventh grade, they could never prepare their students for the matriculation test that would allow them to go to college, which is how apartheid kept the black Africans down. So in order to combat that, and because I have always been mission driven. I partnered with a lot of different US schools, especially in the Seattle area, and we built a network of educators who then worked with those African educators online to share their best practices, resources, and lesson plans to help them learn so that they could become better qualified.

Then I passed it on to the University of Washington and they took it over. It was nice because through this project, the singer Eddie Vedder had released a couple of his songs to fund the tuition of kids in South Africa to go to school. They have to pay to go to school, which is another barrier. Because of this foundation, we were able to get rid of some of these barriers.

Then I started a company called SynapticMash, which was to bring the cognitive and neurosciences into education. In reality, what we ended up doing was building the first cloud solution for education. We saw that school districts were spending millions and billions of dollars on people running technologies that were old-fashioned, because in those days, they were still using client-based grade books and they had servers in the server rooms in the school district. So I thought, why not build a SaaS [Software as a Service] solution for education? So that's what we built. It was funny because I would have these conversations with superintendents and CIOs saying, "Well, we can take all of your data and run your school system from the cloud." And they said, "What's a cloud?" Now that's all common sense, but I was probably about ten years ahead of time back then.

Newnham: When was this?

Pierson: SynapticMash was early 2000. I then sold SynapticMash to Promethean, which is an English company that had just gone public and had one of the most successful public offerings in London at that time. I guess that was around 2010 or 2011. I served as their chief science officer.

Right before I sold it, I partnered with McGraw-Hill and we built the first personalized learning algorithms. Our algorithms and technology connected students to the right content, at the right time, and connected teachers based on their teaching preference, to students based in the ways in which they learned best. And we were very successful at transforming students' lives. We worked a lot with the gap kids, which are kids that hadn't progressed in math for three years. And within six weeks, we would get them caught up with their age peers. Not because of the technology, but I think psychologically, all of a sudden they started seeing themselves as learners and started to believe in themselves. When you are in the education space, if people treat you as if you are not a learner, you then believe you are not a learner, and you don't go to class and you give up. So we tried to build a system that reinforced kids to believe in themselves. And I think that's what truly changed the future for these kids.

Also, my job there was to take our SynapticMash platform and infuse it with the hardware to create an Internet of Things in the classroom. But I ended up hating working there because they were too slow, too hardware-centric, and they didn't understand that the future was moving into personalized learning and the personalization of experiences. That it was going to be intelligent agents, artificial intelligence, and software that was the future. They kept thinking I was crazy, so I left. And that's when we started Declara. Now those themes I used to talk about are all that you hear about. So I was ahead of Promethean by about five years.

Newnham: That's a good place to be. So tell me more about Declara. What was the mission from the start? And how did you build up your team?

Pierson: So Declara means "declare." The name actually came from Debra, as we had been going on about what we were going to call the business. We were sitting around having Mexican food and a lot of wine, and we started thinking, "Declare your intent." We kept talking about declare your intention with reference to the personalization bit, but also, a lot of our first customers were in Mexico. So then Debra brilliantly said, "Declaro," or "Declara."

Right from the beginning, our mission has been "declare personalization." At first, I thought why not build a concierge of learning? What if we had intelligent agents or bots that helped people learn more efficiently and faster? So that is how it began and that has been our mission—to really look at the skilled labor mismatch and help knowledge workers so that they don't lose their jobs.

When we started Declara, it was after a horrible economic disaster. What was clear was that a lot of jobs—blue collar jobs and other jobs— were disappearing. All the assembly line jobs were being replaced by robots and other people's jobs were being replaced. All of these enterprises didn't have a way to innovate fast enough to keep alive, so a lot of companies were starting to go the way of Kodak, which is out of business, because they weren't innovating fast enough. So how do we help these massive large companies from laying off people and re-skilling their workforce?

So what's been interesting is that our first customers have been nations wanting to reskill their education workforce. As in Australia, their teachers were educating students who were going into the agriculture business or mining business, but all of that is being decimated by global warming, so they are asking, "How do we change what we are teaching kids so that they become knowledge workers and inventors of technology?" And so that meant shifting all the teaching professional standards and curriculum standards. It's a massive undertaking for a nation to take on. Australia was our first customer and they've been using our platform to do that for the last four years. Then we went to Mexico and Puerto Rico, and now we're in 3M, Renault, and other big enterprise companies. We have also just won the State of California.

Newnham: Congratulations. When you started Declara, was it always the plan to approach nations?

Pierson: Yes, we did. Oddly enough, I think I wanted to focus on Latin America first but because it's going through a rapid transformation; it was very hard. I learned a lot of lessons even though we won the deal with the largest teachers union in the Western hemisphere—SNTE [Sindicato Nacional de Trabajadores de la Educación] in Mexico. Latin America is going through a transition where they are all moving into a knowledge-based workforce and we're trying to get there, but you have to drive through a lot of corruption and bureaucracy, which is very difficult for a startup. So after working with Mexico and staying true to our mission and our core values, we decided we needed to really focus in on global companies and come home a little bit. That's how we won California and that's why we are working to move into other states in the United States. And, at the same time, we are also starting to get some inroads into Europe, because it is also going through a transformation.

There is a lot of work that is starting to be done over there, and abroad, around planning for smart cities. We are doing some work with University of Technology Sydney [UTS], who are trying to think through how we build smart nations, smart cities, smart states. UTS has bought licenses for their university. I'm thinking of bringing them in on a partnership for some work we are doing with Bristol University that's working on planning smart cities in the UK. So we are trying to position ourselves as partners—of being a global research platform to help universities and innovators across cities, states, and nations to create intelligent cities so that people become life-long learners.

Imagine that you can walk through a city, and you walk past a museum, and the content of the museum is fed out to you so that you know what is happening in all these different places and you can access this content anywhere you are. Or let's say you have a heart attack, God forbid. The intelligent agents are able to change the traffic lights so that the ambulance can get to you. Or traffic gets redirected if there's a fire somewhere. So intelligent cities are going to be the future, but to get there, there has to be multiple steps. The first step is helping knowledge workers who are planning this to get smarter so that they can connect all the data and build standards across all of these products. The next step is to roll out across all the content sources within a nation. In Australia, we are connected to five different content stores that we feed to people based on their behaviors. What we've done is build a CognitiveGraph—our own IP—on every person who's on our platform so that we can anticipate what their needs are for learning.

Newnham: How does your CognitiveGraph work? Is it based on what they are reading learning and uploading?

Pierson: Yes, what we are doing is building a knowledge learning graph that's dynamic. We're looking at what you read, who you interact with, what you search, and the knowledge that you have been sharing with others. By doing that, we start to be able to anticipate what you're contextually trying to learn. So let's say it's Debra and she's trying to run our social media. She's also trying to do research around Russian banks, because we might have a customer in the Russian bank space. So you have to shift content learning and understanding based on your learning needs that day. What our algorithms do is to try to understand and anticipate what you need. We deliver content and expertise based on your behavior. So if you create a team on our platform and you invite a bot into your team, the bot will start reading all the content that you have brought on and will start searching the web. We have them pointing at all the research, government-funded research initiatives such as NSF, NIH, CDC, and FDA, so that the bots will bring in content to help you learn faster.

Renault uses us to figure out how to build the next-generation fuel cell car. Our bots are actively looking at what MIT is building in the fuel space or at Stanford University, and its bringing content to them. And they have their researchers interacting with all of that information so that they can build the next-generation technologies.

What is underneath all of this is a recommendation engine that is intelligently trying to help you access content, information, and crowdsourced insights to help you learn more efficiently.

Newnham: Education and tech are two major factors in all that you do. Where do you see the future of education going?

Pierson: You know it's interesting because one of the other verticals we're working heavily in is health care, because health care is intertwined with learning and education.

But in terms of education, I think that education now is moving into a space of personalization and that you are going to see a lot of bots or robots interacting with educators and education. As an educator, you can't know everything all of the time, but you have to teach your students how to be twenty-first century learners. And being a twenty-first century learner isn't about memorizing anymore—it's about anticipating and inventing that future. So you provide those teaching learning skills to students. It's a shift in the educators' position in the classroom—from not just being the facilitator of learning but to helping your learners actually be innovators of new thought or novel ideas themselves.

Newnham: What are some of the major obstacles you've faced, in terms of funding, or in terms of scaling the business?

Pierson: Right now we're in that terrible stage. It's like being a teenager. Before you are a teenager, you're in middle school. You've got zits, you're verging on becoming something, but yet you're still lanky. Your arms are too long. So we're at that point where we're about to start to really break even and be profitable, but we are also at that stage where we actually need funding to get there, but we can't get the funding unless we get there. So it's the chicken-and-egg scenario. It's like skydiving, and right before you hit the ground, your chute comes out. So that's why it takes a lot of grit and fearlessness to run a startup.

Also, the first few years were really tough. It felt like rolling boulders up a hill and people shooting at you at the same time. So I think if, as a startup, you can survive long enough, you start getting enough traction. And then it really starts moving and all of your hard work is starting to pay off. But boy, you have to have the grit and you have to stay on it daily.

Newnham: What advice would you give women who are looking to get into the tech field?

Pierson: I think it's interesting because a lot of women have moved out of tech. For a while, I had a lot of women in my development team. And then all of sudden, some really great female engineers decided that they wanted to shift their career, get into writing or doing anything but technology. So I think that if women are coming into technology, be aware that it's very male dominated still, but technology needs women because women surface ideas and approaches that men don't think of. And women seeking to get into the technology space can be highly successful. You just need the grit to persevere. It's a male-dominated field, but like the Marine Corps for me when I was younger, you just have to focus on the joy of the things that you love in your work and not get distracted by the fact that you may be the only woman in the room.

Newnham: You've obviously achieved so much in your life both professionally and personally. What are you most proud of and why?

Pierson: I'm most proud of being married to Debra. It's interesting, mainly because Debra and I have been together almost twenty years. And throughout those years, our relationship hasn't been recognized in various states. It wasn't recognized in California. Then we moved to Washington and it wasn't recognized there. The laws changed in California and so we moved back to California. And then California changed its laws—pulled back marriages—and then Washington passed it. So we kept going and wherever we went, they kept changing the laws. It's funny, but it's also ridiculous that we have people in the United States, and other nations, where they don't think gays and lesbians should be married. They spend millions and billions of dollars blocking it. It's crazy. The fact is that finally the laws changed so that we could get married, but it has almost been as much of a battle to get married as my health.

Newnham: What do you wish your legacy to be?

Pierson: That I have dedicated my life to transforming education and helping people meet their full potential through learning.

Index

D. Newnham, *Female Innovators at Work*, DOI 10.1007/978-1-4842-2364-2

Get the eBook for only $4.99!

Why limit yourself?

Now you can take the weightless companion with you wherever you go and access your content on your PC, phone, tablet, or reader.

Since you've purchased this print book, we are happy to offer you the eBook for just $4.99.

Convenient and fully searchable, the PDF version enables you to easily find and copy code—or perform examples by quickly toggling between instructions and applications.

To learn more, go to http://www.apress.com/us/shop/companion or contact support@apress.com.

Printed in the United States
By Bookmasters